THE ARTS AND EMERGENT BILINGUAL YOUTH

The Arts and Emergent Bilingual Youth offers a critical sociopolitical perspective on working with emergent bilingual youth at the intersection of the arts and language learning. Utilizing research from both arts and language education to explore the ways they work in tandem to contribute to emergent bilingual students' language and academic development, the book analyzes model arts projects to raise questions about "best practices" for and with marginalized bilingual young people, in terms of relevance to their languages, cultures, and communities as they envision better worlds. A central assumption is that the arts can be especially valuable for contributing to English learning by enabling learners to experience ideas, patterns, and relationship (form) in ways that lead to new knowledge (content).

Each chapter features vignettes showcasing current projects with emergent bilingual populations both in and out of school and visual art pieces and poems, to prompt reflection on key issues and relevant concepts and theories in the arts and language learning. Taking an asset-based stance about language and culture in English learners' lives, this book shows the intimate connections among art, narrative, and resistance for addressing topics of social injustice in school and community settings.

Sharon Verner Chappell is Assistant Professor, Department of Elementary & Bilingual Education, California State University, Fullerton, USA.

Christian Faltis is Dolly and David Fiddyment Professor of Education and Director of Teacher Education, School of Education, University of California, Davis, USA.

THE ARTS AND EMERGENT BILINGUAL YOUTH

Building Culturally Responsive, Critical, and Creative Education in School and Community Contexts

Sharon Verner Chappell and
Christian J. Faltis

Routledge
Taylor & Francis Group

NEW YORK AND LONDON

First published 2013
by Routledge
711 Third Avenue, New York, NY 10017

Simultaneously published in the UK
by Routledge
2 Park Square, Milton Park, Abingdon, Oxon OX14 4RN

Routledge is an imprint of the Taylor & Francis Group, an informa business

Library of Congress Cataloging in Publication Data
The arts and emergent bilingual youth: building culturally responsive,
critical and creative education in school and community contexts/
edited by Sharon Verner, Chappell, and Christian J. Faltis.
  p. cm.
  Includes bibliographical references and index.
  1. Education, Bilingual—United States.   2. Arts—Study and
  teaching—United States.   3. Multicultural education—United States.
  I. Chappell, Sharon Verner, editor of compilation.   II. Faltis, Christian,
  1950– editor of compilation.   III. Cahnmann-Taylor, Melisa. Knowing
  your students, becoming a culturally responsive teacher.
  LC3621.A78 2013
  370.117—dc23
  2012040373

ISBN: 978-0-415-50973-2 (hbk)
ISBN: 978-0-415-50974-9 (pbk)
ISBN: 978-0-203-12468-0 (ebk)

Typeset in Bembo and Stone Sans
by Florence Production Ltd, Stoodleigh, Devon, UK

SUSTAINABLE **Certified Sourcing**
FORESTRY   www.sfiprogram.org
INITIATIVE   SFI-01234
SFI label applies to the text stock

Printed and bound in the United States of
America by IBT Global

To the artists, arts-based researchers and educators who do brave work with emergent bilingual youth, their families, communities and schools . . .

To our children and grandchildren who teach us to be and become responsive to their complex and precious lives . . .

Every day.

CONTENTS

IMAGES

FOREWORD

In the midst of the many high profile local, national, and transnational conversations about global migration, cultural diversity, and citizenship, there are few serious and compassionate engagements with the question of how educators might more effectively create multilingual environments for children and youth in schools. Bilingual and multilingual environments are not only a recent result of globalization, but are also a longstanding feature of human cultural experience. How do visionary teachers address new language acquisition, as well as facilitate the bilingual learning processes of those children and young people who are moving from place to place, and language to language? What strategies do they teach us all for promoting and maintaining linguistic diversity, and further, cultural diversity, in our societies? These questions are urgent. The presence of children in schools who come from elsewhere—whether this be a distant location or a different historical and cultural lineage in the same location—and who speak one or more languages other than the dominant language of the schools they are in, is now commonplace around the globe.

These children necessarily represent a challenge to the dominant forms of knowledge—the epistemes—of conventional schooling, based as it is on archives of knowledge that are marked by monolingual barriers. Even with the growing accessibility of multilingual knowledge archives on the internet, conventional forms of pedagogy in schools rest on normative habits of monolinguistic dominance. Bilingual and multilingual children and young people are perhaps the most important face of the present. No matter what the disposition is of a school community towards these children and their families, their presence and its challenge signal the possibilities of a radical plurality of forms of knowledge, and bilingual, multilingual and hybrid vocabularies and pedagogies. In short, these competencies may be understood as key to the peaceful cohabitation and exchange of knowledge between global human communities.

But bridging the gap between the realities of teaching bilingual or non-dominant language speaking children and youth, and the positive and epistemically generative possibilities of the co-presence of diverse languages and cultures, is not easily accomplished. This is where this book comes in. The authors have created a multivocal and multivalent text that captures some of the pedagogies and epistemic ruptures resulting from creative commitment and risk-taking attitudes of excellent teachers who are working with "emergent bilinguals" in the context of U.S. public schools. These teachers embrace the challenge of those whom the authors aptly frame as "emergent bilingual" youth, and embrace the youth themselves—their own, in-process, emergent humanity. They understand themselves and their students as mutually dependent and co-determining. Not only are the students emerging as bilingual, or sometimes multilingual, in the stories told by the book, but the teachers are also in a process of becoming bilingual or multilingual, as creators of new codes and as knowledge-producers. Learning alongside their students, they open themselves up to the cultural experiences and world views and in the process develop expanded vocabularies of knowledge and pedagogy.

The book itself is organized as an exercise in understanding multiple worlds of language and experience. The authors passionately frame questions of bilingual education with solid data and historical research, while also leaving central questions open for readers to debate using our own experience and priorities. They begin with a nuanced discussion of the recent theorizations of language acquisition, setting the tone for an evocative exploration of language, knowledge, the arts, and culture. The book proceeds with an arrangement of the voices of practitioners, framing vignettes from teachers' experiences in the classroom. These are deployed as opportunities for further engagement and rigorous questioning. They continuously provoke further relevant connections and queries in the reader. The authors ask us to consider our own instinctive responses, to assess our own situations, and to add to the conversation. Putting into practice a critical pedagogy as writers and teachers, they invite our traveling to the worlds of the teachers and students in the book, as well as self-reflection. This dialogue can then lead to more effective and appropriate practice in our own contexts, a practice that nurtures our own emergent humanity.

Telling stories and being understood is a crucial element of shared human experience. The recognition and affirmation that results from sharing stories and experiences becomes a potent rationale for the role of the arts, as evidenced by the multiple experiences represented in the book. The arts provide a set of vocabularies for exchange across differences, enhancing self-realization, communication, and ultimately, community. As the authors write, "Emergent minoritized bilingual children . . . are sometimes perceived by schools and popular media as having "no language at all" with parents who don't care about education or literacy at home." The question of being without language, unspoken and unspeakable, is one that is addressed potently by the arts in the vignettes in this book.

The arts provide a language at a crucial moment in "emergent bilingual" children and young people's lives, when they are otherwise (mis)understood as being mute and under-developed, with their strengths and individuality invisible. The discussion of the arts intersects productively with the terminology offered by the authors, importantly the phrase "emergent bilingual," which produces a sense of expanded bilingualism that includes communication through the arts. This approach elaborates a broad understanding of the intersection of the arts, communication, and learning. Communication through the arts can be seen as a powerful avenue, and yet one that remains undervalued and under-utilized in schools.

The book also opens an important intersection between the arts, bilingual education, and critical pedagogy, or education for liberation. Throughout the history of public education in the United States, cultural and linguistic differences have been understood in a narrative of racialized developmentalist thinking that undervalues the knowledge and cultural experiences of students who speak languages other than English. These philosophies and pedagogies in fact derive from legacies of colonialism and global racial hierarchy. John Dewey, perhaps the most important theorist and architect of American public education, believed that the world was ordered on a continuum between savages and civilization (Fallace, 2011). According to Dewey, children's earliest stages of development could be correlated with the cognitive abilities of the "savages" of Africa, Asia, and Latin America. This correlation of a lack of intelligence with languages and cultures that are not Anglo-American still orders the contemporary understanding of linguistic diversity in schools. Rather than understanding the different linguistic abilities of children in the United States as assets, this suggests that their attachment to other forms of cultural expression, including language, are signs of intellectual weakness. Pedagogies that value other visual, verbal, and written languages provide the possibility for the radical co-presence of difference and the grounds for the liberation of people who have been systematically oppressed by educational systems that are designed to subjugate their knowledge and culture.

This is an important time to again reach beyond a racialized hierarchy and assert the value of the rich cultural milieu of the United States, including its multiple languages, migratory national affiliations, and cultural practices. These constitute the knowledge base of contemporary U.S. public schools. Rather than as a problem to be solved, this should be understood as an asset, and nowhere is this clearer than in California. It is no accident that this important book emerges from California, where, as the authors report, "Nearly 1.6 million pupils in the kindergarten through grade twelve (K-12) public educational system in California, or one in four, are English learners (ELs) and emergent bilinguals. This represents almost one-third of the ELs in the nation." California is a global laboratory and a battleground for questions of public education and cultural and linguistic difference. It is the birthplace of the first higher education programs in Ethnic Studies, Asian American Studies, Native American, and Chicano Studies, and has been the site of ongoing contestations regarding how the public education curriculum and enrollment policies incorporate and address the experiences of these diverse communities. This book gives readers the opportunity to learn from those experiences, and at the same time, it opens up the conversation to teachers and students around the U.S. It is clear that, in many diverse locations, and even in the worst conditions, bilingual communication, new relationships, and communities, can grow. As referenced by authors in this book, Tupac Shakur (1999) writes, ". . . surrounded by toxic conditions where a thriving life should not occur, it still did. And not only did life occur, but it was beautiful. It was a rose." In each of the stories and voices in this book, we find hopeful signs of vibrant, bilingual life, courageously growing in places where they are not supposed to grow.

Dalida María Benfield
Cambridge, Massachusetts

References

Fallace, T. D. (2011). *Dewey and dilemma of race: An intellectual history, 1895–1922*. New York: Teachers College Press.

PREFACE

The Arts and Emergent Bilingual Youth offers a critical sociopolitical perspective on the issues that contextualize working with emergent bilingual youth at the intersection of the arts and language learning. This book utilizes research from both arts and language education to explore how these interconnected approaches contribute to emergent bilingual students' growth and development. Featuring model arts projects, the book raises questions about "best practices" for and with marginalized bilingual young people, in terms of relevance to their languages, cultures, and communities as they envision better worlds. A central assumption is that the arts can be especially valuable for contributing to English learning in tandem with young people's home languages by enabling learners to experience ideas, patterns, and relationships (form) in ways that lead to new knowledge (content). The form and content featured in this book is uniquely situated in the lives of emergent bilingual youth, as they navigate the social and educational policies affecting their communities.

This book is intended for school and community-based educators interested in reforming pedagogy (curriculum and instruction) for emergent bilingual youth through an arts-based lens, as well as credential and graduate students in arts and second language/bilingual education in such courses as English language learning methods, arts methods, culture and curriculum, curriculum theory, community-based arts practice, and teaching artist methods.

Each chapter features visual artworks, poems, and vignettes showcasing current preK-12 projects with emergent bilingual communities both in and out of school. Each chapter begins with an introductory section, framing the theoretical, historical, and practice-based contexts for the narrative vignettes that follow. Then, each chapter presents stories of model arts projects accompanied by reflection questions that relate the content to readers' own professional lives as teachers and artists. The chapters focus on thematic commonalities among the featured vignettes and highlight relevant critical theory and research in the arts and language learning.

Chapter 1 builds theoretical and pedagogical contexts of second language learning, social inquiry as an arts community of practice, and critical turns with emergent bilingual youth through the arts both in and out of school.

Chapter 2 explores the complexities of culturally responsive teaching in the contexts of working with emergent bilingual youth, such as understanding (im)migration, indigeneity and other communities in which families participate, as well as building culturally and linguistically responsive pedagogies based on family funds of knowledge.

Chapter 3 explores collaborations with families and communities in all their local diversity, such as through curricular projects in science and language arts, and through local decision-making projects with families that lead to community development.

Chapter 4 explores the importance of play in the lives of emergent bilingual youth, and the ways that language, literacy and the arts provide for being creative and critical.

Chapter 5 emphasizes the value of living and telling stories through various arts processes. We highlight culturally and linguistically diverse narrative structures, as well as alternative arts modalities as mediums for storytelling about bilingual, bicultural issues.

Chapter 6 explores a variety of approaches for reading and responding to literature with emergent bilingual youth. We provide guiding characteristics for readers interested in building such critical, responsive literature projects.

Chapter 7 addresses the ways emergent bilingual youth communities might respond critically to world events, particularly as these events relate to their lives and their rights, roles and responsibilities as socially engaged young people.

Chapter 8 addresses how bilingual youth talk back to political, social, cultural, and educational systems through new media production, including social networks, web building, and digital storytelling.

Chapter 9 emphasizes the importance of counter-narrative practices at school, even among the intense pressures of high stakes testing, featuring the power of professional learning communities among teachers with critical, culturally responsive facilitators and guided inquiry.

Chapter 10 suggests ways of building sustainability in our projects in/with various bilingual communities, such as through continued curriculum development, lifelong learning about being and becoming bilingual, as well as guiding direct cultural action and local decision-making projects.

The book contains two appendices to support educators in the implementation of a critical, creative, caring education with emergent bilingual youth. Appendix A outlines a process of planning, implementing and evaluating projects through a series of questions and action steps. Appendix B contains a list of resources for educators of organizations and websites in arts education, multicultural and social justice education, and family and community partnerships.

When taken as a whole, these chapters build a framework for critical, creative, caring education with emergent bilingual youth. From an asset-based stance about language and culture in the lives of communities, this book demonstrates intimate connections among the arts, narrative, and resistance for addressing social (in)justices in school and community contexts.

ACKNOWLEDGMENTS

We owe deep gratitude to the combined efforts that have supported and strengthened this book:

- To the contributing authors for the wisdom they share through their stories
- To Naomi Silverman, for her enduring editorial guidance
- To the reviewers for their constructive criticism
- To Drew Chappell, for his keen editorial eye and his willingness to drop everything and offer whatever support we needed during the completion of the manuscript.

1

INTRODUCTION

A monolingual, white seventh grade teacher answers the knock at her classroom door. The principal walks in and introduces Yanira, a student who has immigrated from El Salvador a couple of days before. Yanira looks around shyly and sees a sea of faces staring at her. She hides behind her notebook and thumbs through her bilingual dictionary, anxious to learn the pronunciation of a few words and to find someone who speaks her native language.

A bicultural teacher with some second language experience examines her class roster and learns that four of her students have been designated as English learners for the last six years. The group of students clusters together and alternates between English and their home language carrying on conversations bilingually. The students debate about movies they have seen and then switch to stories of their older siblings and cousins living across the border in México.

A third grade teacher, who is bilingual, learns from the district office that she can no longer use the children's home language for classroom instruction because of a state law that mandates English only. Her students are forced to whisper to each other in their home language (also the native language of the teacher) in order to ask questions about class assignments.

In the above examples, teachers and students struggle to negotiate the complexities of a bilingual or multilingual school environment. Now consider what might happen when they work through the arts to understand these complexities.

The teacher in the first example designs a curricular unit in which the students create identity boxes using collage and popular culture to explore cross-cultural interactions. The teacher guides the newcomer Yanira to explore her impressions of living in the U.S. and the impact of this new culture on her life. Yanira smiles for the first time as she works on her identity box, with a self-portrait of her hands over her eyes inserted into its center.

The second teacher instructs her long-term English learner students in the use of ethnographic interviewing techniques (questioning and photography) to gather family stories, which they compile into a class performance along with pictorial images. The students negotiate the placement of stories in order to convey emotional arcs of characters and thematic issues of living within two cultural groups in the Southwest.

The third teacher selects bilingual poetry to integrate into her social studies unit on immigration and assimilation. Although under an English-only mandate, she learns that the students can work in multiple languages as long as her whole group instruction is in English. She speaks individually to students using both languages, and they begin to build confidence including their native language in their own poetry compositions. The teacher learns how to use both languages to reinforce the development of bilingualism, as well as how to intertwine aspects of culture with language development.

Purpose of the Book

These scenarios point toward the purpose of this book: to explore the power of interrelating the arts, bilingualism, second language learning, and critical inquiry about the world. As teachers and artists, we can work toward understanding the experiences of emergent bilingual youth (labeled English language learners [ELLs] by the state) and how they are affected by curricular practices in and through the arts in school and community-based settings. This book is one such effort, requiring that we forge diverse connections among the fields of the arts disciplines, art education, English language development (ELD), and bilingual education in educators' personal arts practices and pedagogical strategies with bilingual youth. Among the questions explored in this book are:

- How do teachers and learners engage in the arts to explore school and community topics while both enriching their primary language and acquiring English as their second language?
- How do teachers' personal arts practices facilitate understanding of issues affecting emergent bilingual students?
- How do drama, visual arts and media tools help students develop bilingually (including acquiring English as a second language) in various settings, such as in formal schooling, community centers, and afterschool sessions?
- How does arts-based learning tie into what is understood theoretically about bilingualism and second language acquisition in and through young people's life experiences?

As authors, we come to this project with personal and professional experiences that position our beliefs about the imperative of both the arts and social justice in the educational lives of emergent bilingual youth. Sharon grew up in a suburb north of Los Angeles, aware of the presence and absence of bilingualism and biculturalism in her life:

> We drive past the groves on the way to a play with my dad. After seeing the Great White Witch and Aslan the Lion battle over good and evil, we stop at a roadside stand. I am between worlds. I inhale the sweet perfume of oranges and watch as a big pulpy glass is poured, freshly squeezed by the man behind the counter. I say "gracias" and nod, because I don't know how to say much else in Spanish. I see a girl packaging sugared rolls and try to place her. I think she goes to my school. But she is not in my classes. Now I realize that few of the bilingual students were. Where did the school put them? Why weren't we together? I could have learned a lot from her. But we weren't and I didn't.
>
> (Chappell, 2009, p. 15)

Sharon identified teaching as the space where she could explore what it means to live, work, and learn across borders. She has struggled to learn Spanish as her second language throughout her K-8 arts and language teaching career, and she has shared this humbling process with her emergent bilingual students in Texas and California. Sharon's degrees in English, Women's Studies, Arts Education and Curriculum Studies inform her approach to teaching at California State University Fullerton. She writes poetry and creates artist books as an integral part of her university teaching and research practice. Her role as a mother of a young child also influences her drive to conceptualize creative, critical, caring education.

Chris's early years of life were spent living between Northern California and México, where he studied in elementary school in Morelia, México City and Hermosillo, and became bilingual and identified as Mexican as a child. The son of a Spanish teacher and artist, Chris went on to study Spanish as an undergraduate, and eventually went on to earn a Master's in Chicano Studies, and a doctorate in bilingual education in the early 1980s. A political activist throughout his life, Chris turned to art while in Arizona as a faculty member at Arizona State University. During the late 1990s and early 2000s, conditions for Mexican immigrants worsened in the state, as anti-immigrant hate groups became increasingly emboldened in their efforts to deny basic human rights to Mexican children and families, regardless of their legal status. In 2005, Chris created the persona of Simón Candú to promote his political art aimed at portraying through what he calls "visceral realist art," that portrays Mexican immigrants' lived experiences in Arizona, intensified by visceral emotions about their mistreatment in schools and society.

Our biographies inform the organization, content, and ideological positioning of this book. We work to clarify our own values, beliefs, and practices in our daily efforts to become more culturally and linguistically responsive educators, researchers, and artists. This book is a tangible artifact of our ongoing process.

Overall Organization of the Book

In each chapter, you will read two to three narrative portraits from practicing artists, teachers and researchers who work with emergent bilingual young people particularly around issues of social and cultural importance. As editors, we will reflect on particular practices, tools and theories related through these stories that enhance English language learning and native language development for critical social inquiry. Each of the stories is comprised of: a narrative focusing on a key turning point in the project; the goals and objectives of the project; a description of project participants and context; arts and language strategies utilized in the project; and suggestions for future applications of these strategies. We end each chapter with reflection questions and suggested activities for applying relevant concepts and theories in the arts and language learning to your own teaching practice. You will also find two Appendices in the back of the book. Appendix A outlines a process of planning, implementing and evaluating critical, creative, caring projects with emergent bilingual youth through a series of questions and action steps. Appendix B contains a list of resources for educators of organizations and websites in arts education, multicultural and social justice education, and family and community partnerships.

In this chapter, we lay a foundation for the importance of a balanced interdisciplinary approach to arts and language education, as well as highlighting key concepts and terminology regarding the education of *emergent bilingual youth*. We use this term to portray the potential development of both languages in young people in the United States who come from homes speaking languages other than English. The most common term used by the state to identify this preK-12 student population is English language learners (ELLs or ELs). Older terms include limited English proficient (LEP) and language minority students. The term *emergent bilingual youth* (García and Kleifgen, 2010) emphasizes an asset-based stance about languages and cultures in young people's lives, and reminds us all that bilingual youth are much more than passive recipients of English instruction; they are developing dual languages and literacies from a social and cultural base of home and community language practices.

Our primary goal is to articulate the potential of current practices to become more culturally and linguistically responsive, critical, and creative. We are interested in moving toward arts processes and products in educational settings that focus on resistance and counter-narration, taking a stance about language and culture in the lives of emergent bilingual youth against political domination (Freire, 2000; hooks, 1995; Pacheco, 2012). Given the past twenty years of restrictive language and immigration policies in the U.S., adults and youth alike have utilized art-making as a means to portray the life stories of bilingual and immigrant youth, as well as to raise questions about how language, identity, culture and power intersect in their lives. This book is significant because it forges intimate connections among art, narrative, and resistance, addressing topics of social (in)justice that have been virtually silenced in mainstream educational conversations and research (Olsen, 2008; Suárez-Orozco and Suárez-Orozco, 2002). We hope that making art and discussing it through specific analytical approaches such as those in this book can produce dialogue toward social change in, with and by emergent bilingual youth communities.

Contemporary Contexts of Teaching Emergent Bilingual Youth

In order to appreciate the importance of becoming culturally and linguistically responsive as an educator, we include the following contemporary contexts of teaching emergent bilingual youth. Currently, over one hundred languages other than English are spoken in homes and communities across the United States, solely and/or bilingually. The most common of these languages used for daily communication is Spanish, although there are some states in which Spanish is not the most common second language. It is predicted that there will be approximately 15 million students with Limited English Proficiency (LEP) enrolled in U.S. schools by 2026 (Gollnick and Chinn, 2004) and 40 percent of the K-12 school age population nationwide will be comprised of children whose first language is other than English by 2030. In California alone, nearly 1.6 million pupils in the kindergarten through grade twelve (K-12) public educational system, or one in four, are English learners (ELs) and emergent bilinguals. This represents almost one-third of the ELs in the nation.

Among those LEP children, the Hispanic population shows a marked increase (Lucas and Ginberg, 2008). ELL/LEP students are more likely to be at risk in terms of performing poorly academically than English speaking counterparts (Verdugo and Flores, 2007). The dropout rate of Latina/o students is disproportionately high, reaching 44.2 percent in the year 2001, compared with 7.4 percent among non-Latina/o student population (Gollnick and Chinn, 2004).[1] Verdugo and Flores (2007) argue:

> Although the challenges posed by ELL students are significant, it is less clear what strategies and programs educators can use to improve the educational experiences of this population. Much of this ambiguity is due to the lack of research and information, inappropriate educational policies, and the inability of educators to understand ELL students and their backgrounds.
>
> (p. 168)

As researchers and teachers, we suggest ways of educating emergent bilingual youth with pedagogy divergent from the technical, test-driven, discrete skills, English-only curricula that confront educators on a daily basis in the classroom. In this book, you will see projects and approaches that engage the critical and creative alternatives that lead to complex knowledge building in communities of language learners.

There have been numerous efforts in the history of U.S. public education to legislate the programs of instruction for emergent bilingual students. In California alone, these efforts include:

1976—Chacón–Moscone Bilingual Education Act establishes legal framework for mandatory bilingual programs.

1987—Legislators allow the Chacón–Moscone Act to sunset but maintain support of the bill's principles.

1997—Proposition 227, "English for the Children," passes which generally bans instruction in California schools in any other language than English. Yet many bilingual programs survive as a result of parental waiver demands for instruction in such languages as Spanish, Vietnamese, Chinese, and Korean. Similar bills followed in Arizona and Massachusetts.

2002—The current authorization of the Elementary and Secondary Education Act (ESEA), known popularly as NCLB or No Child Left Behind. This policy effectively removes any mention of bilingual education as a program model, language of instruction, or office of leadership in the federal government. Instead, NCLB and state departments of education use the terms "limited English proficient," "English learner," and "Structured English Immersion" to describe the learners and classroom setting. Importantly, the new policy frames the discussion of educating emergent bilingual youth as a schooling effort to improve their English proficiency without the consideration of home language or culture as either an educational tool or necessary context of these young people's development.

In response to NCLB's discursive practices that exclusively emphasize English language learning, this book recursively portrays the vitality of emergent bilingualism: the potential development of both languages in young people who come from homes speaking languages other than English (often along with English), and who live in wider bilingual communities.

ARTS ARTIFACT ONE

NWCLB (No White Child Left Behind)

Simón Candú, contemporary artist/activist/teacher

What actions do you see in this painting? What themes, emotions, and issues does this painting raise? Do you agree or disagree with the stance taken by the painter about issues of culture and language in schooling, as influenced by social policies and practices? (*See* Figure 1.1)

FIGURE 1.1 *NWCLB* by Simón Candú

What follows is an overview of the intersecting concepts in the areas of second language learning, arts education, and critical social issues in bilingual education that inform this book.

The Importance of Promoting Bilingualism

We take the strong position that second language acquisition is most effective and connective to the extent that it relates to the development of a child's or adolescent's home language and culture, and that second language acquisition always develops from—and in relation to—a home language. To this end, it is important to acknowledge the value of teaching and learning in the language a child or youth understands and uses for making sense of the world, alongside adding a second language. It is axiomatic that children and youth who become literate in the language they understand are in the best position to acquire a new language because they already have much of the literacy understanding that is needed to make sense of text in the new language, once they have cracked the code and developed oral proficiency to a level where the written language maps on to their developing oral language.

In the following sections, we briefly trace some of the major ideas in second language acquisition. The purpose of these sections is to show how elements of second language acquisition parallel arts-based teaching and learning. We note that in the field of second language education, concern for the development of the home language is essentially absent. Accordingly, as you read these sections, it is important to consider that what is traditionally written about second language acquisition assumes that the learner is proficient in the home language and, in many instances has already acquired literacy in that language.

The Black Box

From the late 1960s to the beginning of the twenty-first century, the field of second language learning was dominated by theoretical frameworks that envisioned the process of acquiring a second language as something that occurs inside a "black box" metaphorically located inside the head of learners (Long, 1980). MIT linguist Noam Chomsky had just begun to map out his universal generative theory of language competence, and cognitive science was in its infancy. In the developing field of second language acquisition theory, cognitive theorist Larry Selinker (1972) identified five central processes involved in second language learning: language transfer, transfer of training, strategies of second language learning, strategies of second language communication, and overgeneralization of rules in the language being learned. The first and last of these were psychologically based; the other three were matters of teaching and learning experiences. He argued that most second language learners develop an "interlanguage," an internal system of language constructed by the learner, based on cognitive and linguistic interactions between the first and second language, coupled with how the learner experienced learning. The implication for bilingualism is that children and youth rely on their home language as they develop their second language or interlanguage (Baker, 2011).

Some ten years later, former language teacher and applied linguist Stephen Krashen (1981, 1985) developed the Monitor Theory, claiming that second language learning depends on two separate cognitive systems, acquisition and learning. Acquisition of a second language happens subconsciously when learners internalize language based on comprehension of meaning, akin to how children acquire their home language. Learners are then able to produce language at their level of ability based on what they understand in the new language; from this perspective, understanding precedes production. Language learning, on the other hand, happens when learners pay conscious attention to the language, in an effort to understand and internalize rules about how the language works. Learners who rely on learning call up the rules and the vocabulary they have memorized to produce language on demand. For Krashen, and his followers, acquisition is what leads to communicative abilities; what learners learn consciously and explicitly about language may not turn into acquired language that can be called on for communicative purposes.

Language Acquisition as Creative Construction

Krashen (1981), drawing on research that viewed language acquisition as a "creative construction" process (Sharwood Smith, 1994), argued that learners acquire a second language in ways that are similar to how children acquire a first language, where children creatively construct meaningful utterances by receiving comprehensible input and organizing that input into an accessible communicative system which is used to produce meaningful language. Creative construction was defined as the existence of universal cognitive mechanisms which enable learners to discover the structure of a second language system to communicate meaning, based on the need to express meaning to others (Dulay and Burt, 1975). Evidence for the creative construction process was taken from the language learning errors learners produced as they moved toward increased proficiency. For Krashen, the focus on creativity in making meaning results in fluent language use because the learner intends to communicate ideas using the developing language available whenever the need for communication arises. When learners are asked to learn the rules of language production and produce errorless language, creative construction is thwarted. Moreover, attention to linguistic form over language meaning signifies that learners can talk about linguistic form in their primary language, giving them some cultural capital as "educated learners," but such talk yields little if any return with respect to fluency when learners attempt to speak the new language.

Krashen's theoretical work spurred a longstanding debate in the field of second language learning about the role of explicit attention to language rules and form for the development of communicative ability in a second language. On one side were those whose research and personal evidence supported explicit instruction of language forms, arguing that attention to form speeds up language acquisition, enables learners to produce error-free language, and helps learners understand about language as a system. Some advocates of this perspective have argued that a language learning focus on acquisition, as defined by Krashen, means that learners will always produce language full of errors as they progress toward proficiency. Teaching for acquisition is often viewed as intellectually lazy, because it means that teachers don't necessarily have to know much about the complexities of language structures in either the home language or the new language (see Gregg, 1984) or have much pedagogical content knowledge about teaching language.

In contrast to such criticism, language teachers who saw value in privileging meaning-making over focus on form began to experiment thoughtfully inside their classroom settings, seeking out and engaging students in more authentic experiences where learners could use their creative construction process to communicate meaningfully in the new language. For these individuals, pedagogical content knowledge meant understanding how language is acquired holistically, what language errors reveal about how learners are progressing, and how encouraging authentic, communicative experiences is most likely to lead to acquisition.

Many began to look to developmental errors as a novel means to "see" the acquisition process as it was transpiring, rather than what is wrong with the learner.

Input, Interaction, and Output

By the 1990s, much of the work in second language acquisition in the U.S. had shifted from a focus on teaching language forms to an emphasis on Input, Interaction, and Output (IIO) model (see Gass, 1997) as the favored theoretical explanation for how people (children, youth and adults) acquire communicative abilities in a second language. However, instructed second language acquisition approaches, in which students were asked to learn and memorize vocabulary and grammatical systems, continued to be offered in many schools and foreign language classrooms.

The IIO model expanded Krashen's Monitor Theory, with its focus on comprehensible input and the creative construction process, to include interaction and output. Interaction was crucial for language acquisition because it enabled learners to engage in two-way conversations, where adjustments are made for linguistic form, conversational structure, and content, until the participants achieved some level of understanding (Gass, 1997; Krashen, 1985). The role of output in conversation, once again revered for its creative aspects, was viewed as a means for stretching the language capacity of learners, forcing them to creatively construct meanings syntactically and semantically to carry on the conversation with more capable speakers or writers (Swain, 1993, 1995). Learner output, in the form of speech and/or writing, also engendered new comprehended language input within the context of two-way conversation, where the more capable speaker or writer responded bilingually or in the new language to the meaning of the learner output in ways that encouraged comprehension.

The focus on interaction within the IIO model helped move the field of second language acquisition to a broader view of language as means of negotiation for meaning within the structure of two-way conversations for getting things done and typically where there was an information gap between the learner and more capable speaker. This focus too had its challenges, mainly that its overemphasis on cognition ignored the role of language play and the sociocultural nature of second language acquisition.

Language Play and Second Language Acquisition

As the IIO model began to take hold in the field of second language acquisition, a number of scholars expressed concern that language is about much more than instrumental oriented-conversation. Cook (2002) and Rampton (1999), for example, argued for the role of language play, or ludic talk, in second language acquisition. For these scholars, ludic talk enables learners to try out different roles as language learners, to be playful with their new identities, and to go beyond information gaps to express language artfully and with élan. Playfulness in language, they argued, provided a delightful venue for language acquisition.

In language play, language learners have opportunities to try out multiple meanings of words and expressions, and formal features of language can be manipulated for emotion, humor, and expressions of affinity identities. In first language acquisition, it is easy to see that language play is critical to promoting mastery of the language systems, and for in-group membership and identity formation. For second language learning, language play is less understood and recognized as integral to becoming bilingual.

In this book, we view language play through arts-based learning as essential for supporting learners' efforts to make sense of the world, and to be able to laugh and cry at what their experiences bring them as bilingual youth, using their home language and learning a new one. Accordingly, a significant part of being recognized as an able member of any speech community entails knowing how to negotiate one's identity across multiple settings, in and through different language varieties. As we intend to show throughout this book, arts-based learning affords opportunities to emergent bilingual youth for language play, humor, emotional response, aesthetic quests, social positioning, and critical commentary about the world.

Language Acquisition as Social Positioning for Solidarity and Support

ARTS ARTIFACT TWO

Buying Time

Marilyn Dike-Dunn, 2010

> English is too big,
> So I buy some time,
> I know where to start . . .
> "You start here on number one Mrs. Langston says"
> So then I try,
> But when my pencil touches the paper,
> My English is erased,
> So then I buy some time,
> I sharpen my pencil like this; the point breaks, so then I sharpen it
>   again,
> This time I'm extra careful,
> Perfect and ready,
> I grab a ruler,
> To write English, I need straight lines on my paper,

English is a big job,
It must be done right,
I gather the courage to write again,
Ready to write the most perfect sentence in English,
"Clean-up please," Mrs. Langston protests,
So then I put my English away,
In my "unfinished work" folder,
All my English goes there.

In this poem, how does the student experience being in English? What classroom instructional practices affect the student's learning? How might the teacher encourage the student's playful use of language, in English and home language?

In recent years, second language acquisition scholars have questioned the referential/transactional nature of the IIO conception of language learners, arguing that the process of interaction between learners and speakers of a language is much more than the transmission of information. Instead, these scholars emphasize the sociocultural construction of knowledge as key to understanding how people acquire a second language in the real world, where, in addition to the transmission and molding of ideas and information, social positioning is necessary to developing communicative abilities in language. That is, beyond information exchanges, language learners need opportunities to take stances, challenge ideas, provide support for others, pose and solve problems that matter, and build relationships with others to contest injustices. New language patterns emerge from these kinds of social interactions that support, challenge, and question ideas and content.

Language learners need to negotiate for meaning beyond transactions with more capable speakers of the language, such as supporting other language learners and building solidarity with those who share similar positions about what ideas count and whose voices are silenced or heard in schools (Aston, 1993). Support-based interactions involve empathizing with the plights of one another, or sharing affinities using humorous, endearing or complimentary language. Solidarity interactions involve clarifying one's perspectives and ideas about the world, and finding ways to show solidarity for their own positions and against others. In both cases, the ensuing language is reliant on the personal and experiential involvement of others, with the goal of building new relationships of shared positionality, and with an eye toward interaction that builds solidarity among voices that challenge the status quo (Dryden-Peterson, 2010). In the poem above by Dike-Dunn, the student feels isolated in her use of English, rather than in relationship to others who also experience English as an additional language.

Second Language Acquisition and the Arts

From our perspective, then, second language acquisition entails much more than cognitive processing, and gains little from a focus on predetermined grammar study and incessant error correction. For us, children and youth are in a position to acquire English as an additional language and become thoughtful bilingual youth when their efforts to communicate are supported by teachers and peers within authentic experiences, in ways that stretch learners' abilities to use language for expressing their understandings, questions, emotions, positions and communities. The arts are one of the most authentic ways for bilingual youth to interact with others and take positions on aesthetic content and form, asking and responding to questions about who they are, and how their families and worlds interact with the art they encounter. This kind of interaction builds a community of learners who engage in what Barone (2000) calls *conspiratorial communions* where students come to discussions around arts-based work to inquire deeply about possible and desirable worlds.

According to Barone (2008), an artwork can "engender an aesthetic experience in its readers or viewers, [in which] empathy may be established, connections made, perceptions altered, emotions touched, equilibria disturbed, the status quo rendered questionable" (p. 39). Whether in written form, presented visually on canvas or film, or performed by actors, musicians and dancers, the arts provide a context for emergent bilingual youth to express complex meanings about their lives, the world and their education. These meanings include taking stances in solidarity with or against others, using creative construction of language play, communicating emotions and expressing multiple perspectives and voices, as well as expressing polyvocal interpretations of artworks. With pedagogical intention, arts-based processes can assist emergent bilingual youth in questioning the monovocal master narrative about the hegemony of English and monocultural expressions that pervade schooling.

It is commonly understood that the arts deal with form and content at the level of composition. The form of an artwork may involve lines, shapes and colors that, when combined with the content, create an image for viewers to interpret with meanings they bring to the art and which the artwork suggests to them. Each of the forms used in an artwork is imbued with meaning, as the artist chooses the form to interact with the content of the work. In this manner the form and content are interdependent for generating and expressing meaning to the audience that experiences it.

Yet, an artwork's form and content must be viewed in its social and cultural context, understood as a tool or resource produced as part of a community of practice (Wolff, 1993). When bilingual youth interact with artworks, they have authentic opportunities to negotiate with others for the meaning and emotion they bring to and take from the artworks. They can focus on the form of the art, the content, or both, evoking their position toward the art, what it means to them and their social and personal circumstances as learners. Moreover, in many of the artworks we present in this book, the students themselves are active participants in the creation of the artworks: taking photographs, planting gardens, writing poems, singing songs, playing a musical instrument, performing plays. Arts-based learning offers emergent bilingual youth not only rich opportunities for English language acquisition, but also authentic ways of building solidarity and support for personally relevant issues, topics, and linguistic repertoires in response to a system of learning that maintain a narrow status quo of what counts as legitimate knowledge (Apple, 2004; Pacheco, 2012). Students engaged as creators and/or spectators in action, are in a position to pose questions, generate answers, and ultimately to interrogate master narratives about history and the contemporary world.

Teachers of the Arts and Emergent Bilingual Youth

Teachers who use the arts to engage emergent bilingual youth for purposes of critical consciousness development and conspiratorial affinity are much more than arts educators. These teachers are part of a counter-narrative educational community who believe English language learners need multiple opportunities to use their home language and developing new language not only to learn content, but also to question what they are learning so they can become critical learners and engaged citizens of the world (Boyle-Baise and Zevin, 2009).

The overwhelming majority of bilingual youth in the U.S. are from economically poor living conditions (with almost 60 percent of ELLs qualifying for free and reduced lunch at school as compared to 30 percent of English proficient students [Ballantyne et al., 2008]), and many have come to the U.S. to improve their living conditions based on the impacts of globalization, war, and poverty (One America, 2010). Moreover, many of the children designated as English learners were born in the U.S. to immigrant parents, living within discriminatory structures that produce inequitable access to economic and cultural capital (Anyon, 2005). These children come into a system of schooling that—in the majority of states—was structured for monolingual English speakers of European heritage. In states such as Arizona, California, Georgia, Massachusetts, Nebraska, Ohio, and South Carolina, bilingual youth identified with less-than-fluent proficiency in English are mandated to attend English immersion classes, with no instruction in their native language. This program model demands that English learners acquire vocabulary and grammar in isolation, and receive English phonics instruction until they can score highly enough on an exit English proficiency exam.

These students have few, if any, opportunities to engage in discussions in their home language or their new language about art, history, mathematics, music, or science, to touch and feel content, to argue for or against the beauty of a poem, to experience the joy of trying out an experiment where they have posed critical questions. More often than not, with the focus on achievement scores, English learners are excluded from art and music, placed instead in intervention classes and pull-out tutoring.

The numerous artifacts and vignettes in this book show how teachers and artists facilitate the creativity of bilingual youth on topics of personal interest and social relevance, using counter-narrative strategies to question and actively transform the status quo of English-only schooling and assimilationist, deficit-oriented world views toward bilingual families and communities. Consider the following autobiographical reflection by a teacher about a photography project she facilitated with elementary students.

VIGNETTE ONE

Through My Lens: A Child's Perspective

Elizabeth Renner, Omaha Public Schools

As a new teacher, I often felt overwhelmed attempting to teach the district-mandated curriculum while simultaneously engaging my curious first graders in meaningful learning activities. For young children, so much is new and exciting, yet our schedule mandated hours of preset instruction from a reading series with minimal connection to my students' rich life experiences. Jonathan Kozol (2007) writes, "the possibilities for leaving open space and open time in which our children can reveal their secrets and unveil their souls have been diminished too greatly in too many of our schools" (p. 234).

Seeking a way to unite our linguistic and cultural differences and to ignite the children's imaginative curiosity and creativity, I developed a photography project that combined picture making, writing, and artistic expression. In the context of the vibrant neighborhood surrounding our classroom—parks filled with young families and *paleteras* selling ice cream, streets lined with *carnicerias* and Latin groceries, and cars throbbing with the rhythms of *el Radio Lobo*, first grade English language learners transformed into expert photographers. The project flowed like water, slowly eroding the canyon walls of our regimented curriculum—making "open space" for a river of curiosity and wonder. As moving water exposes the beauty and history of the rock formations, our project opened time for students to "unveil their souls" and tell their stories. The photographs were a common language, the language of art. It was our meeting place, from which we ventured to the unknown and found ourselves united together in the open space and open time of creative thought.

I planned with the intentions of connecting to my students'[2] personal experiences, exposing them to the creative process, and engaging the surrounding community. Like most seven-year-olds, my students were keen observers of everyday life. Squirt, a praying mantis, became a member of our classroom after careful eyes spied her on the playground. Our rock collection quickly expanded as students began spotting the asphalt chunking off our ice-laden streets. I sought to harness the innate awareness and provide my students with tools to apply their discoveries—disposable cameras. I contacted a local artist, Amy La Grange, to join us as a partner in the project. She agreed to visit our classroom each week to teach basic camera skills and support students throughout the photo editing. Including Ms La Grange as an "Artist in Residence" conveyed the value of creativity and artistry, bringing a sense of urgency and importance to the children's work.

To celebrate the start of the project, I read Wendy Ewald's *The Best Part of Me* and the students reflected on the "best part" of them. Ms La Grange photographed the children's "best parts," allowing them to explore and hold her camera. We printed the photographs and the children placed their photos in their writing folders, referring to the images as they wrote narratives about their "best parts." The students were enamored with the photos, studying details carefully, and becoming aware of their special features. Patty wrote of a freckle "2 inches away from [her] eye," while Elisa detailed the way her strong hands make tortillas with her *tía*.

Knowing that each child would independently take pictures with disposable cameras, I guided students through the planning process and taught basic camera functions. As a class, we created a list of things the students might want to photograph. Next, each child developed an individual picture plan—a list of at least ten photographs that they would capture. Ideally, the ten-picture plan would serve as a guide on their picture-taking adventures. While each camera had twenty-six photos, planning ten would start students on a path of careful thinking while allowing for the freedom of the creative process. Students devoted a great amount of time and energy to their plans—their careful thinking was evident as they begged for more time. I included a record sheet with space to record, using pictures or words, each of the twenty-six photos they took.

Ms La Grange taught an overview of camera basics—taking care of your camera, using the flash, lighting, and perspective. We showed many examples of pictures taken from diverse vantage points and discussed the effect these had on the final work. A picture shot in the dark without a flash and a picture taken directly into the sun were important non-examples that illustrated the concept of lighting. We introduced camera vocabulary using a labeled diagram and encouraged students to use the new words in conversation as we pretended to set up shots with imaginary "viewfinders"—fingers forming a circular window. Amidst doubts of others—"You're giving cameras to first graders? You're sending them home?" I sent the cameras home with beaming children ready to explore.

As I expected, all of the children returned the following Tuesday with knowing grins on their faces that seemed to say, "I am talented, I am an artist." Maria entered the classroom, peering through her camera's viewfinder, finger on the shutter button, "I saved my last picture for you, Miss Renner!" Later that day, I sat in the Walgreen's parking lot in awe, sifting through hundreds of photographs. The photographs of family members, bedrooms, favorite toys, and neighborhood life provided insight into my students' knowledge.

The following day at school, the students laid their photos across their desks—admiring the artwork. We moved throughout our "museum" on a gallery walk. Students were eager to share the stories behind their photos and explain their creative process—"I took this one from behind my fence!" Later, students sorted their photos into two piles, (1) I Have a Story and (2) Save for Later. The "I Have a Story" photos were stored in writing folders, and over the next month students transferred their stories to paper during Writers' Workshop. Students who struggled to write one or two words previously were writing sentences, lots of sentences! I encouraged their use of native language, particularly in cases where students were having a difficult time translating a concept to English.

The project opened a way of being with the children, listening to the children, which cannot be defined in terms of "research-based" or "standards-based." It was a conversation exploring our shared human experience. Students "unveiled their souls" as they shared thoughtfully planned photographs and told their stories—sometimes silly, sometimes serious, always providing insight into personal challenges and exposing layers of individuality. Elisa captured her fourteen-year-old sister, elegantly stretched out on the front steps. She told her story in a wise voice, noting the warnings she gave to her sister about her father taking the computer away: "I tell her no talk to the boys, my dad take the computer."

As the exploration of photographs and writing progressed, I knew they needed to be shared. I contacted Bob Sandler, community leader of an art and community space located down the street from our classroom. I met with Mr Sandler, explaining my vision and the importance of the work my students were creating. Skeptical at first, he questioned the capability of six- and seven-year-olds to produce quality art that others would come to see. When we discussed the implications for our community, he agreed to schedule a show: we would have one weekend in May to display the work. Mr Sandler's donation of space was a valuable opportunity to gather children, families and community members in celebration of art, culture and our shared human experience. Throughout the next weeks, the students continued to write about their photographs. Ms La Grange engaged the students in the digital photo editing process, which was an opportunity to explore with size, shape, and colors and the computer.

The day of our opening reception, the students buzzed with energetic delight—months of preparation and talk about our "gallery show" were coming to fruition. That afternoon, Patty was to have seven of her front teeth pulled. She adamantly expressed that she would be there, although I feared she might not be well. At 6:00 PM on the dot, Patty entered with her four sisters, mother, and a toothless grin—"I told you I'd make it to the gallery show!"

The students' artistry and thoughtful writing brought all cultures and socioeconomic statuses to the "open space." One mother, who was subdued and nervous at previous school events, was beaming and proudly observing her daughter's work. As we share, we learn. The respect and concern we have for one another gains depth and meaning. The Spanish word *desahogarese*, which is literally to un-drown oneself, is used as the expression "get something off your chest." As we snapped photos and told our stories, *desahogamos*, we released thoughts, feelings, questions, and vulnerabilities. Immersed in the aesthetic, creative context, students became careful observers of the familiar, their families, their homes, their neighborhoods. As our reception was coming to a close, the Mayor of Omaha entered the gallery. One of my students, David, extended his hand, "Welcome to our gallery show, my name is David, what is your name?" The photographs brought us together, no matter the language, no matter the name, no matter the title, more water flowing through, eroding boundaries of the canyon wall.

⋆   ⋆   ⋆

Questions to Consider

1. What did the teacher learn from her experiences with her students through this photography project (about their lives, about herself as a teacher)?

2. How did the students engage specific tools and techniques of photography to accomplish their goals?

3. What language acquisition skills and processes did the students engage as they created their artworks?

This book brings you unique stories like the one above throughout its chapters. We solicited stories from across the United States and have included the perspectives of artists, K-12 teachers, university students and researchers who write individually, collaboratively, and with young people themselves. We have organized the book based on the intersecting themes of these stories and provide discussion around them.

Chapter 2 explores the dynamics and complexities of knowing your emergent bilingual students and becoming a culturally and linguistically responsive teacher.

Chapter 3 explores principles of collaboration with families and communities in all their local diversity. Chapter 4 explores the dialectic of playing with language and playing through the arts in critical, creative projects with emergent bilingual youth. Chapter 5 emphasizes the value of living stories and telling stories through various arts processes. Chapter 6 explores critical responses to literature, while Chapter 7 addresses how communities of learners might respond critically to world events. Chapter 8 addresses how bilingual youth are talking back to political, social, cultural and educational systems through new media production. Chapter 9 addresses the creation of counter-narrative practices at school, even among the intense pressures of high stakes testing. Chapter 10 raises questions about building sustainability in/with multilingual communities. Appendices A and B provide resources for teachers. Taken as a whole, these chapters build a framework for critical, creative education with emergent bilingual youth that we hope will fuel your own work as teachers, artists, and researchers for years to come.

Notes

1. We thank vignette author Masakazu Mitsumura (see Chapter 9) for his contribution of these demographic statistics.
2. All names are pseudonyms.

References

Anyon, J. (2005). *Radical possibilities: Public policy, urban education, and a new social movement.* New York: Routledge.

Apple, M. (2004). *Ideology and curriculum*, 25th anniversary 3rd edition. New York: Routledge.

Aston, G. (1993). Notes on the interlanguage of comity. In G. Kasper and S. Blum-Kulka (Eds), *Interlanguage pragmatics* (pp. 224–50). Oxford: Oxford University Press.

Baker, C. (2011). *Foundations of bilingual education and bilingualism.* Clevedon, UK: Multilingual Matters.

Ballantyne, K. G., Sanderman, A. R., and Levy, J. (2008). *Educating English language learners: Building teacher capacity.* Washington, DC: National Clearinghouse for English Language Acquisition. Available at http://www.ncela.gwu.edu/practice/mainstream_teachers.htm.

Barone, T. (2000). *Asthetics, politics, and educational inquiry: Essays and examples.* New York: Peter Lang.

—— (2008). How arts-based research can change minds. In M. Cahnmann-Taylor and R. Siegesmund (Eds), *Arts-based research in education* (pp. 28–49). New York: Routledge.

Boyle-Baise, M. and Zevin, J. (2009). *Young citizens of the world: Teaching elementary social studies through civic engagement.* New York: Routledge.

Chappell, S. (2009). A rough handshake or an illness: Teaching and learning on the border as felt through art-making. *Journal of Curriculum and Pedagogy*, 1, 10–21.

Cook, V. (2002). *Portraits of the L2 user.* Clevedon, UK: Multilingual Matters.

Dryden-Peterson, S. (2010). Bridging home: Building relationship between immigrant and long-time resident youth. *Teachers College Record*, 112(9), 2320–51.

Dulay, H. C. and Burt, M. K. (1975). Creative construction in second language learning and teaching. In M. K. Burt and H. C. Dulay (Eds), *New directions in second language learning, teaching, and bilingual education* (pp. 21–32). Washington, DC: Teachers of English to Speakers of Other Languages.

Freire, P. (2000). *Pedagogy of the oppressed*. New York: Continuum.

García, O. (2012). "City University of New York–New York State Initiative on emergent bilinguals vision statement." Unpublished paper.

García, O. and Kleifgen, J. (2010). *Educating emergent bilinguals: Policies, programs and practices for English language learners*. New York: Teachers College Press.

Gass, S. (1997). *Input, interaction, and the second language learner*. Mahwah, NJ: Lawrence Erlbaum Associates.

Gollnick, D. M. and Chinn, P. C. (2004). *Multicultural education in a pluralistic society*, 6th edition. Upper Saddle River, NJ: Pearson Merrill Prentice Hall.

Gregg, K. (1984). Krashen's monitor and Occam's razor. *Applied Linguistics* 5(2), 79–100.

hooks, b. (1995). *Art on my mind: Visual politics*. New York: New Press.

Kozol, J. (2007). *Letters to a young teacher*. New York: Broadway.

Krashen, S. D. (1981). Bilingual education and second language acquisition theory. In Office of Bilingual Bicultural Education, Department of Education, California (Ed.), *Schooling and language minority students: A theoretical framework* (pp. 51–79). Los Angeles: National Dissemination and Assessment Center, California State University.

—— (1985). Input and second language acquisition theory. In S. Gass and C. Madden (Eds), *Input in second language acquisition* (pp. 377–93). Rowley, MA: Newbury House.

Long, M. (1980). *Input, interaction, and second language acquisition*. Ph.D. dissertation, University of California, Los Angeles.

Lucas, T. and Ginberg, J. (2008). Responding to the linguistic reality of mainstream classrooms: Preparing all teachers to teach English language learners. In M. Cochran-Smith, S. Feiman-Nesmer, D. J. McIntyre and K. E. Demers (Eds), *Handbook of research on teacher education: Enduring questions in changing contexts* (pp. 606–36). New York: Routledge.

Olsen, L. (2008). *Made in America: Immigrant students in our public schools*. New York: New Press.

One America. (2010). *Root causes of migration—Fact sheet*. One America: With Justice for All. Retrieved July 19, 2012 from http://www.weareoneamerica.org/root-causes-migration-fact-sheet.

Pacheco, M. (2012). Learning in/through everyday resistance: A cultural–historical perspective on community resources and curriculum. *Educational Researcher*, 41(4), 121–32.

Rampton, B. (1999). Dichotomies, difference, and ritual in second language learning and teaching. *Applied Linguistics*, 20(3), 316–40.

Selinker, L. (1972). Interlanguage. *International Review of Applied Linguistics*, 10, 209–31.

Sharwood Smith, M. (1994). *Second language learning: Theoretical foundations*. London: Longman.

Suárez-Orozco, C. and Suárez-Orozco, M. (2002). *Children of immigration*. Cambridge, MA: Harvard University Press.

Swain, M. (1993). The output hypothesis: Just speaking and writing aren't enough. *Canadian Modern Language Review*, 50(1), 158–64.

—— (1995) Three functions of output in second language learning. In G. Cook and B. Seidlhofer (Eds), *Principle and practice in applied linguistics: Studies in honour of H. G. Widdowson* (pp. 125–44). Oxford: Oxford University Press.

Verdugo, R. R. and Flores, B. (2007). English-language learners: Key issues. *Education and Urban Society*, 39(2), 167–93.

Wolff, J. (1993). *The social production of art*, 2nd edition. New York: NYU Press.

2

KNOWING YOUR STUDENTS

Becoming a Culturally and Linguistically Responsive Teacher

Introduction

Children and youth in today's pre K-12 schools and classroom are increasingly likely to be from cultural and linguistic backgrounds that differ in meaningful ways from your background as a teacher. Whether you teach in a school where a majority of the children and youth are emergent bilinguals, English learners who speak a particular variety of language (e.g. Arabic, Chinese, Spanish, Pakistani, Russian, Urdu, Vietnamese, Zapotec) or speak particular varieties of English (African American Vernacular English, regional dialects of English, non-standard dialects of English), the chances are high that you are someone who teaches and communicates regularly in standard varieties of English.[1] Moreover, because you were probably educated as a teacher in a university setting, you bring to your classroom a particular set of ideas about how children learn, what children need to know, how children should behave, and most importantly, which cultural practices are indispensable for success in school, regardless of children's ethnicity, social class, and language backgrounds (Sleeter, 2001). These ideas have been informed by your own memories of being a child in schools, your family background, your teacher education program and student teaching experiences.

What might surprise you as a teacher, however, is that most people are unaware of how our ideas about children and youth and their language abilities impact our interactions with them, whether our students' cultural practices and experiences are different from or similar to our own. In this chapter, we identify aspects of our world views (Spradley and McCurdy, 2008) that inform pedagogical decision-making, which we call *cultural and linguistic ways of teaching*. Our language interactions with people and our interpretations of these interactions are culturally constructed, in the sense that they are produced through socially negotiated interactions within communities of practice that share rules, values and beliefs, and resources. Most often our language-based cultural practices go unnoticed and critically unchallenged by us, but they are not fixed behaviors and ideologies. With reflection and analysis, our cultural and linguistic ways of teaching can become dynamically responsive to the diverse students in our classrooms.

To give you an example of how invisible cultural practices can be, think about walking toward someone you know vaguely. At what point do you provide a socially appropriate acknowledgement of that person, such as a "hello" or a smile? Many of you will find that at a distance of about six feet, you will likely greet the person if you are going to make contact. If you don't wish to acknowledge the person, what do you do? Do you keep your eyes down? Most likely, no one taught you explicitly how to greet people; you learned these cultural practices by being part of a community that uses them for social interaction on a daily basis. If you were taught how to greet people, your instructions or guidance might have differed based on the teacher (a caregiver, teacher, sibling, or peer). So even the most basic language practices do not have an assumed norm, but develop through repeated practice in local social and cultural contexts (Pennycook, 2010).

In classrooms, how you interact with children and youth and what you "know" about them is a function of how you have been socialized to understand and interact with children and youth in your cultural and educational upbringing. For example, it is not uncommon in schooling to assume that "normal" children enter school with 5,000 words, experiences with books, and knowing the English language alphabet with parents invested in education. Yet, adults making educational decisions sometimes perceive emergent bilingual children as having "no language at all," with parents who don't care about education or literacy at home (MacSwan, 2005). These language and cultural assumptions go unchallenged because they are part of what we have been taught to believe about bilingualism[2] and minoritized bilingual families. Some teachers accept uncritically the idea that emergent bilingual children need to "perfect" their English before they can have school time allocated toward "extras" like art, music, and science. Artists and arts educators, however, know that all students should participate in the arts because creativity is intertwined with language and culture, critical thinking, and holistic growth and development (Chappell and Cahnmann-Taylor, 2013). Emergent bilingual youth bring to school a historically accumulated wealth of community cultural knowledge that the arts allow them to express through multiple modalities and literacies. These funds of knowledge (Moll et al., 1992; Vélez-Ibáñez and Greenberg, 1992), or cultural-based ways of transacting and expressing knowledge, are the source of the arts-based practices we share in this book.

As you read, we want you to suspend any deficit-based notions you may have heard and understood about emergent bilingual youth and their families, particularly regarding what they are capable of learning, doing, and expressing while they are learning English. Deficit thinking refers to the ways society frames bilingual, minoritized youth in terms of what they don't have, what they don't do, what they lack. Examples of this thinking include, *"A student just arrived from México and speaks no English," "My students get no support from home," "They come to me with nothing," or "We could accomplish so much if there wasn't a language barrier."* We want you to assume children come to school with deep cultural knowledge about how to interact, express ideas, and transact knowledge. We ask you to learn about your students and their language and cultural funds of knowledge through the arts, using an approach called *culturally and linguistically responsive teaching* (Gay, 2000; Lucas, 2011). Our approach to culturally and linguistically responsive teaching through the arts asks you to do two important things:

1. Acknowledge and incorporate your students' prior knowledge, language abilities, social experiences, and performance styles in your arts-based curriculum; and
2. Help students pose critical questions about what they learn, experience, and do in school and in their lives, with an understanding that artistic expressions are culturally constructed and politically positioned.

Consider the following poem by Melisa Cahnmann-Taylor, who writes about the relationship between her students' experiences in Pinewood Trailer Park and her reflexivity as an artist and teacher of poetry.

ARTS ARTIFACT THREE

Pinewood Estates Trailer Park

Melisa Cahnmann-Taylor, University of Georgia

> *Adriana*
> *Leo*
> *Yellow Shirt*
> *Dinosaur Boy*
> We meet after school
> in the library trailer
> and talk about gum
> stuck to a shoe, fuzzy
> baby chicks, the movie
> screens in our mind
> when I play *Billie Jean*
> or *Miss Thang*, to write
> without scratch-outs or look
> backs or do overs or I can'ts
> but from shivers and loves
> like Yellow Shirt who comes

late, and leaves
to show his mother
his poem.

Angel
Orlando
Mariela
Martín
Angel messed up. Yessica
didn't want to share. Dinosaur Boy
wrote about Tyrannosaurus
Rex. Martín wrote every word
that went with baby brother:
stroller, baby carrier, fever, crib.

Yéssica
Wilfredo
Ana
Gabriel
We read a poem
about what Moms do
and Dads do and they write
how some Dads speed
and get sent back
to México, some do cocaine
and *I knew a boy once*
who had white stuff coming out
his nose and mouth and he died.
Grass, some smoke that
and a seven year old raises
an invisible joint to lips. *Not*
my dad, says Yéssica,
but some Dads
do.

Marta
Alejandro
Sandra
Guillermo
They keep making lists
like gasoline on Dad's hands
or the sight of his big
muscles digging a shovel

into face-dirt, a Dad
reading dinosaurs with his son.
Leo has glasses. He doesn't
stop writing. He wins
candy for coming. He leaves
behind his poem

What parts of this poem make you uncomfortable? What parts make you hopeful? Why? How does this poem help you think about deficit-based thinking and the funds of knowledge of culturally and linguistically diverse students?

We ask that you engage in culturally and linguistically responsive teaching through the arts as a window into what students know, what is important in their lives (their funds of knowledge; González et al., 2005), and how they express themselves as members of a complex, culturally diverse society. As an educator, the arts help you move from cultural and linguistic ways of teaching (a culture of teaching that is relatively unexamined) to culturally and linguistically responsive teaching—an approach to teaching that honors knowing about students' languages, cultural practices and knowledge, that encourages students to express their voices, experiences and styles, and that facilitates students' own empowerment through critical, creative expressions. Arts-based experiences from this perspective encourage reflection (*why does this matter to me?*), critical thinking (*whose perspectives are told and who benefits from the messages in artworks?*), and action (*how can artistic processes change the status quo?*), taking seriously the points of view and cultural and linguistic experiences of children and youth who have been systematically left out of the curriculum.

Consider your own experiences as a child in school. Can you identify a moment when you felt left out, ignored or invisible? Who did not see you? What stories did you not tell because your friend, teacher or family member did not provide the space, or seek connection with you, to understand your experiences? How might the arts have helped you to express your own narratives that ran counter to the dominant one told in those moments in school? How might the support of a peer or adult, encouraging your artistic expression in whatever form without judgment of its "greatness," have helped you in those moments? Understanding your past—as a child and young adult—will help you build stronger connections with your students. Through a reflexive teaching practice, you can develop a foundation for using the arts to help you know about your students' cultural practices and knowledge, especially if they speak a language variety that you don't use or understand.

The stories in this book show how educators and artists facilitate arts-based work with emergent bilingual youth. As you read, consider how you might incorporate such processes into your classroom as a way to learn more about your students, and to help your students develop agency to critique and expand their understandings of what they are learning in school. Clearly, if you teach in a self-contained classroom with thirty children, you are in a much better position to learn about your students' cultural knowledge, language abilities, social experiences, and performance styles (the way they express themselves through the arts, orally, aesthetically, and physically) than if you are a secondary teacher who works with upwards of 150 students a day. If you teach five classes of thirty different students each day, getting to know each and every one of your students is daunting, but not impossible, especially if utilizing the arts and arts-based experiences become an integral part of your classroom community.

Throughout this book, you will encounter multiple examples of teachers and teacher educators who tap into their students' cultural knowledge, experiences, and performance styles through an array of arts-based experiences. Each of these experiences is a result of getting to know who students are and what they bring culturally from their homes and communities to school. In addition, these arts-based examples illustrate ways to use the arts critically, posing questions about social inequities and about whose language and cultural identities count in school and society. The previous poem and the vignette that follows seek to understand the human experiences of their students, to help them develop the agency to express what their lives are like living in poverty, living in the shadows. In the following vignette, Dafney Blanca Dabach uses photography with undocumented immigrant youth, and the camera becomes a tool for students to document the "legality" of their lives, using tones and lights, and the metaphor of shadows to portray who they are.

VIGNETTE TWO

Documenting Dreams: Immigrant Girls' Aspirations through Shadow Portraiture

Dafney Blanca Dabach, University of Washington

> The first time Maricela, Beatriz, and Yanira Ochoa[3] came to the United States, the three sisters were happily surprised by gifts of candy from strangers. It was Halloween and the girls (then ages six, nine, and ten) had just arrived from México. They later recounted that they did not know how to say "trick or treat" in English. Quickly socialized into this tradition, they spent their first evening in the U.S. walking home with bags of candy, ecstatic at the generosity of strangers in a new land. Seven years later, as adolescents on the cusp of adulthood, the sisters encountered a different experience. "There's a lot of racism and bad treatment," says Beatriz. "A lot of people think that we want to take away their jobs." Beatriz continues: At school "others call us 'illegal' and they tease us, saying that they will throw us to the *migra* [Immigration and Customs Enforcement[4]]."

Beatriz, Maricela, and Yanira are part of a larger community of youth in the U.S. and around the world who are undocumented minors—youth who live within a society where they do not have residency or citizenship rights. As undocumented youth, they face unique challenges as a result of their legal status. In addition to the threat of deportation and separation from U.S. family members, they are also faced with an impending limitation once they finish secondary school. According to current U.S. law (as per the Supreme Court Decision *Plyler v. Doe*) all youth, regardless of documentation status, have a right to attend K-12 public schools. However, once undocumented youth complete high school, they may not have authorization to work legally, subjecting them to more limited positions.

As a researcher observing the Ochoa sisters' transition over six years, I wondered: how do the girls imagine their futures given the obstacles they face? Also, in a climate of vitriolic rhetoric and inflammatory imagery surrounding immigration (Chávez, 2001, 2008), how might the Ochoa sisters define their *own* representations of their future aspirations?

"Documenting the Undocumented" Project

The goal of the "Documenting the Undocumented" project was to creatively humanize, voice, and engage with the experiences of youth who despite poor treatment and a lack of legal options make the U.S. their home (Abrego and Gonzáles, 2010; Gonzáles, 2010; Suárez-Orozco and Suárez-Orozco, 2001). To that end, Maricela, Beatriz, Yanira, and I embarked on a project that was part photographic essay and part symbolic portraiture, in order to capture their experiences and aspirations. In addition to our art-making, interviews formed a vital part of the project; each participant articulated her histories, current experiences, and future hopes.

I had first met the girls in 1998 when they became participants in a longitudinal research study about the adaptation of recently arrived immigrant youth (see Suárez-Orozco et al., 2010). Over the years, even when the research project had finished, we still remained close. In 2004 we collaborated on this new project as a response to the waves of anti-immigrant sentiment that were already palpable well before the May Day strike for immigrant rights in 2006. The sisters were ages thirteen, fifteen, and seventeen at the time of their participation.

As a researcher, educator, artist, and child of immigrants myself, I brought particular perspectives to the work. As a researcher, I had questions about how the sisters saw themselves and their future options, especially given the distinct social forces within their transitioning worlds. As an artist and educator, I brought with me the idea that all people deserve a space for expression, and that sometimes artistic forms of expression can be transformative, by creating opportunities to imagine or articulate something previously internal using a form, and then with the externalization of a form, potentially engage in dialogue with others that counter silences. As the child of immigrants in a time of rising anti-immigrant sentiment, I also felt compelled to engage with others in a way that provided a new generation of immigrants a space to envision, express, and voice their own perspectives and counter-narratives.

The Art: Shadow Portraits

I asked Maricela, Beatriz, and Yanira to create symbolic portraits of their future selves through the medium of shadow. They used light, shadow, and a concrete sidewalk canvas, and I used black and white film and a photographer's lens to document their art. The choice of using shadows as a medium may seem ironic or paradoxical. With so many undocumented people living "in the shadows" (Chávez, 1992), why use *this* medium? The art of creating shadows is probably as ancient as storytelling around a fire. Different cultural examples of the use of shadow art abound: Java, South India, China, France. As an art form it is fairly accessible; all that is really needed for shadow art is an idea, a source of light, an object to block light, and a surface as a backdrop. Although potentially simple, shadow art still allows for fundamental arts-learning opportunities such as envisioning and expressing (Hetland et al., 2007). It also employs the elements of design seen in other silhouette-like art: the use of line, form, and shape.

In addition to these reasons, it serves a dual function in relationship to undocumented people. On the one hand it allows for portraiture that conceals identities. On the other hand, it is also a play on image and meaning—shadows have lives too. They are animated and expressive. They tell stories. If there is a way to take back and re-purpose words that were formerly derogatory and hurtful, why not take back the shadows too? Through shadows, the sisters carefully constructed symbols of their desired futures in ways that were unlike the playful burst of shadow hand-puppetry that sometimes accompanies a teacher's classroom projector beam. With deep thought, the sisters contemplated how to translate their ideas into shapes that could be represented in two dimensions, made with available materials, and that would convey meaning tied to self-representation.

Maricela created an eerie symbol of her dream to become an FBI agent: an eye, symbolizing the organization's surveillance. Meanwhile, the swell depicted near Yanira's abdomen revealed her desire to become a mother. Beatriz decided to represent two distinct careers that vied for her attention: hip-hop dancer and U.S. Army soldier; first she struck a hip-hop pose in the shape of the letter "B" for her first initial, and then her body transformed to attention with the traditional army salute. Interestingly, both of Beatriz's careers had

FIGURE 2.1 *Eye of Surveillance*, photo by Dafney Blanca Dabach

FIGURE 2.2 *Hip-Hop Dancer*, photo by Dafney Blanca Dabach

FIGURE 2.3 *Army Soldier*, photo by Dafney Blanca Dabach

ties to her school context. At school they offered hip-hop classes she enjoyed a great deal, and U.S. Army personnel would come to visit: "Right now, at school, they are giving a lot of information about the Army and the Navy. There are soldiers that come to school to talk about their experiences, and give flyers and stickers."

Their aspirations reveal a story of cultures in flux: FBI special agent, mother, hip-hop dancer, and a U.S. Army soldier. What might their portraits have looked like had they remained in México? How will their lived futures compare with their carefully constructed symbols?

Considerations of Future Applications

In thinking about how this work might translate into other settings, I offer a few observations and questions. First, the nature of my relationship with the sisters and their family over many years meant that we could honestly discuss the issues raised in this project. One question that emerges is: What types of relationships exist between potential participants of arts-based learning? On a cautionary note, for some undocumented youth the topic of their aspirations may be too sensitive. And, for family involved, having a camera around may be daunting because of issues of risk associated with the potential for identification. The nature of our relationship changed these dynamics: members of my family had been undocumented, and the Ochoa family knew that.

Another set of considerations surround the art-making process itself. Shadow portraiture is technically accessible, low-cost, and yet still allows ample opportunities for deep thinking. It also offers a sense of protection—under the cover of darkness, a way to still tell a story. At the same time, there may be other forms of portraiture, for example developing iconic images of future selves using other media such as paper (*papel picado*, silhouette cut-outs, etc.). An additional set of questions also emerges after the completion of the art-making: What now? Is the purpose to publicize the art for greater awareness of undocumented youths' perspectives? If so, what venues to select? How does one ethically maximize the impacts of such a project? Also, how might the photographs themselves benefit the artists, aside from the benefits that emerge in the process of art-making? Perhaps fine photographic prints can be made to sell in order to raise money for youth who currently may not access funding for higher education. In our case, we displayed prints at a local gallery, and images were made available in other publications (Dabach, 2006).

Conclusion

Many undocumented youth struggle when it comes to broaching the issue of what their future holds because of the acute barriers of their legal status. Additionally, depending upon their geographic and neighborhood contexts, they may face additional challenges. Instead of resigning to a life in the shadows, we engaged with shadows to create a different vision, tapping into the imagination of future selves. However, unless we as a society collectively address the limits and structures imposed on undocumented youth, not only will they suffer, but we will too, missing out on all that they might contribute.

★   ★   ★

The poem and storied vignette in this chapter speak to the forms and functions that the arts offer to culturally and linguistically responsive education with emergent bilingual youth. Such rationales point to humanizing, integrated purposes for arts education in schools that examine the very heart of learning: Why do people create, question, desire, interact, and make meaning in the world?

In their review of the research on arts education with and about minoritized communities, Chappell and Cahnmann-Taylor (2013) highlight such rationales to support your work as an arts-based teacher:

- The arts engage imagination and agency (Davis, 2008; Greene, 2000).
- The arts focus on emotion through expression and empathy.

- The arts emphasize ambiguity through interpretation and respect for multiple points of view.
- The arts engage complementary thinking practices, also called "studio habits of mind" (Hetland et al., 2005): developing craft, engaging and persisting, envisioning, stretching and exploring, and understanding art worlds.
- The arts are a form of inquiry and reflection, also called "qualitative problem solving" (Ecker, 1963): sense-making, building patterns, developing insights and raising questions, judging the work, and discerning its wider impact.
- The arts engage, respond to and critique social, cultural and political problems.

Arts-based teaching strongly complements culturally and linguistically responsive teaching, as they both emphasize inquiry and expression founded in the inter-actions of self, community and world. The arts are cultural, and language and culture are expressed through the arts. Culturally and linguistically responsive, arts-based teaching recognizes that students bring to school a set of socially con-structed ideas, beliefs, and practices (the ways they talk and interact; the language[s] they choose for expressing their friendships, emotions, understandings; their prefer-ences in dress; their localized identities). Moreover, emergent bilingual students, like all students, use their languages and cultural experiences as a lens for guiding their behaviors, values, and understandings of social and academic experiences. In this way, culturally and linguistically responsive teaching through the arts does not define bilingual students on the basis of their broad cultural and language group membership, in which students necessarily hold a set of ideas, beliefs and practices simply because they belong to a particular ethnic or language group. Rather, culturally and linguistically responsive teaching works best when you learn from students' local knowledge and experiences, and use what you learn from them as resources in your curriculum (Gay, 2000; Pennycook, 2010).

Learning from your students and becoming culturally and linguistically responsive to their local knowledge, experiences, and performance styles comes from:

- talking with students about their interests in and out of school, who their friends are, and what they like and don't like about school;
- building from what students know about topics that interest them, guiding them in how to ask critical questions about what they know and want to learn about the topic;
- offering students a range of ways to listen to adults and their peers through creative expression, ranging from photography, sculpture, visual arts, and vocalizations, to acting, musical compositions/rhythms, creative writing, and poetry;
- taking observation walks, where students are invited to observe, discuss, and interpret, moving from form (color combinations, design features, familiar

and unfamiliar shapes, lines, and perspectives) to content (social interactions, values and beliefs, ethical questions) in what they see in their surroundings;
- encouraging students to see the arts in everything they do, from how they talk, walk, arrange their school work, dress, sing, dance, and wear their hair, to how they express their personal emotions, desires, hopes and dreams.

In the next chapter, we extend the goals of culturally and linguistic responsive teaching beyond the classroom, and into building school–family–community partnerships through the arts.

Questions to Consider

1. Think about your own childhood. What experiences in your childhood best prepared you for school? How similar or different are your childhood experiences from those in the poem and vignette in this chapter?

2. What are the cultural and linguistic identities of your own students? What assumptions have you made about them, their families and communities? Which of their languages do you speak? When you hear your students speak a language you don't understand, how do you respond?

3. What goals can you set that will help you to learn more about the lives of your students, and incorporating their funds of knowledge into the classroom?

Notes

1. All of us in teaching use our localized varieties of spoken, standard English, and depending on the level of formality and purpose, also blend in informal and non-standard varieties, age-appropriate slang, and specialized vocabulary. Children and youth do the same thing. Oral language in the classroom is always a mixture of many different varieties of language. As we move from oral to written language, we tend to use more standardized forms, and insist that students do likewise. But talk around the written standard is also varied.
2. Some people believe unknowingly that bilingualism means having two languages, with each language being judged by a monolingual norm of what is correct and appropriate for certain age groups. Some children come to school and are found to have "low proficiency" according to language assessment tools that are based on those monolingual norms, rather than bilingual norms. These students are erroneously labeled "semilingual" (MacSwan, 2000). This label, based on misinformation about emergent bilingualism, positions students as having deficits in language, and leads to watered-down instruction that focuses on learning grammatical structures and isolated vocabulary.
3. Names used are pseudonyms.
4. ICE was formerly the Immigration and Naturalization Service (INS).

References

Abrego, L. J. and Gonzáles, R. G. (2010). Blocked paths, uncertain futures: The postsecondary education and labor market prospects of undocumented youth. *Journal of Education for Students Placed at Risk*, 15(1), 144–57.

Chappell, S. and Cahnmann-Taylor, M. (Forthcoming 2013). No child left with crayons: The imperative of arts-based education and research with language "minority" and other minoritized communities. *Review of Research in Education*, 37.

Chávez, L. (1992) *Shadowed lives: Undocumented immigrants in American society*. New York: Harcourt, Brace, Jovanovich.

—— (2001). *Covering immigration: Popular images and the politics of the nation*. Berkeley, CA: University of California Press.

—— (2008). *The Latino threat: Constructing immigrants, citizens, and the nation*. Stanford, CA: Stanford University Press.

Dabach, D. B. (2006). Documenting the undocumented. *Five Fingers Review: Intersecting Lines*, 24, 212–16.

Davis, J. H. (2008). *Why our schools need the arts*. New York: Teachers College Press.

Ecker, D. W. (1963). The artistic process of qualitative problem solving. *Journal of Aesthetics and Art Criticism*, 21, 283–90.

Gay, G. (2000). *Culturally responsive teaching: Theory, research, and practice*. New York: Teachers College Press.

Gonzáles, R. G. (2010). "On the wrong side of the tracks: The consequences of school stratification systems for unauthorized Mexican students." *Peabody Journal of Education*, 85(4), 469–85.

González, N., Moll, L., and Amanti, C. (Eds) (2005). *Funds of knowledge: Theorizing practices in households, communities and classrooms*. Mahwah, NJ: Lawrence Erlbaum Associates.

Greene, M. (2000). *Releasing the imagination: Essays on education, the arts and social change*. San Francisco: Jossey Bass.

Hetland, L., Veenema, S., Palmer, P., Sheridan, K., and Winner, E. (2005). *Studio thinking: How visual arts teaching can promote disciplined habits of mind*. Cambridge, MA: Harvard University Graduate School of Education.

Hetland, L., Winner, E., Veenema, S., and Sheridan, K. (2007). *Studio thinking: The real benefits of visual art education*. New York: Teachers College Press.

Lucas, T. (Ed.) (2011). *Teacher preparation for linguistically diverse classrooms: A resource for teacher educators*. New York: Taylor & Francis.

MacSwan, J. (2000). The threshold hypothesis, semilingualism, and other contributions to a deficit view of linguistic minorities. *Hispanic Journal of Behavioral Sciences*, 22(1), 3–45.

—— (2005). The "non-non" crisis and academic bias in native language assessment of linguistic minorities. In J. Cohen, K. T. McAlister, K. Rolstad and J. MacSwan (Eds), *Proceedings of the International Symposium on Bilingualism* (pp. 1415–22). Somerville, MA: Cascadilla Press.

Moll, L., Amanti, C., Neff, D., and González, N. (1992). Funds of knowledge for teaching: Using a qualitative approach to connect homes and classrooms. *Theory Into Practice*, 31(2), 132–41.

Pennycook, A. (2010). *Language as local practice*. New York: Routledge.

Sleeter, C. (2001). *Culture, difference, and power*. New York: Teachers College Press.

Spradley, J. and McCurdy, D. (2008). *Conformity and conflict: Readings in cultural anthropology*, 13th edition. Boston, MA: Allyn & Bacon.

Suárez-Orozco, C. and Suárez-Orozco, M. (2001). *Children of immigration*. Cambridge, MA: Harvard University Press.

Suárez-Orozco, C., Suárez-Orozco, M., and Todorova, I. (2010). *Learning a new land: Immigrant students in American society*. Cambridge, MA: Harvard University Press.

Veléz-Ibáñez, C. and Greenberg, J. (1992). Formation and transformation of funds of knowledge among U.S. Mexican households. *Anthropology and Education Quarterly*, 23(4), 313–35.

3
BUILDING FAMILY–COMMUNITY–SCHOOL PARTNERSHIPS

In Chapter 2, we discussed the importance of becoming a culturally and linguistically responsive educator who facilitates critical, creative pedagogy with emergent bilingual youth. In this chapter we explore family–community–school partnerships as a vital dynamic in culturally and linguistically responsive teaching. Throughout the chapter, we explore ways that artists and teachers have engaged in asset-based, arts-based approaches to collaborating with bilingual families and communities in all their local diversity toward academic knowledge and skill development, as well as community-centered education.

In your journey as an artist/educator, you will often collaborate with bilingual families and communities, or you may seek out such collaborations as part of broader school–community initiatives. Yet, the school system often seeks family involvement[1] in classrooms, afterschool interventions, and community centers in a limited fashion: so children will become more "academically successful" or "get off the street," for example. Administrators and grant funders will likely be interested in increased test scores or statistics about decreased dropout, drug use, and teen pregnancy rates. Your work as an arts educator is often aimed at helping these decision-making bodies "target" the problems they have identified in their student population. These problems frame minoritized families in terms of what they "lack" and what schools and community centers should "fix" in those communities. One such intervention program focused on minoritized communities is the federal 21st Century Community Learning Centers (CCLC) program grant, which includes both academic and enrichment programming. Yet, the rationale for granting federal funding to minoritized communities is increasing student achievement via improved test scores rather than equitable distribution of resources and localized community decision-making. Chappell (2006) discusses the limitations of such an "at-risk" frame when developing, implementing, and evaluating programs. In particular, such a frame diminishes creative and critical thinking about the role of schools in communities and communities in schools.

By contrast, this book focuses on family–school–community partnerships from an asset-based, responsive community perspective. Such a perspective responds to the ways schools marginalize bilingual families from participation via practices and policies about homework, curriculum and instruction, language of instruction, definitions of family involvement, as well as school site committee governance. We want to encourage full family collaboration in sustainable educational reform, a perspective that requires us to acknowledge how schools actively (yet perhaps unknowingly) participate in social inequities that impact bilingual, minoritized families.

We can analyze the purposes, modes and effects of community partnerships with bilingual families utilizing a lens of linguistic and cultural responsiveness. A series of questions can help teachers reflect during all phases of our partnership work:

- What are school-based assumptions about what young people need to be healthy and happy, to be academically successful?
- When are young people "at risk," and when are they "at promise" (Swadener and Lubeck, 1995)? Who defines these constructions?
- What do schools assume families should be and should provide for their children?
- What social and cultural capital should young people have? Where do schools believe this capital comes from?
- What are good ways for children to spend their time before and after school?
- How should families participate in and support schools?
- How should schools support families and communities?
- How do current school practices impact lower-income and/or bilingual families?

Reflection on these questions shifts the conversation from a technical one (*how do we close the "achievement gap"?*) toward a critical, sociocultural one (*what issues of power and social dominance are at work in my school?*). Framing students as "at risk" distracts from an analysis of the systems that produce inequitable access to economic resources (such as how the money flows through schools) and cultural capital (such as how schools position particular knowledge and language as valuable). Further, reforms to close the "achievement gap" rarely encourage teacher/administrator reflection about school participation in the structural inequities that affect emergent bilingual youth.

As you develop partnerships, we ask you to think expansively about the relationship between the racialization of people, the economic/social classes in

ARTS ARTIFACT FOUR

La Noche

Louisa Castrodale and Luis Fausto, Palm Springs High School, California

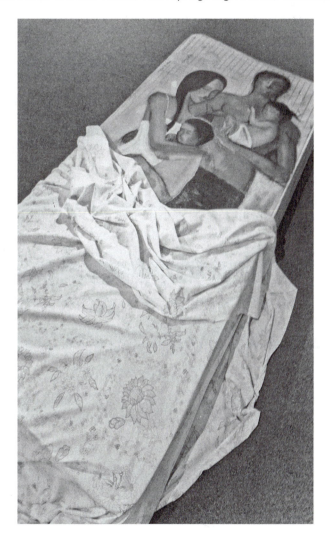

FIGURE 3.1 *La Noche* by Louisa Castrodale and Luis Fausto.
What is the significance of this artwork being painted on a mattress?
How do the family's experiences inform their funds of knowledge?
What resources might the children painted on this mattress bring
to the classroom?

which they live, and being placed "at risk" in schools. We believe that there is a strong interrelationship between the two categories (being viewed as at risk and labeled as ELL), between the two experiences (what it feels like/looks like to be "at risk" and an "ELL" at school), and in the relationships built between schools and families. The power of family–community–school partnerships is their potential to reconceptualize the norms of success for young people, a good education, and productive relationships across cultural and language practices (Apple, 2004). Typically, these norms depend on cultural capital (the knowledge and resources used by schools) that marginalizes the funds of knowledge of the families of students who are labeled and treated as at risk and categorized by their English language proficiency, income levels, or citizenship status. We propose that partnerships shift from fixing the individual "failures" and deficits of families and students to collaborating with families in the celebration of local language and cultural practices, identification of structural inequities that families and schools can address in partnership, and promotion of community-based visions for schools through the arts (Jasis and Ordoñez-Jasis, 2004).

Most partnerships address two broad goals: academic development and/or youth development in and out of school. As you plan collaborations with academic development goals, you will likely hear school-based concerns about raising test scores, meeting state standards in core subject areas, or teaching families how to help their kids learn the skills used in the classroom. These concerns could sidetrack any well-intentioned critical artist/educator (Picower, 2011) who wants to be culturally and linguistically responsive. Yet, you *can* use the language of schools (e.g. developing academic skills) toward asset-based collaborative purposes, as we will show in the chapter. Fortunately, state and common core standards have been broadly conceived to enable local decision-making about curriculum and pedagogy. In this way, you too can interpret standards and engage content-based ways of doing school in critical, creative ways.

For example, you can use community mapping and family interviews to learn about family funds of knowledge and then utilize those resources, knowledge and talents in the curriculum. You can use inquiry models to situate students as investigators into the conditions of their own world. As critical, creative educators, you can re-envision homework and family nights as opportunities for collaborative inquiry, focusing not only on school-based ways of learning and knowing but also on ways in which young people and their families can take on a teaching role. In the vignette that follows, the emergent bilingual students in Shannon Burgert's third grade class develop confidence and leadership as they publicly present their learning about science through different arts processes.

A Matter Party: Celebrating Science and Deepening Understanding

Shannon Burgert, University of Denver

Project Description

Approximately 480 students, kindergarten through fifth grade, attend Fireside Elementary School in Louisville, Colorado. Fireside is a magnet school for English language learners, and altogether our students speak more than seventeen languages. Fireside also has a free-and-reduced lunch population of a little over 20 percent.

Each fall in my third grade classroom we hold a Matter Party to celebrate and share what we've learned about matter and energy. At the party, students present a project that they've prepared to extend their learning outside the classroom and to demonstrate something they learned in our unit (there's always someone interested in antimatter or non-newtonion fluids).

I explain to students that they can choose how they want to present what they learned. I give them examples of past projects and possibilities, encouraging the arts but also welcoming more traditional forms of presentation. Examples include an ice sculpture with an explanation of what happens to the molecules as they change states; a song about all the things around us that are made up of matter; a newspaper article describing a new form of matter; an advice column from a solid to a gas; demonstrations of various properties of matter, such as gas taking up space; a poem about where all energy comes from; and a short scene about where energy is stored. Students must turn in project proposals, and they may work solo or in pairs. I provide resources and support for students to work on the project at home. Parents and siblings are invited to the party.

Students choose the medium to represent their science learning. What is appropriate depends on their experience and the level of risk that they want to take. Giving students choice leads to their enjoyment and engagement while they work on their projects. Such a choice is helpful to second language students because some mediums, such as painting or sculpture, rely less on oral and written English to illustrate understanding. At the same time, students build language and content knowledge as they work on their projects, working side by side as bilingual learners and native English speakers. Elliot Eisner (2002) writes:

> Meaning is not limited to what words can express . . . The arts provide a spectrum of such forms—we call them visual arts, music, dance, theatre —through which meanings are made, revised, shared, and discovered.

> These forms enable us to construct meanings that are nonredundant; each
> form of representation we employ confers its own features upon the
> meanings we make or interpret.
>
> (p. 230)

Students learn from the various forms of representation their peers use—they
gain further depth through words, images, and actions.

Through this project, students use what Uhrmacher (2009) calls the aesthetic
dimensions of learning: risk-taking (by presenting to the class and trying new
forms of representation), making connections (finding relevance to their own
lives), imagination (they are creating rather than singing lines or coloring in
the lines created by someone else), sensory experiences (tasty treats and gooey
forms of matter all enhance the experience), active engagement (students
choose, create, and present a diversity of projects), and perceptivity (the more
they see, the more they know—as my students prepare their projects, they
spend lots of time with their topics, building deep understanding). Uhrmacher
suggests that these dimensions of learning contribute to memory retention,
knowledge, creativity, active engagement, and relevance between school
learning and students' lives.

FIGURE 3.2 *Angel Presents a Comic about Matter that He Worked on at Home with His Family*, photo by Shannon Burgert

FIGURE 3.3 *Atharv Uses a Labeled Diagram to Explain the Water Cycle,* photo by Shannon Burgert

Story

We have pushed desks to the perimeter of our classroom, and third grade students sit on the floor while parents sit in chairs at the back and sides of the room. Everyone is quiet. I welcome the guests to our Matter Party and introduce the first presenters: "We now have Dr Diaz and Dr Mendoza to present their findings on different examples of energy." Two students giggle and don white lab coats.

"Drs" Diaz and Mendoza, who speak Spanish as their primary language, use a poster with cut-out magazine pictures to show forms of energy. They take turns describing their poster, which has labels to support their oral presentation. "We get energy from eating," Dr Diaz says as she points to pictures of the digestive system and various foods. "Doing sports is energy," says Dr Mendoza, pointing to half a dozen pictures of people exercising. Dr Diaz points to pictures of trees. "Trees and wind have energy too," she says, finishing their presentation. Kids and parents clap, and our matter "experts" grin.

For the next presentation, two native English speakers, "Drs" Webb and Byers, excitedly get into their lab coats. Received with many oohs and ahhs, the students demonstrate what happens to dry ice when they pour water over it, and they follow it up with a rap:

> Introducing Drip-drop-hip-hop! It's all about water.
> Water, water, **drip drop**, ice . . . **brrrrrr**.
> Let's go gas.

Water is everywhere around the globe,
down in the ocean and up above.

There are three main states that water has,
solid . . . liquid . . . and gas!

Ice is the solid because it is frozen
when it melts a liquid appears

All it takes is a whole lot of heat
for a gas to form and disappear

Water, water across the nation
evaporation
condensation

water in the sky is called
precipitation

you don't drink enough you'll get
dehydration

water water, word
H2O Yo!

The third presentation is by "Dr" Nelacanti, a native Hindi speaker, who suits up in the white lab coat and reads us a letter she's written, from Solid to her friend Liquid.

Nov. 5, 2009

Dear Liquid,

I would like to introduce you to my good friend of mine Gas.

There are some similarities between us, to list a few:

- We all take up space and have mass.
- We all are made up of atoms and molecules.

We also have differences to list a few:

- I have a fixed shape, you take the shape of the container, but Gas fills whole container.
- My atoms are very close to each other, your atoms are spread out, but the atoms in Gas are far more spread out.

Let us all meet and have fun together.

Your friend,
Solid

Then we pass around a polymer ("gak") that "Dr" Kim has made, and while students giggle at the way it oozes, she explains that it is neither a solid nor a liquid—it has properties of both.

Right before an intermission, it's time for a presentation by a new, shy English learner from El Salvador. "Dr" Guevara has made a poster with a drawing of a root beer float, labeled with the solid, liquid, and gas components of the float. I explain to the audience that I am the assistant for Dr Guevara. (This student chose to have me support him rather than work with other students, to increase his comfort in front of our audience.)

I point to the ice cream on the poster and say, "The ice cream is a . . ."

"Solid!" he says.

I point to the root beer. "The root beer is a . . ."

"Liquid!"

Finally, I point to the gas bubbles on the drawing. "The bubbles from the carbonation are . . ."

"Gas!" Dr Guevara grins as the other students clap enthusiastically.

We take a break from presentations to enjoy root beer floats, which parents have dished out in the back of the room. After intermission, "Dr" Muñoz, a native Spanish speaker, reads an illustrated letter that she's written about how we experience matter through our five senses. ("One thing you can taste is a popsicle.") Other projects include a PowerPoint presentation on changing states of matter, a volcano (with an explanation about how lava changes states), a song about where matter lives, a song and dance about different forms of energy, two comic strips, a poster presentation about water by a girl dressed as a water fairy, and a matching card game reviewing matter and energy concepts. In the final presentation, a student shares her multimedia painting of her family's favorite Maine coast. She points out the water, clouds, and rocks that illustrate different forms of matter on Earth.

We finish off our party outside, watching the higher-than-our-heads fountain reaction of Mentos dropped into a Diet Coke bottle. After kids gasp and squeal at the reaction, we head inside to follow up with a YouTube video of elaborate Coke and Mentos experiments. I note that using variables—different liquids, for instance—in the Mentos experiment is a possible science fair project. We clean up and talk about what we learned from each other during our celebration.

Then, I celebrate: my students have deepened their understanding of the scientific language and concepts we've studied, both through their own exploration as well as through exposure to the different forms of representation created by their peers. These different art forms reveal different perspectives and provide greater meaning, relevance, and depth of understanding—a sculpture might be able to help students see and feel what a solid is, for instance, while the words of a song might detail the solids a student sees in daily life or explain that solids are made up of many molecules. The students have also had an engaging, fun, celebratory experience with science. And, with such knowledge and positive associations, my bilingual students have gained greater access to science—becoming a step less science shy (Fort, 1993) and a step more empowered.

★   ★   ★

The vignette above focuses on a school partnership toward academic development in a specific subject area. The culturally responsive elements include encouraging students to make connections to personal interests, ask their own questions about the world, build affinities and relationships with other emergent bilingual youth through multiple languages, and share their knowledge with their families through a community gathering.

In partnership work with bilingual families, we can build positive cross-cultural participation, reciprocal knowledge, shared status and value across partners, common goals, and institutional support (Cox-Petersen, 2010). This requires us to engage with families and communities through the funds of knowledge they possess and utilize in their daily lives and work through the arts (González et al., 2005). Further, we invite you to imagine extending an asset-based, empowerment approach to the level of community-based analysis of the social, political, and economic structures *they* identify as perpetuating barriers to their full participation (Ada, 1995; Morrell and Duncan-Andrade, 2008; Noguera, 2005). In the Matter Party vignette, for example, teachers could survey families about their experiences with science and science teaching in schools, leading to family-based investigations of scientific questions they are concerned about.

Arts-based, culturally and linguistically responsive engagement requires that artists and educators use simultaneous critical and creative thinking, with an openness to dialogue and a flexible social commitment to community agency (Greene, 2000). As we work across cultural practices, it is important to move beyond tokenism and cultural tourism, such as the typical multicultural celebrations of food and ethnic dance associated with a month or holiday (Black History Month, Chinese New Year, Cinco de Mayo). Often, these school events are the only mention of the contributions, traditions, and stories of diverse groups, and—as "have-a-nice-day" celebrations—they are the "stuff of colonizing fantasies" (hooks, 1994). We call for family–community–school collaborations to provide authentic opportunities to engage deep questions of personal, local relevance throughout the school year.

For example, imagine how you might interact with families around the question of developing bilingual and bicultural identities in the United States, or attending school as a bilingual person in an English-only environment. You might discuss how schools treat the home languages of families, how pressures to "be American" have impacted home cultural identities, and how modes of public participation in cities and schools have constrained or empowered bilingual youth and community development. These difficult questions can be explored through art-making around focused themes such as identity, place, home, family, and borders. In the vignette that follows, Dorothy Abram, facilitator of the Refugee Theatre Project, shows her struggles to consider family contexts in relation to the goals of the project: using theatre to support refugee community development and individual student English language development.

VIGNETTE FOUR

The Older Sister: Beyond ELL Pronunciation to Performance and Purpose

Dorothy Abram, Johnson & Wales University

"I am BEAUTY!" said Nagwida, a fourteen-year-old refugee from the civil war in Burundi. Her spoken words were not an insistence on her survival after escaping the genocide in central Africa, or against the odds in the refugee camps of Tanzania. Nagwida simply was proclaiming her new role in our AWARE Alliance Refugee Theatre (AART) play, *Three Purple Plums: Exploring the Dimensions of Hope for Children and HIV/AIDS in Africa*. Her proclamation, however, was life-affirming for her new identity as a refugee and early language learner in Providence, Rhode Island.

Nagwida's experiences in our ELL-refugee theatre must be put in context. She would have been illiterate and uneducated in Burundi, as the daughter of an impoverished farmer in the hilly countryside of Africa. The role of children in agricultural economies is to work the land and help with the survival of the family—not to become literate or attend college. Reading and writing in a radically different language in her new cultural setting of the United States was a formidable challenge for Nagwida. It seemed to me that she had little hope her new life in the United States would surpass the goal of survival that she held through her years in the refugee camps of Tanzania.

I asked myself if I was expecting too much of Nagwida to perform in a theatrical drama with all that such a production entails: reading, memorization, interpretation, presence, and performance. Nagwida's involvement in *Purple Plums* enabled me to realize that children of all backgrounds not only respond and rise to expectations, but also feel affirmed and honored by the personal care and individual attention that such performance brings. "I am BEAUTY" was Nagwida's statement of a new-found hope and promise for herself.

Because I viewed Nagwida's blossoming with such delight, I was caught off-guard when, as our performance date approached, she told me that she could no longer attend practices or perhaps the performance. Her older sister, Revokata, the oldest daughter in the family, had enrolled in a special program that required her to live away from home. Because of Revokata's absence,

Nagwida was placed in the cultural and familial role of "oldest daughter" to care for her seven other siblings, including older and younger brothers, little sisters, and an infant—babysitting, cooking, and cleaning.

This change of role and responsibility within her family resulted in a visible change in Nagwida. In the role of Beauty, Nagwida had become the character, coordinating her clothes according to color, pattern, and texture, and grooming her hair evenly beneath an intricately twisted Burundian head-dress. Nagwida seemed to shine in Beauty's delight and pleasure in life. Now, it seemed Nagwida had to renounce her theatrical role for the reality of fulfilling the needs of a demanding household.

With this change, our group and I needed to examine our purpose of the Refugee Theatre project. If we abandoned Nagwida to the necessities of her cultural family requirements, were we also abandoning her growth and achievement? What about our responsibilities to Nagwida as a person? Theatre gave her the stage to perform beyond her abilities that the classroom couldn't match. What was I to do—for Nagwida and for our performance?

I contacted a past student who had been involved with an earlier refugee project, and, to my surprise and delight, Lizzie eagerly offered to work at home with Nagwida, tutoring her in her lines from the play, while babysitting the children. Little did we know that Lizzie, being significantly closer to Nagwida's age than I am, would become her "new older sister" and mentor, and fit a familiar cultural category of meaning for Nagwida. The bond went beyond the shared love for performance and into an enduring friendship. With this relationship, Nagwida could continue performing and fulfill her family's urgent needs.

Beauty was a luxury to be afforded even in the face of necessity. How could our play embody such possibilities? These questions go to the heart of the AWARE Alliance Refugee Theatre project. The project started as my response to the cynicism expressed by my university students about the possibility of ending genocides in the world. How could it be, I wondered, that our youth were so disillusioned about social change and global justice—especially living amidst such privilege? With such diverse populations of refugees living in Rhode Island, could I accept the students' complacency as just another generational trait? Perhaps the four walls of the classroom were insufficient in providing the awareness that my students required to engage in our global world.

AWARE enabled my students, refugee children and youth, and local participants to build a community of awareness, compassion, and creativity with our focus on human rights, in particular with refugees of genocide. In this way, our AWARE Alliance Refugee Theatre celebrates the cultural knowledge and historical experience of our local refugee and immigration populations through diverse public presentations and performances. These refugee children were invited to prepare and perform a dramatic presentation titled *Three Purple Plums: Exploring Dimensions of Hope for Children and*

HIV/AIDS in Africa for an AIDS benefit. As part of this greater community of global awareness, the refugee children were as excited to perform the stories of others as their own. These children had seen other recently arrived refugees on stage in powerful theatrical renditions of their cultures and histories that celebrated them as refugees. Together, through these diverse performances, they built a consciousness, consensus, and community of awareness and compassion.

Refugees of war, genocide, and exile—in Liberia, Burundi, Rwanda, Somalia, Haiti, Cambodia, Bhutan, Iran, and Iraq—the children were eager to participate in the staging of the dramas of others. Often dismissed as nothing more than refugees or immigrants in their everyday lives, the children transformed their identities through theatre into a source of strength and insight. They often spoke about how their personal experience of hardship and suffering related to the play's characters they represented. Finding purpose fueled their motivation to articulate their lines, deeply understand their characters, and create a spectacular performance. Moreover, by creating a community with other children of shared experiences, they now had an interconnected global network in their local community. Figures 3.4 and 3.5 capture the spirit of this community.

The evening of the performance, Nagwida was Beauty incarnate when she entered the room, preparing for her final bow. As the only young person in the group who knew—from her cultural background—how to balance a basket without motion on her head, Beauty was given a long, luxurious walk through the audience to her entrance on the stage where the others were waiting.

FIGURE 3.4 *Exclamations*, photo by Dorothy Abram.

FIGURE 3.5 *Beauty Praying*, photo by Dorothy Abram. (From left to right) Nagwida Ntibagirigwa, refugee from Burundi; Myken Milsette, immigrant from Haiti; and Jasmine Randolph, student, Johnson & Wales University in *Three Purple Plums* (a play by Dorothy Abrams about HIV/AIDS and child-headed households in Africa).

She and the other refugee children held hands together to accept their ovations. As they took their final bows, they affirmed my sense of possibility, promise, and purpose in our conflict-ridden world.

★ ★ ★

Building partnerships requires deep consideration of the contexts of family and community life in relation to the goals of the arts project. This includes learning about the ways that families already participate in artistic expressions, such as through cultural arts practices (Moriarty, 2004). In the vignette above, the teacher realized through active, ongoing reflection that her original intentions and goals for the project did not attend adequately to the needs of her students. So, Abram introduced Nagwida to another girl who had participated in performance and also understood her particular cultural, familial context. This relationship proved vital to Nagwida's ongoing participation in the theatre project, and, more importantly, to her sense of connection between the content of the theatrical performance and her life.

Educators can also learn about the variety of cultural arts practices that bilingual communities—such as immigrant and refugee families concentrated in particular regions—have established for a variety of purposes. These funds of knowledge can enrich your family–community–school partnership tremendously. Local art-making is the result of a rich network of social and cultural capital, such as the relationships and resources families utilize for regular, creative gatherings in public and private spaces. For example, in a study of immigrant communities in San Jose, California, Moriarty (2004) suggests that cultural arts practices are forms of participatory civic engagement, through which emergent bilingual youth and their families bond within their cultural communities and build bridges to other communities.

As you read this book, we would like you to reflect on the ways that your own partnerships might engage community networks, resources, and local creative practices (Chappell, 2005). We would like you to consider engaging local language and cultural experiences as well as families' multiple perspectives in the design and implementation of family–school–community partnerships. Such an approach reflects the hybridity and complexity of community cultural identities and produces rich creative exchanges, strong intergenerational relationships, and more permeable borders between school and home.

We also encourage you to utilize the language of schools (academic standards and skills) in critical, creative projects with youth and community development goals. These goals include helping young people develop identities as active, engaged cultural workers, who investigate problems of their own concern and design arts-based responses to express their findings about those issues. For example, arts educators have conducted participatory action research with youth (such as using ethnography and digital media techniques to research how schools track youth by English language proficiency and limit A–F requirement offerings for students in ESL classes; Noguera et al., 2006; Oakes et al., 2006). Other arts educators have facilitated youth production of hip-hop performances and recordings (as in the Reyes' vignette in the Epilogue; and Wang, 2010); documented refugee youth identities and intergenerational community relationships through photography (see the KEEP Photovoice Research Project); mapped the history of young people's public housing communities through oral history and multimedia book production (see Voices, Inc., 2000); and created murals and graphic novels about being migrant (see the Rodríguez-Valls' vignette in Chapter 6).

While these approaches may interest and inspire you as an educator, you might still have reservations. What if you don't come from the communities with whom you work? What if you can't speak your students' home language(s)? What if you don't have enough experience in an arts medium to help them produce anything "good"? We suggest that rather than needing to be *the* expert in a partnership, the artist/teacher becomes a co-facilitator of the process. While this role contains much uncertainty, you will become increasingly empathetic as well as develop rich relationships with community members who will help you guide the process (White and Sadanandan Nair, 1999). In this way, each member of the collaboration becomes a student and teacher of languages, cultures, and local practices (Freire, 2000).

The vignette that follows features a mutual teacher/student learning process as the partnership builds. Artist and teacher Saskia Stille explores how a family/ school gardening and video project engaged newcomer students in the question: how can we grow food sustainably utilizing community resources?

VIGNETTE FIVE

Making an Edible School Garden with Multilingual Children: Engaging Linguistic, Cultural, and Community Resources

Saskia Stille, OISE/University of Toronto

Project Description and School Context

This case describes a project involving newcomer and Canadian-born English language learners at the elementary level. Working collaboratively with the teacher and students, I assisted students in researching the curriculum topic of urban and rural communities, focusing on issues of food and sustainability. This work culminated in the production of a digital film documenting the students' creation of an edible school garden. Through work in the garden, the students ruptured and re/made their space and place of learning, inviting a performance and expansion of their identities, and increasing the ground on which they could stand and enact their identities in school.

The setting for this project was an elementary school in a large Canadian city. The school serves 2,000 students from kindergarten to grade five. Ninety-five percent of the students speak a language other than English at home, and the majority of families have arrived in Canada within the past five years. This project took place in a third grade class in which the students and/or their families had come from Afghanistan, Pakistan, Iraq, India, Kuwait, and Sri Lanka. The study was part of a larger school–university research partnership designed to engage multilingual children at the elementary level in literacy activities that draw upon the full range of their cultural and linguistic knowledge.

The positioning of students' cultural and linguistic resources plays an important role in the literacy accomplishments of students in school. As such, the project explicitly brought students' prior experience and background knowledge into classroom activities. Although instruction was in English within the classroom, students' knowledge of other languages was recognized and they were encouraged to draw upon this knowledge by using both English and their home language (L1) during activities including class discussions, reading and writing activities, and oral presentations. This use of students' L1 in the classroom scaffolded their learning in English by helping them to develop concepts and formulate ideas for their writing, resulting in stronger literacy than if students had used English alone, and sending a positive message to students about their identities (see Cummins et al., 2005).

Researching Communities

Because many of the children in the class were newcomers to Canada, we used the curriculum topic of urban and rural communities to connect with their prior experience and cultural knowledge. Students conducted research about our local community, and about communities where they or their families had lived previously. The school textbooks had little information about these communities, so we used digital media and information and communication technology tools to facilitate this work. For instance, we used Google Earth to look up places where the students were from and to document features of different kinds of urban or rural communities around the world.

The day we looked up Kabul using Google Earth was during Ahmed's[2] second week of school. Ahmed joined the class midway through the year, just after arriving in Canada from Afghanistan. Ahmed was fluent in Dari and Pashto, and had had interruptions in his previous schooling because of war in his home country. Like many new English language learners, Ahmed was often silent during class activities. On this day, I set up my computer and a laptop projector to display Google Earth on a large screen for all the students to see. Filing back into the classroom after recess, the students ran to the carpet, eager to see these technology tools used in their classroom. Students raised their hands in excitement when they understood what we were doing together. They called out the names of their hometowns, places where their cousins lived, and places where they wished to go. We clicked on photos that people had uploaded from these places, and students tried to remember if they knew the names of all the places that the pictures showed. They wanted to see them all. During this excitement I made sure to show Ahmed's city, Kabul. He was mesmerized, but soon after he left the carpet and returned to his desk. After some time, I asked the teacher to take over and I went to sit with Ahmed. He was crying.

Ahmed didn't have the words to talk to me about his feelings. I felt terribly that this activity had caused him to cry, and his tears were a stark reminder to me of all that students bring with them into the four walls of the classroom. As the project continued, I worked to create ways in which Ahmed could participate alongside his peers in the class. For instance, as we drew maps of the local community, Ahmed worked with precision to make a very accurate and detailed map. I held up his work to share with the class, and asked him to circulate around the room and help other students with their maps. As the weeks passed, Ahmed began acquiring the language of the classroom, repeating common expressions and teacher instructions. When we did writing activities, we encouraged him to use his home language rather than English so that he would be able to write more than he was capable of writing in English.

Students produced narrative writing such as stories, raps, letters, and poetry about communities, and engaged in expository reading and writing activities such as searching for information and images about food and sustainability on the internet, and preparing PowerPoint presentations to showcase what they had learned. Working with a partner, students chose topics for these presentations, which included ideas such as Overpopulation in India and Pakistan and All About Rice. Ahmed in particular took to using the computer easily. Typing words in English was easier than writing them on paper, and produced a more polished version of his text. Working with his partner, Ahmed memorized the parts of the presentation that he would deliver, and he stood in front of parents, administrators, and students in other classes in the school library to present his work.

Digging into the Garden

Students also interviewed one another and their parents to learn more about their community, finding that children in their community lacked access to nature. Many of the students lived in a cluster of large apartment buildings. At the time of the project, the local community center and the public library had been closed for two and a half years for renovation, and there was one small playground in the neighborhood. Interviewing their parents and fellow students about the community, the students found that many families had come from rural areas and had a great deal of experience in farming and agriculture. Students described growing dates and pomegranates; they told about taking care of chickens and sifting rice by hand with their mothers. One student described the banana trees that grew near her home, explaining: "Three children can fit under a banana leaf . . . when it rains, we use it as an umbrella." Another student shared his favorite memory of gardening, when his uncle lifted him high up onto his shoulders to pick apples. Now living in apartment buildings, the students and their families no longer had access to land for gardening. We decided to create an edible school garden to create such a space, a place where parents could work with their children and pass on knowledge and skills about food, agriculture, and sustainability.

Working together, we prepared the ground to make a garden. Figure 3.6 shows two students conducting a survey of the garden area, where they recorded what they saw, heard, smelled, and felt in the garden space.

Students used large sheets of art paper to record what they found in the garden. They taped down artifacts such as weeds, garbage, or bits of dirt to their paper, and did rubbings with charcoal to record impressions of surfaces found in the space. Ahmed found a very large maple leaf and taped it to his

FIGURE 3.6 *Students Surveying the Garden Area before Work Begins*, photo by Saskia Stille

paper. He ran to find a red crayon and colored the sides of the page to make a Canadian flag (see Figure 3.7).

Because of school board and union policies, we were unable to use any machinery to till the garden, and the caretakers were not able to help us. The students put in long hours to prepare the ground by hand, and parents eagerly

FIGURE 3.7 *Ahmed's Picture of a Canadian Flag*, photo by Saskia Stille

joined in day after day, enjoying the opportunity to work in the soil with their children. In the garden, Ahmed worked hard. He worked his own garden plot and then moved on to help others. When the time came to add new soil to the garden plots, Ahmed carried the heavy bags to each of his friends. I asked Ahmed about his enthusiasm for work in the garden, and he explained that he had a garden in Afghanistan where he helped his family grow vegetables.

Digging into the garden created an opportunity to understand how students' identities, their investments, and learning were constructed within the school and community context. In an interview at the end of the project, a student named Harshani reflected on her feelings about making the garden: "Sometimes children can be smarter than grown ups. I wish that all the students in this school could be smarter than grown ups." Harshani's comments suggest that she learned something about her capabilities in the context of this project, and the possibilities and potentials of learning.

Implications

Re/making a portion of the school grounds in the form of a garden enabled students and their families to position themselves as agentive subjects and produce new relationships of power, identity, and learning. As both a product and process of learning, the garden rendered students differently, including through their relation to the school space, and the meanings made through their encounters with their teacher, their parents, and other students in the school. Schools are not neutral social spaces, but constituted by particular structures, practices, and relations which organize students' experience and activities and index what counts as powerful knowledge and literacies (Leander, 2002).

Teachers can play an important, agential role in contesting and disrupting what counts as school-based learning. Teachers can extend learning activities to include a consideration of and engagement with broader social realities relating to the school community, and these learning activities can be connected to curriculum objectives. For instance, creating an edible school garden grounded learning activities in the social, cultural, and political context of the students' lives and the collective life they shared in school. The garden activity taught curriculum expectations across multiple subject areas, including mapping and measuring the garden to connect with mathematics objectives, teaching about soil composition and the life cycle of plants to connect with science objectives, and writing persuasive fundraising letters to connect with literacy objectives.

The creation of the garden enabled students to draw positively upon their cultural knowledge and prior experience; it affirmed students' identities, and extended language learning across the curriculum. These instructional conditions promote high levels of literacy engagement and attainment for culturally and linguistically diverse students (Cummins et al., 2011). Students showcased their learning, and re/made the ground on which they could stand and enact their identities in school.

*   *   *

The vignettes in this chapter attend to the need for diverse culturally and linguistically responsive collaborations with emergent bilingual families and communities that share several core principles:

- A shift from a deficit perspective to an asset-based, empowerment approach to working with bilingual families.
- A reflective analysis of the labels, norms, and assumptions employed by schools when planning policy, curriculum, and pedagogy for/with minoritized youth.
- A stance that the language of the schools (such as subject-area standards and academic skill building) should engage families and communities toward mutually identified goals grounded in their lives.
- An emphasis on utilizing the funds of knowledge and cultural capital in communities through an art-making process.
- An encouragement of multiple perspectives: asking teachers, students, and families to listen and empathize with one another, to become critical partners in transforming their environments.
- An inclusion of multiple purposes for art-making already at work in communities, such as art for sake of family, building networks, sharing resources, and celebrating cultural traditions.

These principles engage dynamics that artist/teachers know well. The arts require the use of shared spaces, the exploration of complex themes, the shifting of student identity from worker to contributor, and an interrelationship between process and product. These art-making dynamics can be used in empowering ways when working with emergent bilingual youth and their families. Together, such partnerships can build critical consciousness about community and schools as we work through reciprocal exchanges, shared decision-making, and a critical analysis of cultural contexts and structural influences. In this way, family–community–school partnerships no longer need to claim that the arts save lives or raise test scores. Instead, as Greene (2000) puts it, the arts can build a collaborative wide-awakeness about and in the world.

Questions to Consider

1.   Think about your childhood. What experiences did you have participating in community organizations or groups? How do your experiences relate to those of the students in the chapter vignettes?

2.   In the vignettes of this chapter, how do the facilitators engage their students' funds of knowledge, as well as those in their families and communities? What are some ethical issues that teachers should consider based on the dynamics you saw in these vignettes?

3.   Based on what you read in this chapter, how can you get to know the families and communities of the emergent bilingual youth with whom you work?

Notes

1.   We use the term "family involvement" rather than "parent involvement" to value the diverse family structures contributing to the education of young people and to practice the use of inclusive, mindful discourse as part of cultural and linguistic responsiveness.
2.   All names are pseudonyms.

References

Ada, A. F. (1995). Fostering the home–school connection. In J. Frederickson (Ed.), *Reclaiming our voices: Bilingual education, critical pedagogy and praxis* (pp. 163–78). Ontario, CA: California Association for Bilingual Education.

Apple, M. (2004). *Ideology and curriculum*, 25th anniversary 3rd edition. New York: Routledge.

Chappell, S. (2005). How immigrant arts can inform the classroom community. *Teaching Artist Journal*, 3(1), 58–62.

—— (2006). Children "at risk": Constructions of childhood in the Community Learning Centers federal after school programs. *Arts Education Policy Review*, 108(2), 9–15.

Cox-Petersen, A. (2010). *Educational partnerships: Connecting schools, families and the community*. Thousand Oaks, CA: Sage.

Cummins, J., Bismilla, V., Chow, P., Cohen, S., Giampapa, F., Leoni, L., Sandhu, P., and Sastri, P. (2005). Affirming identity in multilingual classrooms. *Educational Leadership*, 63(1), 38–43.

Cummins, J., Early, M., and Stille, S. (2011). Frames of reference: identity texts in perspective. In J. Cummins and M. Early (Eds), *Identity texts: The collaborative creation of power in multilingual schools* (pp. 21–44). Staffordshire, UK: Trentham Books.

Eisner, E. (2002). *The arts and the creation of mind*. New Haven: Yale University Press.

Fort, D. C. (1993). Science shy, science savvy, science smart. *Phi Delta Kappan*, 74(9), 674–83.

Freire, P. (2000). *Pedagogy of the oppressed*. New York: Continuum.

González, N., Moll, L., and Amanti, C. (Eds) (2005). *Funds of knowledge: Theorizing practices in households, communities and classrooms*. Mahwah, NJ: Lawrence Erlbaum Associates.

Greene, M. (2000). *Releasing the imagination: Essays on education, the arts and social change.* San Francisco: Jossey Bass.

hooks, b. (1994). *Teaching to transgress: Education as the practice of freedom.* New York: Routledge.

Jasis, P. and Ordoñez-Jasis, R. (2004). Convivencia to empowerment: Latino parent organizing at *La Familia. The High School Journal,* 88(2), 32–42.

KEEP Photovoice Research. (n.d.). What is this research about? Retrieved June 9, 2012 from http://www.fresno.k12.ca.us/divdept/keepstudents/home.html.

Leander, K. (2002). Locating Latanya: The situated production of identity artifacts in classroom interaction. *Research in the Teaching of English,* 37(2), 198–250.

Moriarty, P. (2004). *Immigrant participatory arts: An insight into community-building in Silicon Valley.* San Jose, CA: Cultural Initiatives of Silicon Valley.

Morrell, E. and Duncan-Andrade, J. (2008). *The art of critical pedagogy.* New York: Peter Lang.

Noguera. P. (2005). Transforming urban schools through investments in the social capital of parents. In S. Saegert, J. P. Thompson, and M. R. Warren (Eds), *Social capital and poor communities,* (pp. 189–213). Thousand Oaks, CA: Sage.

Noguera, P., Cammarota, J., and Ginwright, S. (2006). *Beyond resistance! Youth activism and community change: New democratic possibilities for practice and policy for America's youth.* New York: Routledge.

Oakes, J., Rogers, J., and Lipton, M. (2006). *Learning power: Organizing for education and justice.* New York: Teachers College Press.

Picower, B. (2011). Resisting compliance: Learning to teach for social justice in a neoliberal contest. *Teachers College Record,* 113(5), 1105–34.

Swadener, B. and Lubeck, S. (1995). *Children and families "at promise": Deconstructing the discourse of risk.* Albany, NY: State University of New York Press.

Uhrmacher, P. B. (2009). Toward a theory of aesthetic learning experiences. *Curriculum Inquiry,* 39(5), 613–36.

Voices, Inc. (2000). *Don't look at me different/No me veas diferente.* Tucson, AZ: Voices, Inc.

Wang, E. (2010). The beat of Boyle Street: Empowering aboriginal youth through music making. *New Directions for Youth Development,* 125, 61–70.

White, S. and Sadanandan Nair, K. (1999). The catalyst communicator: Facilitation without fear. In S. White (Ed.), *The art of facilitating participation: Releasing the power of grassroots communication* (pp. 35–51). Thousand Oaks, CA: Sage.

4

PLAYING WITH LANGUAGE, PLAYING THROUGH THE ARTS

The first three chapters of this book synthesized a relationship between second language and bilingual learning, linguistically and culturally responsive education, and collaborations with families and communities. This foundation serves as a lens through which we would like you to consider the remainder of the book. Chapters 4 through 9 are focused on curricular content in arts-based projects with bilingual youth and the instructional contexts that guide this curriculum. The vignettes in this book introduce important topics and genres for critical and creative educational work with emergent bilingual youth: the use of play, storytelling, literature, world events, and new media technologies. Chapter 10 concludes with re-imagining how we can sustain counter-narrative practices for the health, well-being, and life futures of all young people.

To begin our curricular explorations, this chapter focuses on an improvisational process at the core of cultural practice and meaning-making—the process of play. Through play, children and adolescents explore, construct, negotiate, and renegotiate meaning with others in real and imaged spaces—to become anew. Indeed, the concept of "play" is closely aligned with that of "recreation," literally to re-create oneself (Nachmanovitch, 1990; Schechner, 2003). In play, children and adolescents can represent their emotions, humor, and identities through collective interaction with others, through performances, art, music, games, and dance. About play, Berk (2006) says, "Children are active agents who reflect on and coordinate their own thoughts, rather than merely absorbing those of others" (p. 627). As discussed in Chapter 1, play and playing are vital to language development. Creative construction allows for the integration of and experimentation with new linguistic forms, structures, and concepts. Children and youth use language to represent their knowledge and experiences in ways they control, to create and imagine the way they see the world around them.

In this era of high stakes, test-driven accountability in schools, play for the sake of pleasure and play with language are often characterized as trivial, with little potential for improving academic achievement and no overt relation to getting the right answers on tests. In the "culture of school work" (Anyon, 1980), there is little space for play; even in early childhood learning, teachers often guide "play" based on academic learning objectives that may be at cross-purposes with the play worlds children are developing themselves. For example, a Spanish/English preschool teacher might be concerned about one of her three-year-olds, also Spanish/English speaking, who does not talk in class where English is the primary language of instruction. The teacher designs several intervention play experiences to encourage this child to speak and develop her English language. The child chooses not to respond in either language, although she enjoys the games such as finger painting and piecing together a puzzle created from a photograph of the child's face. The teacher consistently talks to the child, prompting English vocabulary about the painting's colors, lines, and shapes. The teacher observes aloud the child's body parts as the child pieces them together in the puzzle. Sometimes the teacher praises the child in Spanish, but all instructional talk is in English.

In this example, a singular focus on academic English language development has constrained this teacher's play-based interactions with her student. How might this child's play and playful language emerge differently if the instruction instead focuses on guiding the child's creativity (in both languages as well as through the child's interactions with the mediums of play, her playmates and her teacher)? For emergent bilingual youth, an emphasis on meaning (communicative competence) developed through play is generally more effective than an overriding emphasis on form (linguistic competence) (Borey and Dahl, 2010).

In this chapter, we argue that playing with language, and playing through the arts are valuable in their own rights, offering unique opportunities for *libratory play* (Chappell, 2010). Play can liberate the speaker or writer from the limited creativity produced in classrooms emphasizing error correction and correct grammar use. With play bounded responsively by personal curiosity and community inquiry, language and literacy become tools for "the having of wonderful ideas" (Duckworth, 2006). As emergent bilingual youth acquire a second language alongside their home language, they need opportunities to make real and imaginative connections about the past, the present, and the future through language play and other symbolic meaning systems.

Further, through resistant and transformational play, emergent bilingual youth need opportunities to navigate mainstream cultural assimilationist restrictions and institutional racism that impacts their developing bicultural identities (Bell and Roberts, 2010). Play is often a way of making sense of power, of navigating roles of dominance and establishing new agential self-worth in response to the double binds—or contradictions between individual experience and expressed community values—produced in a monocultural, monolingual school environment (Pacheco,

2012). We suggest that through the deliberate, thoughtful guidance of a culturally and linguistically responsive teacher, emergent bilingual youth can learn to use language and arts-based play to critique social inequities and develop new collective understandings about their emotions, identities, and perspectives.

What Is Play and How Do We Learn to Play?

In contemporary Western society, play is viewed as central to the development of early language and cognitive functions (McMahon et al., 2005; Sutton-Smith, 1985). In other words, when young children engage in imaginative play, such as improvising stories, dressing up, and playing house, the language and thinking that emerges from these practices fosters the development of more complex language and thinking. In early play, children imitate activities such as caring for toy babies, driving vehicles, and exploring unknown areas. Each of these activities has rules that, early on, children create for themselves in relation to the values, attitudes, and beliefs their communities hold. With age, these rules for play become increasingly explicit and constraining, and include consequences if they are broken: losing a "life" in a video game, incurring a penalty in team sports, being called out for cheating at a board or card game, not winning an art competition or being selected for a school play. In this manner, childlike play (seemingly more expansive with fewer bounded rules) is encouraged in early childhood, but as children mature in age and school grade, play is (generally, in Western society) looked upon as childish. It is not that adults do not play, but they set apart their play (sports, travel, leisure), and typically do not view it as rehearsal for the future, as adults often view the purpose of childhood play (Sawyer, 2001).

In this book, we view play, language development and the arts as intertwined experiences that contribute to children's being in the present as well as becoming toward the future (Lee, 2001). When children and youth play, their language develops because they are using language for real as well as imaginative purposes. When play is combined with arts-based practices, children and youth engage their emotions, thoughts, and language for creative, collective experiences. Play encourages children and youth to laugh, hear rhymes, use puns, and pay attention to the aesthetics of life (such as voice, color, movement, style, form, light, direction), all the while building relationships with others, experiencing feelings and the world around them with a heightened sense of being and belonging.

In the vignette that follows, emotions and narrative become playful ways of developing language, community, and core subject knowledge in the classroom. Research colleagues Mary Carol Combs and David Betts, along with fourth/fifth grade teacher Paul Fisher, tell how emergent bilingual students used dramatic play to express emotions and feelings about who they are. As you read, note how language, community and core subject content—particularly in language arts and social studies—are developed through different arts processes in culturally and linguistically responsive ways.

Acted and Enacted Lives: Language Play, Theatre, and Language Development at the Border

Mary Carol Combs and J. David Betts, University of Arizona; Paul Fisher, Southeastern Arizona Arts in Academics Project

> Play is the source of development and creates the zone of proximal development.
>
> (Lev Vygotsky, 1978)

This article discusses the Southeastern Arizona Arts in Academics Project (SAAAP),[1] an innovative arts and performance-based project designed to help teachers create an arts-based learning environment in which students "perform" their learning through alternative, creative expression. This environment, in turn, improves students' learning and enjoyment of the arts and other academic areas through intensive teacher professional development and collaboration with teaching artists in dance, music, theatre, visual art, and creative writing.

SAAAP facilitated additional achievements through its drama program at Borderlands K-8 School,[2] the focus of this article and the site where one of us (Paul) was an artist in residence for two years. The program encouraged spontaneous and exuberant eruptions of oral English discourse from fourth and fifth grade Mexican-origin English language learners in a Borderlands classroom. The program also provided classroom teachers with a vision of powerful learning in an intellectually stimulating and non-judgmental space filled with sociodramatic language play. Paul's efforts reflect what Giroux (1991) has called a "language of possibility," that is, the capacity of teachers to imagine and implement alternative and joyful pedagogies with young English language learners.

Theatre and Play in a Borderlands Classroom

Borderlands K-8 sits squarely on the U.S.–México international line; from the entrance one can literally look across the wall into Sonora, the northern Mexican state that borders Arizona. The school serves students from the local community as well as U.S.-born students who reside in México and cross the border to attend the school.

When teaching artist Paul Fisher walked into Borderland's combined fourth and fifth grade classroom he faced a room full of English language learners. In prior visits for the Southeastern Arizona Arts in Academics Project, he had observed that students were accustomed to desk-based, stationary instruction and seemed reluctant to participate in interactive group activities. Paul knew he had to help the children feel more at ease, so he began by asking them to stand up for some warm-up exercises.

"Okay, before you sit down, tell me your name and something you like. My name is Mr Fisher, and I like music."

Paul pointed to a boy in front, who said, "Alvaro, baseball." Paul gently asked Alvaro to use a complete sentence. Alvaro replied, "My name is Alvaro and I like baseball." Next Luz, who said, "My name is Luz. I like my dog."

As the children spoke, Paul tried to identify those with performance-based confidence to assist him in modeling the activities throughout the lesson. Then, he placed a chair at the front of the room, explaining that he would ask individual children to walk to the chair showing a *feeling* and then continue showing the same feeling while sitting down. Paul chose Omar, an enthusiastic boy with dark curly hair. After hesitating for a moment, Omar smiled and skipped to the front of the classroom. He smiled widely while sitting in the chair.

Paul exclaimed, "That was great, Omar! Now ask one of your classmates to name that feeling." Omar called to Alvaro, who shouted "Happy!" to the rest of the class. Now it was Alvaro's turn to demonstrate a feeling. He beamed, then frowned and stamped over to the chair. The other children were giggling by now, and more of them participated. "Mad! Mad!" they yelled. As the activity progressed, a few students chose to accompany their friends to the

FIGURE 4.1 *Girl and Boy on Chair*, photo by Paul Fisher

FIGURE 4.2 *Two Girls and a Boy*, photo by Paul Fisher

chair, mimicking their actions. Things were going well. The students participated enthusiastically and enjoyed themselves. They helped each other with
vocabulary challenges.

Then, Paul initiated another activity: "Okay, now I'm going to ask Bobby
to come sit in this chair. Then I want some volunteers to come up and try
to make Bobby laugh. You have thirty seconds to make him react!" The
volunteers made funny faces and sounds. Bobby tried to maintain a straight
face, but he soon exploded with laughter.

Next, Paul asked Luz and Julia to come to the front of the room. He invited
Julia to sit in the chair and asked Luz to try to persuade Julia to get out of the
chair. Luz struggled to find the "right" words in English. Other students began
to offer suggestions in English and Spanish to make Julia stand up. By this
time, all of the students were motivated and eager, getting up without prompting and acting out scenarios.

At this point, the ice was broken and Paul knew he could move on to
more complex language activities. At the end of the lesson, the regular classroom teacher, at first doubtful about his students' willingness or ability to
participate in English, expressed amazement that the children were so active
and verbal.

Creating Zones of Proximal Development for English Learners through Dramatic Play

Powerful learning in conventional school settings can occur in unconventional ways. As the scenario above suggests, theatre arts activities like role-playing and improvisation are engaging to young learners because of their similarity to play. In play, including semi-structured dramatic play, children create imaginary situations, switch between roles, and engage in social interaction with others (Vygotsky, 1978). Indeed, play creates a "zone of proximal development" (ZPD), termed by Russian psychologist Lev Vygotsky as a metaphorical pedagogical space in which human cognitive development occurs through social interaction with others. Vygotsky (1978) defines the ZPD as the "distance between a child's actual development level as determined by independent problem solving and the potential level of development through interaction with adults or more capable peers" (p. 86). The zone, instantiated through play, represents a space where children can grow with a sense of self-efficacy and self-worth.

For English language learners, sociodramatic play can be particularly effective in developing second language abilities and higher order mental processes such as thinking, imagination, intention, and generalized emotions. Dramatic play activities directly engage students' emotions, allow them to express themselves verbally, and help overcome the reluctance to participate in performances by some beginning learners (Ernst-Slavit, 1998). Dramatic play helps ELLs internalize the linguistic patterns of the second language and provides a context into which they can bring locally available bilingual resources (Piirainen-Marsh and Tainio, 2009). In addition, humorous language play can help develop sociolinguistic competence, second language vocabulary and semantic fields (Bell, 2009).

Drawn into a supportive setting by skilled facilitators like Paul Fisher, the English language learners at Borderlands lowered their "affective filters" and made the leap into experimentation with new language and vocabulary.[3] We believe his efforts made possible a zone of proximal development, a creative space in which children engaged in what Courtney Cazden (1981) has called "performance before competence." In other words, students made the leap into experimentation with new English discourse and vocabulary before they were fully fluent in the language. Dramatic and humorous language performance is evident in Paul's activities. Students found an environment where they were allowed to play with language without fear of criticism. Even beginning English learners were able to show off their nascent abilities in the language.

Arts Integration and English Language Learners

Elliot Eisner (2002) has argued that art in its various forms is as intimately connected to education as creative and imaginative play is to learning. Connecting play, learning and language is the role of arts integration. There are many natural places for arts connections in the school setting. As Paul Fisher expertly demonstrates, theatre is language play—and language development. It encourages peer participation in an uncritical context, where being "believable" is valued more than being "correct."

Fisher worked with teachers at Borderlands for two years, encouraging them to take risks and try the various activities on their own. While some teachers were more reluctant to step into the drama unknown, others embraced the addition of sociodrama and language play into their pedagogy, facilitating the "legitimate peripheral participation" by students that Lave and Wenger (1991) describe.[4] Paul reported that gradually these Borderland teachers increased their experimentation with drama activities, overcoming initial trepidation about trying something new. Paul witnessed the tangible benefits: more active student engagement and a developing linguistic independence among English language learner students. As we noted earlier, incorporating drama and play into the ELL classroom may indeed yield academic and linguistic benefits for English language learners. We believe it also creates zones of creative possibilities in which language and cognitive development can occur.

★   ★   ★

Play and the Arts: Hand in Hand

As teachers, you can learn extensively about your students through play and the arts. First, though, we encourage you to relinquish two key beliefs and practices: (1) that you control what students think and do in the classroom; (2) that play diverts attention from the business of learning. Teachers want to control what goes on in a class. Losing control of classroom behavior and learning can be frustrating, no doubt. However, play does have rules, like any social practice, and you can talk with students about the rules: what works and doesn't work, and why. For example, you might place students into groups to discuss and then create a collage depicting a contemporary event, such as election day and bilingual community members volunteering at the voting polls. You might discuss with them how to use play safely and effectively in the art form. In this case, the students might cut out photos of different people from magazines and make composite people using different faces and bodies they find. They could use word play to create dialogue for what the bilingual poll workers might say to people who come to vote—through rhyme, exclamations, found lines of music they enjoy. The limitations you provide (as in specific boundaries set around students' artistic production and play) are often a way of freeing a student's process. Doing more with less lies at the heart of many art forms, as well as the reason that play itself is bounded by rules that the participants create and reinforce.

Moreover, as a facilitator, you can show students that some rules for play and artistic creativity do not need to be followed, that there are times when students can question and even "break" the rules. Resistant play is particularly important as you help students analyze problems in the world that manifest (literally and metaphorically) in games they already play. You can help children envision how to overcome and move through limitations imposed on their play based on assumptions about the rules of legitimate participation (Lave and Wenger, 1991). For example, different forms of Western dance have long defined conventions of able-bodiedness that guide dancers' selection and inclusion in performances. It would be unusual to see a person in a wheelchair or with braces dancing the part of the Sugar Plum Fairy or in the Rockettes kick line on a New York stage. In the last twenty years, disability rights advocates and researchers have increasingly questioned such exclusionary practices that hegemonically value the "abled" body (Risner and Stinson, 2010). By increasing our value of inclusiveness in schools, children's play can become a mode for envisioning new ways to move our bodies, and create new rules and narrative possibilities. With culturally and linguistically responsive facilitation from an arts educator, play can be bounded in terms of a social justice focus on collaborative exploration, experimentation, and collective theory-building (Bell and Roberts, 2010). In this way, the rules of conventional dance, for example, could be broken in order to embody creative expression from multiple perspectives and bodily experiences.

Such libratory play might be focused on the resistance to monocultural, monolingual narratives, practices and value systems that preclude the experiences of emergent bilingual students, their families and communities—past and present—from being legitimate focuses of the curriculum in schools. Play can be a way to access these marginalized narratives: students can engage in a process that is generative, responsive to experience through counter-narratives that bind the imaginative to the real. In the vignette that follows, Jessica Mele and Karena Salmond of the Performing Arts Workshop describe how they utilize "cultural touchpoints," moments of narrative significance to their immigrant students, to play with language and explore the theme of journeying. As you read, note how language, community and core subject content particularly in language arts and social studies are developed through different arts processes. This theme of continued play through language will be explored in Chapter 5 as well.

Journey: Identity and Language Development through the Arts

Jessica Mele and Karena Salmond, Performing Arts Workshop, San Francisco

"San Francisco is sad," a third grade student at Mission Education Center wrote in response to a creative writing prompt, "because I miss my abuela and the salsa verde she made." Students at Mission Education Center have stories to tell. They have been learning to tell those stories through art—writing, drawing and theatre. All recent immigrants to the United States, the students have traveled long distances to reach San Francisco. They are learning how to negotiate a new home and a new life in a new language, English. Arts-based inquiry and arts-integrated curricula can offer a deeper, more meaningful way for students to develop their language skills, because it begins with their own self-identity.

For over forty-five years, Performing Arts Workshop has engaged students from preschool through high school in long-term, sequential arts programming. In the late 1980s, the Workshop began serving an increasing number of English language learners, reflective of the changing demographics in the Bay Area. Workshop Artistic Director Gary Draper, along with fellow artists, developed a teaching pedagogy (the "Cycle of Artistic Inquiry," Performing Arts Workshop and Siegesmund, 2000) that has proven effective at building the language skills of English language learners. The Cycle of Artistic Inquiry leads students through a creative process that begins with perceiving an artistic problem, conceiving of that problem; expressing themselves, and then reflecting on and revising that expression. These key processes—perception, conception, expression, reflection and revision—necessitate that students not only learn how to express themselves (physically, verbally), but also learn how to critique and revise each other's creative work. In other words, by developing students' physical and verbal vocabulary through inquiry-based problem solving in an art form, Performing Arts Workshop teaching artists help students move between their native language and English.

For example, teaching artists use the art forms of theatre, dance, and creative writing to help students develop a rich vocabulary and understanding of basic literacy concepts (metaphor, symbolism). However, they also go one step further to reflect on student expression in a given lesson ("What did you see in that improvisation? Where did you see examples of metaphor? How could that example have been stronger or more clear?"). Students reinforce concepts learned through creative "expression" as they reflect and revise, and therefore develop a deeper understanding of concepts in each lesson. As a result, this type of learning has a more pervasive impact on students' communication skills than standard "English Language Arts" curricula prescribed by the school district. When arts-based learning and targeted ELA curricula work in tandem, the effects on student learning are dramatic.

Since 1992, the Workshop has served all Spanish-language K–5 newcomer students in the San Francisco Unified School District at Mission Education Center. Students at "Mission Ed" come from different Latin American countries and arrive with varying degrees of experience with formal education. For six years, Workshop Artist Mentor Kristin Papania has worked with students and staff at Mission Ed to integrate the arts into the school's curriculum, with the goal of developing students' oral proficiency in both Spanish and English. During the 2009–10 school year, Papania engaged students in a year-long exploration around the theme of "journey" that used culturally relevant touchpoints (the concept of "journey" connecting to each student's own journey to the United States; connections to native Central American art forms, such as *molas*). Through the arts processes, Papania connected the curriculum to students' own cultural history in Central and Latin America. She visited each class once a week for thirty-two weeks and used elements of creative writing, visual art, and theatre improvisation in her teaching.

Papania began the year with a simple task: "write your name." Students examined the lines, textures, and curves associated with their names—tracing the letters with their fingers, using language to describe how the shape of their name changes from letter to letter. From there, students discussed lines across space, embodying those lines in movement exercises across the classroom floor. They drew a line to represent their journey to America, and called on the same themes of line, texture, and curvature in depicting their journeys. Papania connected the story of each child's journey to vocabulary about emotions through writing. Pointing to a point on the "journey" line, students followed the prompt, "I felt _____ here because I had to _____." Students experimented with comparing and contrasting different points on their own "journey lines," as well as those of their peers. Papania then led students to explore their current sense of place with a second writing prompt: "I used to think _____. But now I understand _____."

The evidence of student learning was clear in each student's portfolio. At the start of the year, their oral and written English use was sparse, often limited to one sentence: "I went to the park." By the end of the year, students were engaging the five senses in their writing, describing their emotions, and engaging in peer critique and revision. Students were motivated to expand their own vocabulary in their native Spanish because they were genuinely interested in each other's stories. They learned to ask questions and add more detail in their Spanish language written and verbal communication. This practice in Spanish gave students a larger vocabulary base from which to develop their vocabulary in English.

Across town, students at Stevenson Elementary also showed significant growth in English language development through the performing arts. While Stevenson Elementary does not exclusively serve newcomer students, many of its students are classified as English language learners (a majority of Cantonese speakers). During the 2008–9 academic year, Performing Arts Workshop partnered with Stevenson's classrooms to conduct year-long theatre residencies as part of a study funded by the U.S. Department of Education. Christy Carillo, a fourth and fifth grade teacher, conducted an action research project focusing specifically on the impact that the residencies had on her ELL students. She partnered with the Improve Group, an outside evaluator working with Performing Arts Workshop, to develop research questions and instruments to evaluate those questions in her classroom. Carillo was interested in seeing whether students' practice of the English language in another context outside of the normal classroom structure (e.g. theatre class) aided their language development.

Carillo's findings were clear: first and foremost, the theatre residencies, taught by teaching artist Eric Hoffman, established a safe place outside of the classroom for creative exploration. Hearing another voice speaking English in addition to the classroom teacher's enabled students to hear and engage in discussion with multiple audiences, which provides additional contexts for the development of dialogue and the exchange of ideas. Additionally, the message that there are "no right or wrong answers" in art provided an atmosphere safe for taking risks when using language and expressing creativity.

Carillo found that the ELL students in her classes were generally less comfortable interacting in class using English at the start of the year. The weekly theatre residencies helped them become more comfortable speaking and presenting, dispelling fears of saying the wrong word or line in a dialogue or improvisation. The ELL students carried the confidence they experienced during their theatre work back into the classroom, which further supported their English language development. Acting in tableau or pantomimed formats in addition to improvisations with dialogue gave students new opportunities to express themselves nonverbally. This increased participation and self-confidence, which in turn increased participation in other classroom activities. In Carillo's class, the process of reflection and revision of creative work helped her ELL students develop the expressive language needed for describing what they saw during a peer's performance, and describing what was most interesting or in need of adjustment. In other words, the creative work gave students a purpose for expanding their descriptive and explanatory oral language abilities.

The creation of artwork is a personal experience. At Performing Arts Workshop, we know that this personal form of expression is also a powerful way to learn and to support learning. When students learn to approach a school-mandated curriculum (for example, "genre writing," or "descriptive writing,") through an artful entrypoint, their learning has a purpose, and therefore is likely to be more meaningful and enduring. They become not just good students or English-proficient: they become inquisitive, joyful learners. "I'm not looking for the *right* answer," says teaching artist Kristin Papania, "I'm looking for *your* answer."

The projects undertaken at Mission Education Center and Stevenson Elementary School in San Francisco are reflective of the power of the arts to be culturally responsive—to be the connective tissue between students' own experiences and history outside of school and their lives in school. They are also strong examples of partnership between classroom teachers and teaching artists. Teaching artists are positioned between classroom teachers, community members, parents, and literacy specialists. Community-based artists who partner with schools offer a dynamic way for English language learners to deepen their learning in the classroom, to reinforce literacy concepts, and to expand their vocabulary beyond the standard curriculum. However, examples of true arts integration partnerships between classroom teachers and teaching artists are rare, and difficult to sustain over a long period of time. In order for them to take place, many education stakeholders must change the way they view the arts—as a separate portion of the curriculum, expendable when need be. Rather, artists and activists must articulate the opportunity for the arts to transform teaching pedagogy; and they must do so in partnership with classroom teachers.

FIGURE 4.3 *Performing Arts Workshop Teaching Artist, Kristin Papania, with Mission Education Center Students, San Francisco,* photo by Laurence Jones

★ ★ ★

In the vignette above, playful work with language includes seeing the world anew through arts-based techniques, tools, and languages. Schools do not usually ask students to play with the aesthetic qualities of their names (as in *Ramona Quimby* by Beverly Cleary, where Ramona is chastised for turning her last name's letter "Q" into a cat's body). Through gestures (pantomime) and frozen images (tableaux) created with the body, students in the Performing Arts Workshop began to see their cultural journeys from an embodied, sensory perspective (Springgay, 2008)—improvising the contours of the geography, emotions, and relationships of their stories. Importantly, the focus is on open-ended meaning-making rather than achieving "correct" form. The children played in their bodies with ideas in order to collectively build cultural touch points for the group to observe and discuss. Yet, the teacher did not leave them to "sink or swim" in their use of English to make those meanings. Through careful use of sentence frames and other sheltered content strategies, emergent bilingual youth can feel a sense of success in their new use of English as well as their enriched use of home language.

Implications for Libratory Play in the Content Areas

As you imagine using play in your classroom or other educational context, consider the principles of practice that will guide its pedagogical application. One of the focuses of this book is to examine the effects of dehumanizing and alienating policies and practices on emergent bilingual youth, as they navigate the implications of homogenizing culture and monolingual spaces of power in their lives. Thus, the use of play as curriculum also deserves such critical reflection. Often, play is associated with having "fun," yet left unsupervised and/or unexamined, the fun of play may involve some players wielding power over others via stereotypes, language discrimination and other explicit and implicit forms of social dominance. While schools see some of this play as bullying, they may benignly dismiss other play with responses like: "Those kids," "Boys will be boys," or "If no one's bleeding, I leave them alone." Young people's playing with power is understandable given how little relative decision-making they experience throughout their days. Children need to explore the values and beliefs, questions, struggles, journeys, and positionings of their lives. Yet, how do we structure this exploration in a way that is ethical and safe for all participants? From a stance of ideological clarity about the importance of mindful care and justice (Expósito and Favela, 2003), what should our principles of play be?

We suggest that, as teachers, we examine our own childhoods for moments of play about which we now feel uncomfortable because of the way power was wielded during that play. In a series of interviews conducted by one editor of this volume (Chappell), a white, middle class teacher remembered stuffing bags of popcorn in the cafeteria for a school fundraiser, unsupervised by school faculty or staff, and laughing with a friend who chanted rhythmically "Bag it, faggot" as the popcorn spilled into the bags. In another recollection, the same teacher remembered helping a high school friend steal a street sign because it contained the word play "Wong Way." The teacher remembered feeling uncomfortable about witnessing his friends playing this way, thinking it was "wrong" yet not stopping the play. Another white, middle class teacher remembered being four years old at day care, and chanting "Let's have a picnic on Fadi!" while circling a little Middle Eastern boy. The boy lay in a ball, perhaps crying—she couldn't remember. The teacher knew that at four years old, she had made Fadi feel badly, but she didn't stop until the game grew old.

These stories are examples of what Schechner (2003) calls "dark play," improvisational games in which participants engage (perhaps unwillingly or unknowingly) in "fantasy, risk, luck, daring, invention and deception . . . [in order to] subvert order, dissolve frames, and break its own rules" (pp. 106–7). Such play is not sanctioned by authorities and, accordingly, can be unsafe and hurtful to the player and/or others, as in these examples. These memories exemplify play unexamined in terms of how socially dominating behaviors (re)produce a lack of tolerance or respect for difference (as in sexuality, language, ethnicity, and culture in those examples). Yet, even play sanctioned by authorities leads to unsafe and hurtful results. Dominating play indeed leads to rewarding "the strong over the weak" (though "strong" and "weak" may be defined differently in and by different play experiences), producing as much punishment as reward, both for those who lose the game, as well as for those who celebrate others' loss for their gain (Kohn, 1999).

Schools often respond to prejudice and other forms of bullying with zero-tolerance policies. Yet, such policies also silence rather than unpack the relationship between privilege, prejudice, and the social dominance of difference that occurs between children, cultures and communities throughout the world (Li Li, 2006). Further, the strategies at work in current teacher preparation multicultural education courses have yielded few changes in candidate dispositions toward equitable teaching of culturally and linguistically diverse young people (Dolby, 2012). Understanding power, privilege and social dominance is complex, sometimes isolating, often scary work for teachers to facilitate with their students; yet, it is imperative that we learn to critique dominating modes of play, and then build new libratory models with emergent bilingual youth.

Dolby (2012) suggests that informed empathy, a set of skills that libratory play can help develop, should be positioned at the center of multicultural education. Informed empathy involves learning about the historical and material structures that contextualize people's experiences so that perspective-taking leads to feeling *with* rather than feeling *for*. Libratory play is one way we can develop informed empathy with and about minoritized communities. Through libratory play, participants can develop awareness and critical consciousness, using techniques such as remembering one's own encounters with social dominance; embodying and destabilizing those encounters; taking on the perspectives of others, imagining their lives, feelings, thoughts, and motives for action; informing one's embodied responses in play with information from diverse primary and secondary artifacts that provide depth and information; discouraging stock responses or stereotypes as part of play, and when they arise, being willing to "freeze the play" or return to those moments after play is done to analyze beliefs and actions (Chappell, 2010). As the teacher, you are the bridge to this critical curriculum, and in charge of facilitating a safe environment for its development.

Many artists/teachers have employed libratory play techniques with local communities, such as in devised theatre and dance (Cohen Cruz, 2005; Lerman, 2011); theatre games and activities (Boal, 2002); storytelling (Bell and Roberts, 2010); and process drama (Bolton and Heathcote, 1995). We explore the structure of process drama briefly to illustrate the power of the arts as a medium of play and social critique. In this structure, students can use improvisational dramatic play to make sense of historical as well as contemporary events impacting their lives. Process drama encourages students to work in role to solve planned, yet unscripted, problems around a social theme or event, then debrief the experience out of role. This act of "doing history" becomes a playful investigation into the worlds of the past that builds interpretive schema for understanding enduring human dilemmas (Boyle-Baise and Zevin, 2009; Levstik and Barton, 2010).

For example, a sixth grade teacher might ask her students to engage in a process drama about the U.S. immigration round ups of Mexican Americans in the 1950s and today.[5] She might assign her class the roles of immigrants with different citizenship statuses and migrant histories from both time periods, while she takes on the role of a police officer conducting the round ups. The teacher would identify a problem for the students—as immigrants—to investigate, such as how they would each respond to the police officer when confronted. The students could gather source images, videos and quotations about the two time periods, reflecting on their meaning through drama techniques such as tableaux and pantomime (for more on drama structures, see Neelands et al., 1990). Most importantly, students would call on their own emotions to imagine how their characters would feel. They might generate a drawing, painting, or poem about these feelings and their decision to act. See, for example, the painting in Figure 4.4 created by artist/teacher Simón Candú in response to recent immigration round ups. After the process drama, students might invite speakers to share their experiences responding to the police or immigration officials and relate the students' in-role choices to those made by people facing the same treatment.

ARTS ARTIFACT FIVE

Separated Families

Simón Candú, contemporary artist/activist/teacher

FIGURE 4.4 *Separated Families* by Simón Candú

Asking students to play improvisationally and ethically around issues of social dominance helps them build informed empathy about the lives of diverse people affected by those events. For students whose families were illegally deported in the 1930s, for example, using such a process drama is not only culturally and linguistically responsive but also humanizing. For those students who would otherwise not know that deportations still occur, or for those whose families support restrictive immigration policies to ensure American "safety," such curriculum offers an opportunity to stretch student thinking from new perspectives.

Building a culture of informed empathy means asking young people to imagine what kind of world they want to create, where people connect with one another and work to understand each other without social dominance structuring these relationships (*What would the North American continent look like, for example, without a border fence? Do we need a border fence? Who lives crossing those fences daily?* See Adler et al., 2007). The Center for Building a Culture of Empathy (n.d.) suggests that structured play opportunities can build self-empathy, mirrored empathy, imagined empathy, and empathetic action. Such play can occur with peers, across generations, through the use of new media and the arts, in response to or about enacted relationships, policies, curriculum.

Play does not have to be "dark" in order to resist authority. We can help students ethically identify when sanctioned rules, regulations, policies, and artifacts violate their sense of what is right, good and just for all people. In the U.S., we need only to turn to civil rights movements throughout history to see why such resistance is necessary. Many guerilla theatre, agit-prop, and culture jamming groups utilize play as a resistance tactic with serious messages. Yet, acts of resistance and libratory play do not have to be grand in scale to achieve the goals of critical and creative development with emergent bilingual youth. When the students in Arizona's Arts in Academics Project—featured in Vignette Six of this chapter—physically moved with exaggerated emotion and gesture, they pleasurably resisted the schooling of their bodies, the expectations to be still, rational and contained in school (Chappell et al., 2011). When the students at the Performing Arts Workshop—featured in Vignette Seven of this chapter—talked openly about their journeys from other countries, playing with those memories, they defied an assimilationist ideology of erasing the past and starting anew in America (Olsen, 2008).

Pacheco (2012) observes that minoritized communities in the U.S. regularly re-imagine the use of historically and socially given tools, artifacts and instruments in order to address perceived material constraints (such as working for a better second language learning education or access to college for undocumented youth). The vignettes in this book share examples of ways that emergent bilingual youth re-imagine and play with cultural artifacts (see Rodríguez-Valls' migrant students re-naming graffiti as cultural tags of home and naming [in Chapter 6], and Garcia's high school students' re-tooling the immigrant crossing sign [in Chapter 7]). Rather than produce psycho-social tensions between the colonized and the colonizing culture, as in W. E. B. Du Bois' (1994) notion of double consciousness, the double bind (Pacheco, 2012) experienced by minoritized communities becomes a productive source for social activity, particularly for everyday acts of playful resistance.

Such informed improvisation can re-write narratives that contain, marginalize and erase particular experiences, such as those that say particular bodies can't move, certain language varieties sound strange, or specific communities should leave traditions and histories at the schoolhouse door. In this way emergent bilingual youth can use improvisational acts of play to name their struggles and envision new worlds. When facilitated and defined by a knowledgeable artist/educator, who can keep the experience from being harmful or exploitative, play can help to build new communities of relatedness and empathy. In Chapter 5, we continue to explore play, particularly through the role of stories and storytelling.

Questions to Consider

1. How do you and your students play in your classroom? How controlled is the space of your classroom in terms of student movement during play? In terms of playing with language(s) in use?

2. Watch children as they play on the playground. What kinds of rules for play are they following? How do these rules differ from those in the classroom? How do they deal with rule breaking in the midst of play?

3. How did the facilitators in the vignettes create playful experiences? How was this play limited? How did the pleasure of playing add to the students' experiences?

4. With your guidance, in what ways could play through the arts encourage students to challenge the status quo and to build counter-narratives? How can you guide their ethical development through play?

Notes

1. Southeastern Arizona Arts in Academics is a three-year project funded by the U.S. Department of Education Office of Innovation and Improvement. Participating teachers receive over one hundred hours of professional developing, in-serving, credit and literature. The SAAA website provides a description of its mission:

    Teachers are trained to create an arts-based learning environment which improves learning in the arts and all subject areas through intense professional development and collaboration with master teaching artists in dance, music, theatre, visual art and creative writing. Teachers and artists collaboratively design learning experiences to be rich and complex for all learners, challenging and engaging them in multiple modalities and encouraging them to achieve, learn and grow as citizens. Through the learning tasks designed the project also seeks to create cultural understanding, enrich and empower students, schools and communities.

    (http://saaa.schoolinsites.com/)

2. All names are pseudonyms.
3. Stephen Krashen (1982) has described the "affective filter" as a kind of psychological barrier that second language learners may erect because of low motivation, low self-esteem, or anxiety. He argues that a high affective filter is more likely to impede language acquisition than a low filter. Consequently, appropriate pedagogy for ELLs would include both comprehensible input and an instructional setting that encourages a low filter (pp. 30–32).

4. Lave and Wenger (1991) describe legitimate peripheral participation as the central defining characteristic of learning as a situated activity. Initially, the participation may be "peripheral" (simple, low risk), but it is legitimate and moves a novice learner from the periphery of a "community of practice" to the center. The learner may begin her participation on the periphery of the community of practice, but her participation is legitimate, because she is becoming more familiar with the culture—and language—of the classroom community.

5. See Valenciana (2006) for more on the illegal deportations of Mexican Americans in the 1930s. See Romero (2006) and Kossan and Wong (2011) on contemporary immigration round ups and responses from Mexican American families, teachers, activists.

References

Adler, R., Criado, V., and Huneycutt, B. (2007). *Border film project: Photos by migrants and minutemen*. New York: Abrams Books.

Anyon, J. (1980). Social class and hidden curriculum of work. *Journal of Education*, 162(1), 67–92.

Bell, L. A. and Roberts, R. A. (2010). The storytelling project model: A theoretical framework for critical examination of racism through the arts. *Teachers College Record*, 112(9), 2295–319.

Bell, N. (2009). Learning about and through humor in the second language classroom. *Language Teaching Research*, 13(3), 241–58.

Berk, L. (2006). *Child development*, 7th edition. Boston: Allyn & Bacon.

Boal, A. (2002). *Games for actors and non-actors*. New York: Routledge.

Bolton, G. and Heathcote, D. (1995). *Drama for learning: Dorothy Heathcote's mantle of the expert approach to education*. Portsmouth, NH: Heinemann Drama.

Borey, V. and Dahl, T. I. (2010). Playing with meaning in a Norwegian language immersion village. In D. Chappell (Ed.), *Children under construction* (pp. 63–86). New York: Peter Lang.

Boyle-Baise, M. and Zevin, J. (2009). *Young citizens of the world: Teaching elementary social studies through civic engagement*. New York: Routledge.

Cazden, C. (1981). Performance before competence: Assistance to child discourse in the zone of proximal development. *Quarterly Newsletter of the Laboratory of Comparative Human Cognition*, 3(1), 5–8.

Center for Building a Culture of Empathy. (n.d.). Retrieved June 10, 2012 from http://cultureofempathy.com/Projects/How-To-Build-Empathy/index.htm.

Chappell, D. (Ed.) (2010). Colonizing the imaginary: Socializing (specific) identities, bodies, ethic, and moralities through pleasurable embodiment. In D. Chappell (Ed.), *Children under construction* (pp. 1–20). New York: Peter Lang.

Chappell, D., Chappell, S., and Margolis, E. (2011). School as ceremony and ritual: Photography illuminates moments of culture building. *Qualitative Inquiry*, 17(1), 56–73.

Cohen Cruz, J. (2005). *Local acts: Community-based performance in the United States*. Piscataway, NJ: Rutgers University Press.

Dolby, N. (2012). *Rethinking multicultural education for the next generation: The new empathy and social justice*. New York: Routledge.

Du Bois, W. E. B. (1994). *The souls of Black folk*. Avenel, NJ: Gramercy Books.

Duckworth, (2006). *"The having of wonderful ideas" and other essays on teaching and learning*. New York: Teachers College Press.

Eisner, E. W. (2002). *The arts and the creation of mind*. New Haven, CT: Yale University Press.

Ernst-Slavit, G. (1998). Using creative drama in the elementary ESL classroom. *TESOL Journal*, 7(4), 30–3.

Expósito, S. and Favela, A. (2003). Reflective voices: Valuing immigrant students and teaching ideological clarity. *The Urban Review*, 35(1), 73–91.

Giroux, H. (1991). *Modernism, postmodernism, feminism, and cultural politics*. Albany: State University of New York Press.

Kohn, A. (1999). *Punished by rewards: The trouble with gold stars, incentive plans, As, praise, and other bribes*. Boston, MA: Mariner Books.

Kossan, P. and Wong, K. (2011). Phoenix students walk out, march toward Capitol to protest immigration bill. *The Arizona Republic*. Retrieved June 10, 2012 from http://www.azcentral.com/news/articles/2011/03/04/20110304phoenix-capitol-student-march-abrk.html.

Krashen, S. D. (1982). *Principles and practice in second language acquisition*. New York: Prentice Hall.

Lave, J. and Wenger, E. (1991). *Situated learning: Legitimate peripheral participation*. Cambridge: Cambridge University Press.

Lee, N. (2001). *Childhood and society: Growing up in an age of uncertainty*. Maidenhead, UK: Open University Press.

Lerman, L. (2011). *Hiking the horizontal: Field notes from a choreographer*. Indianapolis, IN: Weselyan.

Levstik, L. and Barton, K. (2010). *Doing history: Investigating with children in elementary and middle schools*. New York: Routledge.

Li Li, H. (2006). Rethinking silencing silences. In M. Boler (Ed.), *Democratic dialogue in education: Troubling speech, disturbing silence* (pp. 69–88). New York: Peter Lang.

McMahon, F., Lytle, D., and Sutton-Smith, B. (2005). *Play: An interdisciplinary synthesis*. Lanham, MD: University Press of America.

Nachmanovitch, S. (1990). *Free play: Improvisation in life and art*. New York: Penguin Putnam.

Neelands, J., Goode, T., and Booth, D. (1990). *Structuring drama work: A handbook of available forms in theatre and drama*. Cambridge, UK: Cambridge University Press.

Olsen, L. (2008). *Made in America: Immigrant students in our public schools*. New York: New Press.

Pacheco, M. (2012). Learning in/through everyday resistance: A cultural–historical perspective on community resources and curriculum. *Educational Researcher*, 41(4), 121–32.

Performing Arts Workshop and Siegesmund, R. (2000). *A cycle of artistic inquiry*. Retrieved on June 8, 2012 from http://www.performingartsworkshop.org.

Piirainen-Marsh, A. and Tainio, L. (2009). Collaborative game-play as a site for participation and situated learning of a second language. *Scandinavian Journal of Educational Research*, 5(2), 167–83.

Risner, D. and Stinson, S. W. (2010). Moving social justice: Challenges, fears and possibilities in dance education. *International Journal of Education and the Arts*, 11(6), 1–26.

Romero, M. (2006). Racial profiling and immigration law enforcement: Rounding up of usual suspects in the Latino community. *Critical Sociology*, 32(2–3), 447–73.

Sawyer, R. K. (2001). Play as improvisational rehearsal: Multiple levels of analysis in children's play. In A. Goncu and E. Klein (Eds), *Children in play, story, and school* (pp. 19–38). New York: Guilford Press.

Schechner, R. (2003). *Performance studies: An introduction*. New York: Routledge.

Springgay, S. (2008). *Body knowledge and curriculum*. New York: Peter Lang.

Sutton-Smith, B. (1985). *Children's play: Past, present and future*. Philadelphia, PA: Please Touch Museum for Children.

Valenciana, C. (2006). Unconstitutional deportation of Mexican Americans during the 1930s: A family history and oral history. *Multicultural Education*, 13(3), 4–9.

Vygotsky, l. (1978). *Mind in society*. Cambridge, MA: Harvard University Press.

5

LIVING STORIES, TELLING STORIES

In Chapter 4, we focused on playing with language and playing through the arts as interrelated processes vital to emergent bilingual youth as they develop identities, knowledge and skills as creative, critical contributors to the world. Senses of possibility, connectedness and place may all be developed through play. This chapter emphasizes the role of stories in play: how we live through stories and tell those stories as a central way of knowing the world (Barone, 2001; Barone and Eisner, 2011; Clandinin and Connelly, 2004; Polkinghorne, 1988). We focus on building awareness of culturally and linguistically diverse narrative structures, as well as using multiple arts modalities and local varieties of English and other languages to tell stories about being and becoming bilingual in all its complexity.

As a teacher, you might be asked to implement a skill-based literacy program in your classroom in which the majority of instruction focuses on mastering discrete language tasks to build a foundation for reading and writing. In part, this skill-based approach emphasizes the acquisition of a generic grammatical structure, a decontextualized, cognitive behavioral act to be rewarded when performed "correctly." However, linguistic competence (with a focus on language form) should be developed through communicative competence (with a focus on meaning-making). An overemphasis on error correction for second language learners creates anxiety and raises their affective filters, preventing creative use of language or even a desire to produce utterances at all in the new language (Krashen, 1987). One can imagine the constraints an error-correction learning environment would place on the storytelling of emergent bilingual youth. Encouraging language development through meaning-making, in particular, storytelling is the focus of this chapter.

In the race to meet adequate yearly progress (AYP), schools might encourage teacher professional learning communities to analyze student performance in terms of testing data that measures discrete language arts skills. With this focus, professional learning communities often deprioritize asking questions about incorporating the principles of culturally and linguistically responsive storytelling into the curriculum. Instead, teachers feel pressure to use district-purchased pre-constructed curriculum (such as workbooks and test prep pages) that constrain the implementation of rich curricular content in the stories and traditions of our students' communities. However, there are many examples of teachers throughout the United States and across the world who have met these constraints with productive resistance (Cowhey, 2006; Igoa, 1995; Picower, 2012), including those who have written the vignettes in this chapter.

As you read, imagine how you might discuss the inclusion of culturally and linguistically responsive storytelling as part of your school's literacy program with your fellow teachers, school administrators, and community members. Emergent bilingual youth need opportunities to engage in socially negotiated uses of language that relate authentically to their lives. They need opportunities to tell personal stories in ways that humanize them and dignify their communities and families. This chapter's vignettes, in particular, show how storytelling can occur through different art mediums—oral story, visual art and drama—in ways that access diverse, local literacy practices. Further, these storytelling processes fulfill multiple state language arts standards that will contribute to students' language development in terms of adequate yearly progress. Our challenge is building professional communities to support the challenging and rewarding work of building a humanizing curriculum that also fulfills the skill-based expectations set forth in the climate of No Child Left Behind (Jordan, 2010).

Stories occur everywhere; they are the human way of constructing what we know, who we are, and how we live (Clandinin and Connelly, 2004). As we read, listen and talk, we relate meanings from our worlds to the stories with which we interact. Stories help us understand our interactions with others, the way that life continues and changes (Dewey, 1938). In this way, as teachers, we can rely on the universal experience of storytelling itself as we construct a creative, critical curriculum for emergent bilingual youth. Yet, the cultural purposes of storytelling, the structures for telling those stories, and the contexts of experience all influence our telling and interpretation of stories. This narrative meaning-making will look different in form and content based on the communities in which one participates. Pennycook (2010) suggests that such knowledge of diversity should be the beginning of our understanding of local language and literacy practices. When encountering the local stories of families, we can examine our own encounters with multiple voices, narrative structures, and modes of reading, writing, speaking and listening. We can reflect on how our cultural and linguistic responsiveness as teachers develops recursively through storytelling in the classroom.

Engaging diverse storytelling practices encourages the development of four dimensions of multicultural education outlined by Bennett (2010): equity pedagogy, curriculum reform, multicultural competence, and social action. In order to create and discuss stories with emergent bilingual youth, we can examine the ways our pedagogy invites student participation: *How do we foster or prevent collaboration among emergent bilingual youth and English speakers in telling stories?* We can analyze our curriculum and supplement or change the texts in use altogether: *Whose stories are told in educational materials and how are minoritized characters constructed in terms of their enacted power and voiced perspectives in those materials?* (Council on Interracial Books for Children, 1994) We can open ourselves to learning more about the cultures of our students and developing our cross-cultural competence: *What assumptions and misconceptions inform our teaching, and how can an examination of these cultural and linguistic ways of teaching lead to more equitable, humane classroom experiences?* Through this examination of the pedagogical environment, we can identify spaces for social action, as teachers and with students and families: *How can our storytelling projects address the concerns and questions at the heart of my students' communities?*

These questions are of particular importance for educators who were raised in white, middle class homes, where the contexts for literacy events likely mirror school-based practices with books and storytelling. In a foundational study, "What no bedtime story means," Heath (1982) found that white, middle class parent and child turn-taking in discussion about books parallels the initiation/reply/evaluation sequence used by most teachers in U.S. schools. These homes pay early attention to books and information derived from books in ways similar to those in school, such as children acknowledging questions raised in books, and, by the age of three, participating in the "listen and wait" structure when engaging in book or story talk.

There is nothing inherently "right" or "good" about mainstream literacy practices because they have been and continue to be preferred by schools (Heath, 1982; Minami, 2008). Instead, all local communities have expectations of legitimate participation in language and literacy events that are reinforced with each new interaction (Lave and Wenger, 1991). Every community engages in ethical examinations of how we "should" behave, what we "should" say and believe about speaking, listening, reading and writing. Assumptions undergirding local practices (such as the idea that boys don't cry—even when reading a sad story—or that people in the U.S. should only speak, read and write English) can be reproduced and/or questioned.

As educators, our authentic engagement in such ethical examinations of practice requires learning about the multiple cultures, languages, and schemas of our students. Schools can and should reconsider and revise curriculum around diverse home-based literacy practices. Schools can ask young people to read, write, and talk about daily activities such as making shopping lists, comparing prices at the store, looking at TV schedules, catalogues and advertisements. They can bring in and compose family letters, email, poems, calendars, and recipes. Further, students can retell stories about "the old days" or "back home," connecting across borders with ancestors, traditions, and family separated by time and place (Taylor, 1997).

Young people's cognitive schemas for telling and interpreting stories are developed through the locally contextualized language and literacy practices at work in their communities. These schemas include interactions between storyteller, story topic, and listener in relation to how the story functions, such as its flow or coherence toward a particular purpose. Minami (2008) found, for example, that English speakers generally structure events in chronological sequence but also spend ample time providing emotional responses and evaluative comments about characters, places and events throughout the story. By contrast, Japanese stories often do not provide such evaluative or emotional commentary, and instead focus primarily on the sequence of action. A mainstream U.S. teacher might think a Japanese American or Japanese immigrant student lacks the ability to tell a good story (from a Western perspective as one containing emotional complexity and moral judgment), rather than realize that the student's cultural schemas have informed her storytelling. The teacher could discuss with her multicultural, multilingual class what a "good story" is from different cultural perspectives, creating inquiry groups that investigate the criteria and examples of stories from different cultural groups across times, places, and voices.

To further complicate matters, cultural differences in storytelling structures are never static. Rather, cultural practices are in flux as new members initiate themselves, and are initiated, into a community. The dynamic, shifting qualities of cultural practices—in this case, storytelling—is a characteristic of sharing, borrowing and combining the knowledge, tools and practices across cultural groups in the U.S. (Paris, 2012). For example, Latin American and Asian Pacific Islander youth often engage with African American language and hip-hop cultures in their own creative expressions and community practices, creating a more fluid story-telling community than one simply defined by ethnic group membership (Alim, 2007; Paris, 2009).

As you read the following vignettes, reflect on the storytelling practices at work. Also, reflect on the schemas used to tell stories and the ways that the artist/teachers utilize culturally and linguistically responsive processes in their storytelling with emergent bilingual youth. In the first vignette, Eva Washburn-Repollo shows how storytelling requires as much listening as it does telling stories. Then, Joo Ae Kim analyzes the use of drawn and sculpted story boxes to tell stories of Korean students' first days after arrival to the U.S. Finally, Daphnie Sicre shares how she used shadow puppetry to tell stories with bilingual children in preschool.

VIGNETTE EIGHT

Conceptual Translations from English Language Learners' Indigenous Storytelling

Eva Rose B. Washburn-Repollo, Chaminade University of Honolulu

Students often hear stories from textbooks about worlds they did not come from. These stories of others need interpretation so they make sense in relation to students' own lives. Words are products of systems of cultural survival and communities in contact with each other. So, when teachers ask English learners to tell their stories in English, students may invent ways to transcend the limits of communicating in a non-native language. They may struggle to achieve a full expression of their thoughts, and the teacher of diverse learners must learn to make the classroom an accessible, safe space to freely share their differences. The key is a teacher who says: yes, I am interested in listening to your story.

As a storytelling teacher, I introduce the students in the beginning of the semester to elements in communication: the study of perception and the use of words to effectively communicate. I ask them to tell a story about something that happened in their lives, working toward clarity and specific details. I tell them that the audience should feel as if they were there when it happened or can imagine what happened. So, we begin by talking about how our experiences and expectations affect reality and how we assign meanings to things, events and people. We share short stories, for example, of what we expect from someone who says they love us. Or what kind of music we perceive the sunrise would play.

For a diverse classroom with students who use English as a second language this clarity and specificity can be challenging. But as a bilingual teacher I believe that their stories, when given the space, will access their local world views. As a storyteller, I support and trust my students and encourage them to use meaning-making in the stories we tell together. I make no judgments about their choices. There is at once a community and a relationship in the expression of their differences. I ask my students to always be mindful that they are telling stories across cultures, which means that I may need to help them translate the local, private and unique symbols (many of these are foreign to their classmates) they use in their stories.

My bilingual students access stories from their homes and cultural experiences, translate them into English to approximate meanings and perform the words with actions for the classroom. The focus of the storytelling activity is to make themselves understood. A few of the guidelines I established include: (1) the story should have a beginning, middle and end;[1] (2) the story told should matter to them as storytellers; and (3) the stories should include vivid descriptions using words that the audience can understand. I asked them to use their senses and to locate their story in place and time. I encouraged them to talk about events from their local experiences and I modelled my own local stories to them.

In this vignette, I share two stories told by my students. This first story occurred in my freshman college class. Many of my students came from the Pacific Islands and had been in Hawaii for a few months. They were eighteen years old and took storytelling with me to learn how to speak in English. Many of the multilingual students had studied earlier in the classrooms of their countries of origin.

Beetle Nut Chewing among the Elders

For his story, Debu chose beetle nut chewing—the pastime of his elders from his island, called Yap. During lectures, the students faced the whiteboard where a longer table for the teacher was located. This is where I stand to speak to them. There is a space next to the table fronting the students where performances such as speeches, dialogues, short scenes and stories are performed. The students stand before their classmates in this space. Not everyone knew about the beetle nut that grows in the Pacific Islands.

Debu began by telling the class that he wanted to tell us about the beetle nut. He described the beetle nut and told the class that everyone in his village loves to chew the beetle nut. Debu often stopped to search for the right word, struggling with actions for words without an exact translation into English. He attempted to explain the Yapese process of harvesting, drying, powdering and chewing with friends of his father, cousins, grandfather and grand uncles.

As I listened, I felt the village in his voice and in his actions; his actions and facial expressions signaled his arrival to the gathering space with people already squatting there. He often repeated the words, "they are always gathered, you know . . . they like this . . . yes . . . they love it!" He acted out how people gathered around the beetle nut. His body crouched in a comfortable fold, with bent knees as if squatting on a mat.

But he did not complete the pose. He returned to his audience to switch as the narrator of the story. He repeated the action and the lines as if finding other ways to tell different parts of the experience. I ventured to assist. My gut feeling was to supply the words. I defined what I saw in his movements as if playing charades. I said, "This is a usual thing, a part of their work day. This is not planned, they just naturally gather and sit." He said, "Yes, yes!" excited to hear that I saw and understood what he was portraying. I offered that back home men and women would gather like this under big, shady trees, or by a hill where they can watch their farms. I suggested that this might be a communal act of bonding and friendship. He added, "Sharing story." I said, "Like lessons to the young." He agreed, " Yes, that is what I mean."

Debu described how the chewing action delivers a chemical that relaxes whoever chews it. The red juices stain the teeth, but this is considered part of the experience. During this description, Debu's pace was incessant, but English words were not available to him to cover the details. Other students unfamiliar with his culture looked at me, felt genuine interest, and asked questions. Debu had built a new sense of community with his audience. And, as a class, we learned that love and friendship are shared in many different ways.

The Passing of a Chief

As part of a cultural self-awareness project, Sifo, a student from the Marshall Islands, told a story about the passing of a chief and what this meant to him and his people. I expressed that I was grateful for his sharing and waited to listen to him. He responded to my interest. This story was both unique and universal at the same time. Sifo talked about a ceremony by the shoreline, in which his people offered their chief's body to the ocean. He said that the presence of the spirit was perceived by those who gathered. He changed his tone to stand as a witness and storyteller, telling his audience that the spirit of the dead chief had arrived to be part of the ceremony. The spirit moved and commanded the winds and the waters. Sifo fumbled with gestures and requested to use words in his native language when he spoke of the spirit and its power. I agreed.

He spoke words in Marshallese.[2] The sounds of the careful words felt deep and spiritual. He looked toward the skies as he spoke of the different names of birds and animals. His eyes shone when he spoke of sea creatures that gathered near the body. His awe was genuine as he said, "This is what my culture is. It is a gift. It cannot be forgotten."

He later explained that the mysterious event happened only because this was a loving and beloved chief. He emphasized that it was not a typical chief burial. He was also the last known chief from a long line of native chiefs before their country was colonized and new ways of doing things encroached upon the Marshall Islands. He translated into English his belief that culture means "gift." This mattered to the story because his death carried away the symbol of what they knew of the past. Sifo had chosen a story about bringing back the past, about making the chief's memory and the ways of the island last. This act of retelling was testimony of its importance as curriculum of school.

Then I asked, "How can this culture be gifted to others other than retelling this story?" He had no answer; he just smiled. Perhaps this is an incomprehensible loss from which he himself cannot find ways to recover. He is after all one of those who left the place. He too had learned the language of the colonizer.

Reflections as a Teacher

In storytelling spaces, students exist between their worlds of past and present. Through a struggle to find words in their non-native language, the students retell themselves and the world they inhabited. As a teacher, I want to address the loss of important relationships with parents and home cultures and provide bilingual students the opportunity to keep their deep pasts alive in an attempt to keep these worlds present in their hearts and minds.

I find these moments of naming the experiences of students into English vital to bilingual classrooms. Students learn there are words without translation because the concepts connected to those words are built from people's experiences, from home. More than the words in English they learn to approximate the experiences of their local world views. Their stories constantly reveal to me the students' struggle to negotiate bilingual spaces. When Debu talked about the men squatting around chewing beetle nut, he introduced not only the process of this pastime but the warmth and comfort of his relatives' company. When spaces are allowed for students to bring these practices into their academic environments, they remain whole. Too often, schools ask bilingual students to separate their academic learning from their home cultures and primary language. Growing up in the Philippines I read and learned about American stories in my textbooks and I separated my Cebuano world from academic learning. I needed to suppress my home, separate from the self I was becoming at school. Debu's stories allowed him to bring some part of his home into the academic setting.

The encouragement I give to bilingual students comes from my own experiences. Sifo showed surprise like other bilingual students when they realize my real excitement about giving them these spaces. Before I became very comfortable about sharing my culture in the classroom, I often found myself searching for exact translations of my experiences into English words. I often felt frustrated, but now I have come to accept that some of my stories from back home may never be told in this new place that I inhabit. My students understand that I know this, as they do. Our stories connect me to their lives, and together we build membership in a classroom community of our making. They trust that my encouragement is not judgmental and I trust that learning has happened when they tell their own stories.

★   ★   ★

Working with Korean Newcomer Immigrant Adolescents in Community Art

Joo Ae Kim, University of Georgia

Introduction

Immigrant newcomer adolescents are separated by the gap between their past and present, their culture of origin and host country culture, their home and school, and their internal and external worlds (Rousseau, 2004). Many immigrant adolescents struggle with assimilation, their parents' own culture, language differences, and school involvement. Though the challenges immigrant adolescents experience are well known, most adolescents do not receive enough support from their communities, and as a bilingual artist and teacher, I wanted to contribute such support.

Description of the Art Project

Living in a college town in the United States, I have met many Korean American immigrant families, many of whom came to the United States for study or research. When I spent time with immigrant families, I heard about their struggles in great detail. In particular, immigrant adolescents face many difficulties living in America. Following my strong interest in immigrant adolescents, I conducted an art program at a local Korean church with Korean newcomer adolescents. The main purpose of this art program was to help newcomer adolescents discover their self-identities through art-making processes. In addition, this community-based art education program reaches out to Korean newcomer adolescents to help them achieve self-esteem, express their self-identities, and understand their own environments. This story is about six middle school Korean students,[3] all recent arrivals to the United States, four girls and two boys. Two of the participants came to the United States two months before our work together. Four students had lived in the United States for six months. All participants were in an acculturation process in the United States and struggling to learn English in school. All the participants were born and reared in Korea with a strong Korean ethnic identity. I designed art lessons so that the participants could express their emotions, interests, or experiences as recent arrival immigrants. In our art-making together, I did not focus on teaching art techniques, but instead gave tips and suggestions to develop the participants' ideas about each project. I gave the students freedom to choose materials, which helped them discover how to express their own personal messages.

Story Boxes from the Memories of the Participants

Over the course of eight weeks, the participants created three works of art. The first work was a story box that described their first impressions or first day at their U.S. school. The participants worked to combine paint, drawing, and collage in the box. The second art project was a pop-up painting with a plaster hand sculpture attached to the canvas that expressed their transitional lives in the United States. The last project was alternative book art through which they creatively expressed their desires and hopes for themselves in their new culture. From past memories to dreams for the future, the participants expanded their emotions and identities through the art-making process and works of art.

We began the first project by sharing early experiences in the United States. Because all the participants remembered the first day at school clearly, I asked the students to illustrate their stories in a cardboard box. The participants created their own scenarios with various materials inside the box. As an introduction, I shared my experiences as a newcomer to the United States, including embarrassing moments. These moments helped me build a good trusting relationship with the participants. After the participants heard my stories, several felt safe enough to share their stories within the group. Christina talked about her arrival at the airport in Atlanta. She was surprised that a middle-aged woman smoked in a public place since it was rare to see women smoking in public places in Korea. I gave participants a few minutes to think about their experiences, and then I focused on how the participants delivered their stories through their facial expressions. I encouraged them to express their emotions

FIGURE 5.1 *Christina's Story Box,* photo by Joo Ae Kim

by drawing pictures of themselves and I suggested that they show their feelings in their drawings though gesture, facial expressions, and various sizes of figures. Christina wanted to make herself look afraid in the drawing and her figure covered her face with her hands. I could sense her fear (Figure 5.1)

After the participants drew the figures, they created a scene in a cardboard box using a variety of art materials. Some participants painted inside of the box first, and then attached the drawn figures later. Other participants did a collage with pictures they selected from magazines, or cut out shapes from construction paper and fabrics. At first, the participants were confused about how to use the art materials because they were usually limited in their choice of art materials in the art classrooms of public schools. I encouraged the participants to think "outside the box" with unfamiliar art materials such as balloons, tiny straw hats, and scrubbers. After the participants completed the story box, they participated in the small group sharing. They actively asked and answered one another's questions; however, their stories were superficial because they were not ready to share deeply personal stories. I hoped that they would build a sense of belonging for deeper stories later. After the participants made a box, I asked each one to film the inside of the box with a camcorder because I wanted them to use all their senses to express their emotions. To establish a creative and comfortable atmosphere, the participants selected music to play during their art-making. Because I saw the possibility of combining music and art during the art-making process, participants chose background music for the video clips they had recorded. The connection between visual art and music brought expressive power to their story box.

Dong's and Eun's Stories

Dong and Eun are siblings, and the length of their stay in the United States was the same; however, their art-based responses to their new culture were completely different. Dong is a sixteen-year-old male student. He was quiet and focused during art sessions. Eun is two years younger than Dong and is a female middle school student. She was outgoing and positive, always visibly happy during art lessons. In their boxes, Dong's self-portrait was confused, while Eun's face was elated.

In Dong's story box, he expressed confusion about the first day of school (see Figure 5.2). He created a circular design as a background and drew many circles in the eyes of the self-portrait. The music that he added in the video clip was very loud and had a fast tempo—a Korean dance song. The music started with a scream, and he showed dizzy eyes first in the video clip. He moved the camcorder in a clockwise motion several times, and viewers could read his complicated emotions. Dong put his drawn figures in the center, and arranged the items that reminded him of the first day of school. The contrast between the red and blue colors increased the tension in the scene. While

FIGURE 5.2 *Dong's Story Box: The Confusing World*, photo by Joo Ae Kim

FIGURE 5.3 *Eun's Story Box: Brand New Day*, photo by Joo Ae Kim

pointing to his story box, Dong shared that, because of the language and cultural differences, he did not know how to act in school.

On the other hand, Eun created a happy moment inside of her box (see Figure 5.3). She drew a smiling face in the bright colored background and used differently colored beads to represent her "American" name, Irene. She covered the edge of the box with rainbow-colored yarn and used pink and yellow to express her happy moment. Her story box helped me to understand her optimistic and energetic personality. Because Eun came to the United States during winter, the Christmas trees in her box reminded her of her day of arrival. In addition, she drew an airplane flying from Korea to the United States. Eun shared feeling excited when she saw her new town in the United States, and created story box figures celebrating these new days.

Conclusion

This visual arts project helped newly arrived Korean youth to share their stories. Opening one's heart to others was not easy for all participants, but as a bridge, the story box helped them to talk about their personal stories and grow in their confidence. Ballbe (1997) found that "by expressing experiences and feelings verbally and through art-making and writing, the immigrant adolescents progressed toward self-awareness and reconciliation" (p. 8). For these students, visual art made invisible values visible (Scher, 2007). Sharing participants' past memories about their first impressions of the United States helped them to communicate their feelings about being in a new land and language. Outside of the traditional school environment, newcomers extend their capability without any pressure from teachers, stress from peers, or worry about grades. Cultural identity is tremendously significant because it is an important factor in establishing self-identity. This art project provided a place both for personal expression and small group sharing about their cultural heritage as Korean Americans. The art programs at Athens Korean Presbyterian Church aided in promoting immigrant adolescents' emotional well-being by connecting the students to their wider Korean American community.

★   ★   ★

¿Y el Caballito de mar, dónde vive? Exploring Science and Literacy through Bilingual Storytelling and Shadow Puppetry with Head Start Children

Daphnie Sicre, New York University

The Puppetry Residency

For the past twelve years, I have taught middle school and high school drama. Prior to this, I had not considered teaching elementary or preschool children. I felt I could relate to adolescents and enjoyed our intellectual conversations. Never did I ever think I would teach preschool children because, in my eyes, I would not be able to communicate with them. When I was first approached about this project, I was very hesitant—who are these little people? What can they do? As a result of my experiences with bilingual preschoolers, I highly urge teachers to take that step forward, and place themselves outside of their usual comfort zones. I believe it only makes us better educators to confront our own assumptions about young people, whatever they may be.

Last spring, I had the opportunity to teach science and literacy through storytelling and shadow puppetry at various Bilingual Head Start programs in New Jersey. I worked for George St Playhouse in New Brunswick, NJ, which had been awarded a grant to work with three Head Start programs in the area. The theatre needed a teaching artist who could teach in both Spanish and English. Spanish is my first language, and I have been teaching theatre for over ten years. I knew I would be a good fit for the position, but having never taught this age group, I did not know what to expect. Sometimes we become very comfortable in our own "teaching zones." We become good at one age group and decide that is it; there is no reason to work with another group. I had to learn to let go and take a risk. Once I was able to do this, I anticipated that the children would be adorable, energetic, and probably difficult to keep on task for more than ten minutes at a time. I thought adding the bilingual factor might complicate my teaching and their learning even more, and I was not sure if I would be spending my time translating between the two languages instead of facilitating the children's creativity.

Needless to say, I was a bit intimidated by the challenges that faced me. After finishing my residency, I am now grateful for the experience and inspired to do more with children of this age group; I want to encourage them, their wonderful imaginations and stories through theatre. I never imagined I would want to work with preschool children, but they filled my days with joy, surprise and love and taught me self-confidence in a completely new way. As an educator, I learned new ways of teaching theatre and overcame my apprehension of teaching in two languages in the process. In *Stories in the*

Classroom (1990), Bob Barton and David Booth both agree that stories allow students to understand new concepts in a better way:

> Story gives children ways of dealing constructively with inner experience, communicating an intuitive, subconscious understanding of their nature . . . Story acquaints children (even those who do not or cannot read) with a variety of language patterns, some of which may be outside their language community. It familiarizes them with literary language, an awareness they will need as readers and writers.
>
> (pp. 15–16)

My preschoolers' engagement with literature and drama is a fitting example of this process.

I started the theatre unit reading one of Eric Carle's books, *Mr Seahorse* (2004), in both English and Spanish. The other teaching artist and I read the book at the same time and in both languages. It was wonderful to see the students' faces light up when I read the book to them in Spanish. The children would giggle as I read certain words they knew. Those children who did not speak Spanish wondered what they were hearing. The other teacher and I would pause after reading a page and take a moment to explain or translate. At times, we would use repetition in both languages, repeating the word in English once, and then followed by saying it in Spanish. Other times, we would use context clues in both languages, start the sentence in English and end it in Spanish or vice versa. We encouraged the students to join us, participate as we read, and say new words aloud using several movement-based games and activities. The beauty of this teaching was that the children learned new words and interacted with each other in two languages.

Then we taught the children about shadow puppetry and the manipulation of light, shadow and character to tell stories. We demonstrated how our fish puppets could live in the same habitats as the fish and seahorse in the Eric Carle story. During our final day of class, the children exchanged stories in both languages, giving them a new voice to express their creativity and move beyond the text. This is when the magical talents of the children's bilingualism began. Many of the students imitated me and the story I created. They grabbed the book and told their version of the story even though they didn't know how to read text. They used some of my expressions and imitated my characterization to re-create the story. But when they were given their own shadow puppets to create their own stories, their imaginations were piqued and their stories unfolded. They shared stories about friendship, fights, and food.

FIGURE 5.4 *Let's Listen to What the Seahorse Has to Say*, photo by Christa Cillaroto

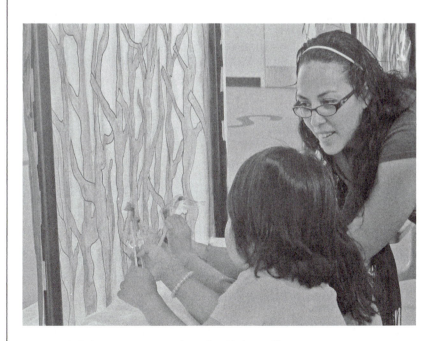

FIGURE 5.5 *What Is Your Story?* photo by Christa Cillaroto

The Creation of the Fish Doctor

As teachers, we had not expected or anticipated what would happen if the delicate puppets broke. We had thought of other circumstances, but never that the puppets would fall apart while the students were using them or how they would react to this happening. When the first class came in with their puppets, ready to learn how to use them, the first puppet fell apart. The glue spots we had used originally during puppet construction were not strong enough to hold the puppets together once the students started playing with them. One by one, the puppets broke. A couple of children started to cry.

My co-teaching artist took one of the broken puppets, and started fixing it, calling her the Fish Doctor. The Doctor became an essential character who helped with each fish that got hurt. We weaved the character in the story we told, and as each fish puppet came apart, we were there with a solution. The Fish Doctor had come to the rescue, bringing the other fish back to life.

The crying quickly stopped. Instead, the children brought the puppets to life, playing and exploring. With each new calamity, we were ready with the Fish Doctor. The students talked to the Fish Doctor, describing what had happened to their fish, in both Spanish and English. They were 100 percent convinced the Fish Doctor was a real fish doctor. And this puppet became a conduit to speak to us in either language.

Final Thoughts

Barton and Booth (1990) share that, "When stories are told by children, our role (apart from listening to them) is to imbue them with meaning. They are not simply anecdotes but appraisals of their experiences. Their confidence grows, and out of it gradually blossoms a cognition" (p. 50). This storytelling experience became a language learning experience for me as well as the preschoolers. They were exposed to new words in a meaningful context, they experienced how science and literature intersect, and more importantly, they created stories drawing on their own imaginations in English, Spanish and in some cases, both languages. Joy (1994) says that storytelling enhances all language and communication skills and supports many other kinds of skills taught in a curriculum. I could see this process happening in my students. They started using words such as "habitat" and "cohabitate" in context, associating scientific terms and settings to the storytelling descriptions we had created together.

After completing the theatre residency, we met with the classroom teachers, and they gave us some wonderful feedback about the children. The teachers shared their own stories of how the students we had worked with kept creating new stories and shared the stories with their classmates. The teachers also expressed that they appreciated looking at a book from a theatrical perspective and, most importantly, that there are other stories to be told aside from those found within the book. I encourage theatre teachers, science teachers, classroom teachers, and *all* teachers to step out of their comfort zone and try teaching a new age group, in new cultural and linguistic contexts. You will be amazed at what you and the children are capable of doing. I also encourage teachers to enable students to explore worlds not only in English but also in their native language. Finally, I implore teachers to use theatre and theatre techniques throughout the curriculum to give children multiple opportunities to expand their creativity and to bring their experiences into the classroom through story and performance.

★   ★   ★

The young people in each of these vignettes—the student who told of beetle nut chewing, the immigrant Korean youth who created story boxes, and the preschoolers who used shadow puppetry—worked through arts-based storytelling processes to reflect on their bilingual, bicultural experiences in the U.S. The teachers in these vignettes reflected on their understanding of their students' emergent hybrid identities, as influenced by the social practices and institutions they encountered.

As a teacher, we hope that you will take this lifelong journey to investigate the worlds of your students through stories. In part, we can do this by connecting with emergent bilingual youth through interacting with the enculturation agents (people of influence) in their lives. Early in the book, we introduced Moll et al.'s (1992) foundational study in which researchers collaborated with teachers to conduct interviews with their students' families in their homes. From these interviews, the teachers designed lessons that accessed specific funds of knowledge, or family-based assets. Similarly, Gail Weinstein (2006) documented how community-based organizations built project-based curriculum with their second language learners' lives as classroom texts. The vignettes in this chapter utilize student assets through storytelling in different art mediums, and students feel valued and valuable through telling their stories. We can extend students' sense of self-worth by collaboratively finding languages to express their struggles with giving up part of who they are, recovering and extending their identities in humanizing and connective ways. We can ask students to think critically about the socio-political and economic conditions that affect their lives, as the vignettes in the next several chapters address.

As we engage in telling and discussing personal stories, we build a critical relationship with the characters and their struggles, which can build critical consciousness about the world (Greene, 2000). Through self-reflection and perspective-taking as teachers and students, we can build empathy as we re-experience our own struggles in relation to the lives of others. While the ways we tell and understand stories will differ culturally, the sensory details and content of our storied lives build bridges and bond diverse people. Stories allow for building multicultural, multilingual classrooms as communal spaces through and because of difference, rather than regardless of it.

What happens when schools don't engage in the language and literacy participation structures used in diverse homes? What happens when the only legitimate self-identity is one formed through the unidirectional development from poverty to the middle class, from immigrant to assimilated citizen, from native language speaker to English only? Stories are particularly powerful ways to reconnect a fragmented curriculum, torn into grammar worksheets and reading comprehension questions in disjointed discipline-based lessons. Stories weave relationships among past, present and future for emergent bilingual youth, reintegrating lives fragmented by restrictive language and immigration policies that separate families and erase cultures. As you embark on your own storytelling journeys with your students, imagine the possibilities of young people guiding the curriculum—learners' lives as texts for learning, being and becoming.

Questions to Consider

1. Think about a typical day in your life. What stories do you tell? To whom? When?

2. What stories do your students tell you? What stories do they tell each other? What do their stories tell you about who they are and what they are interested in?

3. How do you respond when a child tells you a story? What questions could you ask to learn more?

4. Consider the storytelling practices in the vignettes of this chapter. How do the facilitators develop the students' heritage, language, and identities in the process of storytelling?

5. How might you use different arts mediums and modalities for storytelling to build a culturally and linguistically responsive culture in your classroom?

Notes

1. Plot structure is itself culturally constructed. Students can explore this concept, and multiple plot structures, as part of the storytelling process.
2. Marshallese is the name for the language of the Marshall Islands people, named after the colonial explorer John Marshall. The indigenous name is *Kajin Ṃajeḷ*.
3. All names are pseudonyms.

References

Alim, H. S. (2007). "The Whig Party don't exist in my hood": Knowledge, reality, and education in the Hip Hop Nation. In H. S. Alim and J. Baugh (Eds), *Talkin Black talk: Language, education, and social change* (pp. 15–29). New York: Teachers College Press.

Ballbe, T. M. (1997). A group art therapy experience for immigrant adolescents. *American Journal of Art Therapy*, 36, 8–19.

Barone, T. (2001). *Touching eternity: Enduring outcomes of teaching*. New York: Teachers College Press.

Barone, T. and Eisner, E. (2011). *Arts-based research*. Thousand Oaks, CA: Sage.

Barton, B. and Booth, D. (1990). *Stories in the classroom*. Ontario: Pembroke.

Bennett, C. (2010). *Comprehensive multicultural education: Theory and practice*. Boston, MA: Allyn and Bacon

Carle, E. (2004). *Mr Seahorse*. New York: Philomel Books.

Clandinin, D. J. and Connelly, F. M. (2004). *Narrative inquiry: Experience and story in qualitative research*. San Francisco: Jossey-Bass.

Council on Interracial Books for Children. (1994). 10 quick ways to analyze children's books for racism and sexism. In L. Christensen, S. Karp, and B. Bigelow (Eds), *Rethinking our classrooms: Teaching for equity and justice*. Milwaukee, MI: Rethinking Schools.

Cowhey, M. (2006). *Black ants and Buddhists: Thinking critically and teaching differently in the primary grades*. Portland, ME: Stenhouse.

Dewey, J. (1938). *Experience and education*. New York: Collier Books.

Greene, M. (2000). *Releasing the imagination: Essays on education, the arts and social change*. San Francisco: Jossey Bass.

Heath, S. B. (1982). What no bedtime story means: Narrative skills at home and school. *Language in Society*, 11, 49–76.

Igoa, C. (1995). *The inner world of the immigrant child*. New York: Routledge.

Jordan, W. (2010). Defining equity: Multiple perspectives to analyzing the performance of diverse learners. *Review of Research in Education*, 34(1), 142–78.

Joy, F. (1994). Tips for using a simple tale. In National Storytelling Association (Ed.), *Tales as tools: The power of story in the classroom*. Tennessee: Jonesborough.

Krashen, S. (1987). *Principles and practice in second language acquisition*. New York: Prentice Hall.

Lave, J. and Wenger, E. (1991). *Situated learning: Legitimate peripheral participation*. Cambridge: Cambridge University Press.

Minami, M. (2008). Telling good stories in different languages: Bilingual children's styles of story construction and their linguistic and educational implications. *Narrative Inquiry*, 18, 83–110.

Moll, L., Amanti, C., Neff, D., and González, N. (1992). Funds of knowledge for teaching: Using a qualitative approach to connect homes and classrooms. *Theory Into Practice*, 31(2), 132–41.

Paris, D. (2009). "They're in my culture, they speak the same way": African American language in multiethnic high schools. *Harvard Educational Review*, 79, 428–47.

—— (2012). Culturally sustaining pedagogy: A needed change in stance, terminology, and practice. *Educational Researcher*, 41(3), 93–7.

Pennycook, A. (2010). *Language as local practice*. New York: Routledge.

Picower, B. (2012). *Practice what you teach: Social justice education in the classroom and the streets*. New York: Routledge.

Polkinghorne, D. (1988). *Narrative knowing and the human sciences.* Albany: SUNY Press.

Rousseau, C. (2004). Creative expression workshops for immigrant and refugee children. *American Academy of Child and Adolescent Psychiatry,* 43, 235–8.

Scher, A. (2007). Can the arts change the world? The transformative power of community arts. *New Direction for Adults and Continuing Education,* 116, 3–12.

Taylor, D. (Ed.) (1997). *Many families, many literacies: An international declaration of principles.* Portsmouth, NH: Heinemann Trade.

Weinstein, G. (2006). Learners' lives as curriculum: an integrative project-based model for language learning. In G. H. Beckett and P. Ch. Miller (Eds), *Project-based second and foreign language education: Past, present, and future* (pp. 159–66). Charlotte, NC: Information Age Publishing.

6
RESPONDING CRITICALLY TO LITERATURE

In Chapter 5, we discussed playful pedagogies utilizing culturally and linguistically responsive stories and storytelling with emergent bilingual youth. In this chapter, we expand on the importance of children's and families' stories, exploring a variety of approaches for reading and responding to literature with emergent bilingual youth. We provide guiding principles for teachers interested in building critical, responsive literature-based projects as well as vignettes that illustrate these principles. We begin with a likely familiar response to literature, and then move to more critical responses, which challenge readers to ask questions about what cultures assume to be true or common sense and use community knowledge and experiences to talk back to the dominant discourses.

Literature as a Transaction between Readers, Writers and Artists

To begin, whenever we read a text (such as a picture book, painting, short story, poem, photograph, performance, or film), we make sense of that text and the narrative it conveys, from our own subject position, which is comprised of identities, values and beliefs embedded in larger sociocultural and political discourses. Authors, artists, photographers, performers and filmmakers present their texts as whole products, leaving it up to the reader or viewer to reconstruct the piece as created by the text maker, and at the same time, to experience evocatively an aesthetic response to the art. Such an aesthetic, personal response to a whole text is what Rosenblatt (1985) refers to as connections that enable readers to live visually and personally through the experience they are reading, viewing and imagining.

Literature study, driven most often by standardized, depoliticized curricula, rarely asks students to examine their own subject positions in relation to multiple perspectives, and struggles of power within sociopolitical contexts. Yet, through responding critically to literature and other texts, students will learn to decode stories and images as a question-raising, problem-posing process. They will make sense of what they are reading and viewing from an active stance. From this perspective, neither the text nor the reader can claim sole authorship over a text's meaning; instead, meanings are co-constructed or transacted (Rosenblatt, 1978). Asking students to visualize and interrogate literature with their own images, performances, and other forms of art—particularly in relation to their own lives, communities and languages—opens the door to co-construction of the meaning and aesthetic value of the text.

For example, as you read this book, you co-construct meaning informed both by your lived experiences and by those of the various authors, poets, and artists we have included. As editors, we organized this book deliberately to direct your attention to ideas we think are essential for understanding the ways arts-based education can engage emergent bilingual students in co-constructed, meaning-ful, aesthetic, and critical practices that can transform their worlds. Yet, we do not have control over the ways you will interpret this writing, nor do we hope to. The power of literacy is the transactive co-creation that occurs between and through writing and reading. As the reader, you take up these ideas in your own way, interpreted through your experiences within particular communities of practice. And we embrace these many interpretations as the pedagogical strength that comes from multiple perspectives.

Going Beyond a Basic Response to Literature

Many teachers are taught to use strategies for connecting readers to text as a response to literature. The tripartite strategy (Keene and Zimmermann, 1997) of text-to-self, text-to-text, and text-to-world is probably familiar to many readers. In this set of interactions, the goal is to help students respond to literature or other text through making particular kinds of connections with one's self, other texts, and the world. Prompts to make these connections include:

- Text-to-self connections:
    - *What I just read reminds me of something that happened to me . . .*
    - *I can relate to the characters in the story because they . . .*
    - *I agree/don't agree with what I just read because in my experience . . .*

- Text-to-text connections:
    - *What I just read reminds me of another book I have read . . .*
    - *The story is similar to that book because . . .*
    - *The story is different from that book because . . .*

- Text-to-world connections:
    - *What I just read reminds me of something that happened around me . . .*
    - *What I just read reminds me of what is happening in the world right now . . .*
    - *What I just read seems to contradict what is happening in the world right now . . .*

These strategies do have the potential to move beyond comprehension questions within the world of the book, as they emphasize the important transactional relationship the reader builds with the text. As illustrated in the vignettes that follow, teachers can prompt reading connections to students' bilingual worlds, and select literature that is closely related—in visual and storied content—to those worlds. Such cultural and linguistic responsiveness means that students can make more meaningful connections, rather than being told an authorial or teacherly meaning or making superficial, unexamined connections to their lives. With bilingual world connections, emergent bilingual youth can co-construct meaning based on the language practices they bring to school. Students need multiple opportunities to critically examine and respond to text through art, discussion, and performance, all of which require students to talk with one another using familiar language and cultural practices to interpret meanings, and to show connections to their personal and social worlds.

The tripartite response to literature strategy (connections to self, text and world) is one tool among many. Overreliance on a single strategy—particularly strategies that use limited critical thinking or bilingual-world relatedness—will lead students to view literature response as an inauthentic, predictable exercise. This chapter identifies pedagogical strategies that deeply engage local communities and knowledge that students bring to class. Critical literacy involves engaging students in discussions about assumed naturalness of cultural practices, as students examine multiple perspectives and relations of power within the world of the literature and in relation to those in students' communities. As you will see in the vignettes[1] that follow, teachers went well beyond the tripartite text connections to engage students in critical responses to literature.

It is important to underscore here the value of drawing on students' home language and bilingual language practices when responding to text. Many teachers who are monolingual may fear using bilingual strategies in the classroom because they cannot participate in their students' movement between languages. However, with a shift in role, teachers can become learners of their students' home languages and literacy practices in their transactions with text. Such translanguaging reading practices (Baker, 2011) are a hybrid, fluid activity in which conceptual understanding develops in/between both the students' home languages and English. It may be difficult at first for monolingual teachers to trust this practice, but the results will likely excite and astound you—and along the way, as a teacher, you can engage in emergent bilingual practices yourself!

Because responding to text is personal, cultural, and aesthetic, emergent bilingual students need both languages to express their responses to what they read and view. The following vignette tells the story of how young people relate their experiences as migrant working families to their study of literature in the classroom. As you read, notice the role of language and culture when these students respond to Sandra Cisneros' (1984) *The House on Mango Street*—how they connect self, community, text, and the world around them using their home language as a source of meaning and as a critical interpretation tool to read the word and the world they know (Freire, 1970).

VIGNETTE ELEVEN
─────────

Migrant Students Vignette Their Lives: Languages and Cultures Cross the Fields into the Classrooms

Fernando Rodríguez-Valls, San Diego State University-IVC; Sandra Kofford, Imperial County Office of Education; Alicia Apodaca, Central Union High School; Lizett Samaniego, Heber Elementary School

Introduction

Mobility guides the lives of hundreds of migrant students in the Imperial Valley, California. Families often change their homes; parents travel to different cities to work on the seasonal harvesting; and students have to attend different schools. Living and learning for migrant students in the Imperial Valley oscillates between two languages—Spanish and English—which freely coexist among students, parents, and teachers. Yet schools rarely utilize this bilingual richness to supplement their monolingual curricula. Parents, teachers and students constantly cross the México–U.S. border seamlessly bargaining cultures from one side to other side; nonetheless, teaching practices remain framed within one language, English, which hinders the students' bicultural development.

Cognizant of these circumstances, one elementary school teacher, one high school teacher, and a professor at San Diego State University-IVC developed a language *and* arts curriculum for fifty migrant students. This language *and* arts program was part of a Summer Academy created by the Director of the Migrant Education Program in the ICOE (Imperial Valley County Office of Education). The main goal of this Summer Academy was to give voice to the students' experiences by using both languages—Spanish and English—and the arts as instruments for students to think critically about their lives and to provoke in them a lifelong desire for learning. The three teachers developed the curriculum and activities mindful of the findings of Purcell-Gates (1997) in her research of cycles of low literacy, about educators who aim to create culturally responsive and effective practices. First, educators have to understand how students learn and how they read the word and their world (Freire, 1970); and second, they have to create experiences that allow students to analyze and explore the formal and informal sociocultural contexts of school, community, and home where their learning takes place.

For four weeks, from Monday to Thursday, tenth grade high school students critically read, analyzed and interpreted books, poetry, lyrics and videos for three hours a day at San Diego State University–Imperial Valley Campus. Utilizing Habermas' (2001) principles of communicative action, critical reading within this project was defined as a twofold communal activity where readers create their personal meaning while reading the text, to later compare and contrast their meanings with the views of other readers, which helps to construct a common ground for understanding. Following these readings, students wrote poems and designed graffiti walls on long paper to illustrate their lives as migrant students. The main goal of all these activities was to encourage students to examine some of the challenges they encounter in their lives, such as bilingualism, moving from place to place, and the need to fit in. As a result of these activities, we hoped that students would develop awareness of how their bilingual—Spanish and English—and bicultural—México and United States—experiences are constantly being refined, constructing a multidimensional cultural identity.

I am Bilingual and Bicultural

To begin the analysis of their bilingual and bicultural world, teachers and students dialogically read the chapter "My Name" from Sandra Cisneros' book *The House on Mango Street* (1984). Vásquez (2004) defines dialogic reading as the "*why*" reading that goes beyond factual reading. Analyzing how the main character of the story, Esperanza, ponders if her name sounds better in English—Hope—than in Spanish, students and teachers explored the idea of names "getting caught" between languages. During this dialogue, Lizbeth, one of the students, shared, "Esperanza sounds stronger when you say it in Spanish than when you hear it English." Mirna, another student, said, "Sometimes my teachers pronounce my name with an English accent missing the strong /r/ sound. That completely changes my name. I want to tell them '*mi nombre es Mirrrrrna con una ere que suena de verdad* [My name is Mirrrrrna with a /r/ that sounds real]." Listening to Mirna's statement, it is evident that students' names are an important level of their student and cultural identity. Consequently, building cultural responsive practices must begin by recognizing and valuing students' origins. Embracing students' identities fosters learning processes where the participants—teachers and students—treat each other as meaningful protagonists rather than detached antagonists.

Students and teachers further explored Mirna's words by reading the poem "The Rose that Grew from Concrete" written by hip-hop artist Tupac

Shakur (1999); they also watched the video with the same title (www.youtube. com/watch?v=WwURSd_Nj_Q). During this multimedia activity Penelope, one of the teachers, posed the question, "Do you feel like a rose that grew from concrete when a teacher mispronounces your name?" Jumping into the question, Loreta shouted, "*Siento que no les importa* [I feel that they do not care]. I am only a student, my name does not matter." Araceli, another teacher, wrote at the board "I am only a student"; then she pointed to the words and said, "Any thoughts?" Rapidly, Alan responded, "I think sometimes teachers think that we are only students. But, we are more. We are more. I am Mexican American, I am the son of Mateo and María, both farm workers." Diego followed Alan's thought, saying, "They think I am weird because I listen to Metallica all day long. If they would see beyond this, they would find a student who likes to read books and really enjoys writing in English and Spanish." Being part of these dialogues helped teachers realize that culturally responsive teaching requires teachers to know about their students' cultural and personal identities As Penelope, one of the teachers, said, "To teach is to know who your students are."

Students concluded the week of dialogic reading sessions writing and illustrating individual bio-poems titled "Who am I?" describing the distinctiveness of their various cultural idiosyncrasies (i.e. academic culture, linguistic culture) as migrant students previously discussed through the readings. Teachers emphasized the significance of all the different cultures that configure individual cultural identities. Bhabha (1996) defines cultural identity as the "hankie" that holds all the cultures surrounding the life of each individual. An excerpt of Donato's bio-poem titled "*Realidad/Reality*" and illustrated with an anarchist symbol, exemplifies the engrossing and assertive individuality displayed by each migrant student participating in this project:

> *Soy una persona muy anormal, leer y dibujar es mi especialidad; Tengo una personalidad muy particular, no me gusta que me gobiernen, pero me gusta trabajar; soy solitario, callado, e independiente; soy un anarquista, las estupideces de nosotros no me gustan pero me entretienen.* [I am not a normal person, reading and drawing are my strength; I have a unique personality, I do not like people telling me what to do, but I like to work; I am solitary, silent, and independent; I am an anarchist, I do not like our stupidity but it entertains me.]

Donato's bio-poem had an immense impact on all the teachers participating in this project. Penelope reflected, during the daily debriefings conducted by teachers,

> Donato's words are a wake-up call for me. If we teachers have high expectations for migrant students and create opportunities for them to think critically and most importantly value their life experiences, students

will not only be successful but also they will become advocates for others who will follow the same path.

Noé commented after writing his poem:

> This is the first time I was asked to put my ideas in writing and pictures. Writing and drawing about me, I felt like Esperanza—the main character of Sandra Cisneros' book—or Tupac in his poem. Though we are different, the three of us share a story.

His comments confirm the need to develop programs that allow students to link their self-understanding with their ability to call upon a variety of skills to negotiate new challenges (Lee and Bowen, 2006).

We Live in a Bicultural and Bilingual Community

Constructing a cultural identity occurs within a social context; thus, educators have to create activities where students analyze how other groups perceive and value their uniqueness (Lee and Anderson, 2009). After recognizing their uniqueness, students began to analyze the concept of "sharing stories" claimed by Noé in his poetry analysis. Dialogically reading and analyzing another chapter from Cisneros' book, "Those Who Don't," students explored the idea of being stereotyped by other people with labels that oftentimes diminish the linguistic and cultural richness of each group. The dialogue through the readings was guided by the theme, "Our neighborhood, our school . . ." This theme ignited passionate comments among the students. Daniel said, "I have lived in different neighborhoods but all of them looked the same to me. *Siempre vivimos rodeados por Mexicanos* [We always live surrounded by Mexicans]." Penelope, a teacher, asked Daniel, "What about the schools, did they look the same?" After taking his time, he responded, "Schools are different. *En algunas hay más güeros que en otras* [In some schools there are more white students than others]." Tania added, "Teachers always treat white students better than Mexican students." Araceli, a teacher, asked her, "Why do you think that is the case?" She quickly responded, "Teachers are afraid of their parents because they speak English."

Daniel's and Tania's comments exemplify two common traits among all the students participating in the Summer Academy. First, although the migrant students are highly mobile, there is a constancy of their lives. Second, they perceive that students coming from English-speaking families are empowered and protected by the educational system. Araceli, during one of the daily teachers' planning sessions, commented,

> We have to develop activities where students compare and contrast their identities in different environments. It is important for them to

understand that their culture and language enrich the communities where they live and the schools they attend. They have also to realize how other cultures and languages enrich their identity. We have to teach them to construct an identity within society.

The last art project of the Summer Academy implemented the idea of creating a "cultural tag" that defined each student as member of her/his community. Before they designed their "tags," students and teachers watched and discussed the video *Exit Through the Gift Shop* (http://www.banksyfilm.com). The dialogue focused on Banksy's (2005) idea of "a wall and piece," a style where the artist creates a mark on an open space—wall—symbolizing his view on social issues. During this dialogue Daniel said, "Today, I learned that graffiti is not a *'cholo'* [gang] form of art." Penelope, a teacher, responded, "I am glad that you are sharing this idea with us. During the course of your education you will learn and unlearn many concepts. Meaningful learning creates opportunities for you to learn concepts and ideas that are part of communities' preconceived ideas."

To fully experience graffiti as a literary expression, students created a graffiti wall. They began by sketching "individual tags" (Figure 6.1) that represented their uniqueness as migrant, bicultural, bilingual students. After designing these "pieces" in groups of ten they constructed a communal graffiti wall. Transferring their pieces to a large piece of paper (Figure 6.2) displayed on one of the walls at the university's art gallery, they represented the idea of each individual as a unique and important part of society. Once the designs were part of the wall, students reviewed the whole piece and began to cooperatively add new pictures on the empty spots of the graffiti wall. This process symbolized how individual

FIGURE 6.1 *Cultural Tag*, photo by Fernando Rodríguez-Valls

FIGURE 6.2 *Graffiti Wall*, photo by Sharon Chappell

marks act in ensemble in order to construct a whole. Quetzali, reflecting during the art presentation of all the projects, said, "Now that the wall is done, I feel that we have grown together these past four weeks. Friends I already have everywhere I have gone, but you have become my real friends."

Lessons Learned

Migrant students carry their linguistic and cultural richness from place to place, from school to school. Oftentimes, educators overlook these facts; thus, their analysis of why students struggle to adapt, to perform and to fit into the new school is constructed using predetermined notions of students' academic success. Teachers participating on the Summer Academy learned that culturally responsive practices are constructed with three elements. First, *uniqueness*: each participant in the learning process represents an individual with specific needs; thus practices should allow each one to fully express her/his ideas. Second, *flexibility*: meaningful teaching and learning are processes of constant analysis of what just happened to prepare the next step. And, third, *multimedia*: learning to be a cultural human being requires the combinations of different forms of expressions—oral, written, and visual—which combined create a synergy that empower students. Likewise, teaching complex human beings requires offering various media for expression and affirmation of identity.

The migrant students participating in the Summer Academy realized, as Jaime said, "Learning is more than answering questions. We have learned that asking questions makes us think. *Responder es solo complacer. Preguntar es cooperar y crear* [To respond is merely to please. To ask is to cooperate and to create]." Culturally responsive practices should foster questioning as a tool that constantly shapes the students' cultural identity. In these practices teachers are the giving trees for those students who move to learn and who successfully learn to move through the educational system.

*   *   *

In this next vignette, Elizabeth Lewis shares experiences with a migrant youth program, in which emergent bilingual students engaged in a writing workshop to connect personally to literature and multimodal texts, and in doing so to explore their identities as bilingual language users, learners, and writers.

VIGNETTE TWELVE

Young Writers Program for Migrant Youth

Elizabeth Lewis, Dickinson College

This Young Writers Program (YWP) took place through a partnership with the Lincoln Intermediate Unit Migrant Education Program (LIUMEP) in south central Pennsylvania, which serves youth in Adams and Franklin counties. The LIUMEP is an educational organization that hosts a five-week "Summer School of Excellence" program for migrant youth ranging from Pre-K through twelfth grade. The first YWP (Adams County) lasted for two weeks and was held at an intermediate school in New Oxford, PA. It began late June 2010 and ended in early July. The youth served in this program numbered forty-eight in total, came from four different school districts, and were divided into two groups—rising eighth and rising ninth graders, respectively. Though most of the participants were native Spanish speakers from México, some youth were from Vietnam, India, Somalia, and Korea. Correspondingly, these youths' native languages were Vietnamese, Urdu, Somali, and Korean.

The second YWP (Franklin County) took place for one week in late July of 2010. The group youth attending this program was small in number, fourteen in total, and comprised of students from two different school districts. All participants were incoming seventh graders and native Spanish speakers, with the exception of one young girl from Haiti whose native language was French. This group attended the YWP on Dickinson College's campus; an additional programmatic goal for these migrant youth was to bring them to a higher education setting that they could tour, whose college admissions process they could learn, and that would evoke consideration of future post-secondary education in general. In addition, Dickinson College campus afforded participants the opportunity to use cutting-edge media resources with which to create their digital stories.

Structure, Purpose, and Products

Young Writers Programs (YWPs) are summer enrichment programs for youth that have several functions and goals. YWPs provide unique opportunities to work with adolescents to: enhance their writing skills, increase the variety of ways in which they respond to texts, provide rich opportunities for them to explore their own and others' cultural identities, foster in them a sense of empowerment as they develop the identity of *writer* and conveyor of their life stories, and encourage them to contribute to the building of a community without the constrictions that can sometimes be generated by formal academic settings. For the purposes of understanding adolescent ELL literacy and identity development, this YWP was designed with characteristics similar to youth programs initiated by the National Writing Project. A typical day at this YWP included:

- a workshop approach to writing;
- a short opening writing activity with an opportunity for participants to share their work;
- an extended writing activity;
- "Author's Chair"—a more formal opportunity for participants to share their work and celebrate their peers' accomplishments.

Also significant to the design of this program, specifically the textual experiences students had, was a focus on multimodal, multimedia, and multigenre texts. Poetry, excerpts from literature, artwork (i.e. images of paintings, sculpture, drawings), and digital media/images were all used as prompts for both short and extended pieces of writing. In kind, the migrant youth participating at each site composed personal pieces in varied media. Among other forms, they represented their personal identities and experiences through poetry, journal responses, paper/digital collages, drawings, music, and digital stories.

Adams County participants created artwork in the forms of personal collages and drawings. These texts were displayed in the library and school hallways for a varied audience consisting of youth in other grade levels, LIUMEP summer school staff and administration, as well as parents and other family members who visited the school informally on a daily basis—and more formally at a "Family Night" event. Their written work was compiled and published in an anthology. Copies of this book were given to each student to keep and share with family and friends. Franklin County participants created digital stories centered on the theme of "sustainability" and its place in their lives; each student was given a DVD copy of his/her story to keep and share with family and friends after presenting it in the roles of author and director to an audience of peers, family members, and YWP staff at a "Family Day Celebration" held to honor their work.

The overarching goals for the youth who participated in this program included: experiencing the joy of writing as greater than an academic exercise; practicing writing in a variety of genres in the language(s) of their choice; actively participating in and contributing to a community of writers; exploring cultural identities of self and others; and taking selected writing through the composing process to the point of publication (the creation of a YWP anthology/digital story). These goals addressed three research questions: What happens when adolescent ELLs are encouraged to use writing as a means of connecting personally to literature-based and multimodal texts in ways other than solely for academic purposes? What happens when adolescent ELLs are exposed to writing in many genres while developing fluency in English and/or their native language? What is the YWP experience like for migrant youth when they are encouraged to explore their and others' cultural identities?

Through this project, it was my goal as the researcher to understand the perspectives of adolescent ELLs as they write in different genres, related to their varied responses to literature-, multimedia-, and multimodal-based texts; their literacy skills in their first and/or second language; their cultural identities; and their contribution to the development of a writing community with their peers.

Yasmina

"We're worried about Yasmina," Melissa, a regional migrant education director serving as my programmatic partner for the summer, explained to me before I met the rising ninth grader. Yasmina was participating in a Young Writers Program I designed for adolescent English language learners. "When you meet her, you'll understand. She's shy, she doesn't talk much at all. She missed a lot of school last year . . . she just stopped going. Yasmina told me she's bullied a lot by her classmates—that they don't understand her and don't try to. She's more comfortable spending time with her sister and her friends who, like her, are from México."

Hearing this about her the first day of the program, I was anxious for Yasmina to walk through the door of the intermediate school library, a spacious and inviting setting for our writing project. Based on Melissa's description, I recognized her immediately when that moment came. A tall girl with expressive dark brown eyes, Yasmina had a presence about her that she seemed not to have grown into—or used to—yet. She sank into a chair at the corner of the room's U-shaped configuration of tables. From my initial observation, Yasmina appeared to be friends with another young Latina girl sitting next to her, conversing easily with her in both English and Spanish.

Trying to read how comfortable Yasmina felt in this new environment, I watched her as carefully as I could without drawing attention to myself. I introduced the writing program and led students through a short personal writing experience centered on "My Name"—an excerpt from Sandra Cisneros' novel, *The House on Mango Street*. The dual purpose of this writing exercise was, first, to have students introduce themselves to the group by writing about their own names and sharing their pieces if they felt comfortable doing so, and, second, embark on their personal explorations of cultural identity that is the very foundation of the Young Writers Program. Young people, particularly English language learners, are not always afforded opportunities in formal academic settings to engage in identity exploration as a means of discovery and empowerment. With this in mind, I asked Yasmina and her peers to write a response to Cisneros' piece in their native language or in English, or both—whatever felt most comfortable to them. Near silence enveloped the room as then I heard only the scratching of pencils on paper while students reflected upon and wrote about their names. I glanced at Yasmina, her free hand partially covering the journal page as she wrote.

When I asked if anyone wanted to introduce him or herself to us by reading the piece he or she had written, I was taken by surprise when Yasmina's hand shot up first. I invited her to read what she had written, and, after double-checking that she was allowed to read it in Spanish—the language in which, she explained, she had written her response—she began sharing the story of how her mother named her. Though I couldn't understand everything that Yasmina was saying, I became alarmed when she began to cry halfway through her reading. She stumbled through the rest of the piece, covered her face in

FIGURE 6.3 *Final Draft of Yasmina's First Piece of Writing during Workshop,* *"Mi Nombre,"* photo by Elizabeth Lewis

her hands, and wept. Beatrice, the girl sitting next to her who I had first assumed was a friend, reached out and hugged her. Beatrice later explained to me that Yasmina had written about feeling unworthy of having such a beautiful name. Yasmina wrote, "How could such an ugly girl have such a pretty name?"

I was afraid that Yasmina would retreat into herself after having such a strong emotional reaction to writing about and sharing such a personal piece. I only hoped that perhaps she would continue to explore her culture and identity through subsequent writing experiences even if she chose not to share them publicly. My fears about Yasmina were never realized, and I was heartened by the personal journey she experienced through writing that summer. Over the course of the program, I watched Yasmina contribute to the development of a strong peer community, engage deeply in the exploration of her own cultural identity and that of the other young writers, and demonstrate great pride in the pieces she submitted to the final anthology. Though I also observed Yasmina write fervently in both Spanish and English, she favored composing in Spanish. Early in the program she commented, "In school I never get to write in Spanish. It's nice to get what I'm thinking out on paper. Sometimes it's hard to think of the words to write in English when my thoughts are in Spanish." I reflected on Yasmina frequently as I assembled the anthology. I smiled when I received an impatient email message from her that read, "Ms Liz, when's the book coming out? I want to see my published work!"

Yasmina had found her voice, and I hope she never loses it.

★   ★   ★

In this chapter's final vignette, Dan Kelin of Honolulu Theatre for Youth engages Hawaiian student communities in literature analysis about pressures of acculturation and assimilation in their developing bicultural worlds.

VIGNETTE THIRTEEN

Which "A" Will Be? Acculturation, Assimilation, Americanization

Daniel A. Kelin, II, Honolulu Theatre for Youth

The Keapule Elementary English Language Learning program contacted me to design a drama-integrated residency as an alternative way to engage their upper elementary, mixed language students who struggle academically. Honolulu Theatre for Youth annually offers drama-integrated residencies to schools, generally over ten to fifteen sessions, held daily over a two to three week period.

This residency took place in suburban Honolulu, home to a large, fluid immigrant population made up of people from island nations all over the Pacific

Ocean. Keapule Elementary has a population of over 50 percent limited English proficiency with 46 percent of these having no English proficiency, 49 percent having limited English proficiency, and 5 percent being fully English proficient. As a part of its mission, the school "educates children of immigrant plantation families through a Center for English Language Learners, providing ELL students with opportunities for continued growth as they adjust to being in school and assimilating into a new culture." Twenty students in fourth to sixth grade from a variety of Pacific islands participated in the HTY drama-integrated residency, ranging from recent immigrants with almost no English to those comfortable with vernacular English but struggling with academic English. The class met for an hour a day over two weeks in April 2010.

The Keapule sixth grade teacher asked me to address a grade-appropriate social studies theme to help the students explore what it means to be "American." Fascinated as I am by how children define themselves culturally, it seemed that exploring the concept of Americanization would offer them a chance to reflect on how their multiple ethnicities play a role in their definition of "American." I settled on the question, "What should Americanization be?" a question that contained two important concepts—assimilation and acculturation. I defined *assimilation* as a process of sacrificing one's culture to fit into another and *acculturation* as a process of adjusting to a new culture, while retaining aspects of one's own. Students would explore each of the concepts and use them to express what they believe Americanization is/should be. As students are mostly trained through school to seek the "correct" answers or those they think the teacher wishes to hear, I felt it necessary to structure the drama space so all students would want to contribute their *own* ideas. The entire residency could then be a reflective journey guiding the students to understand the three words (Americanization, assimilation and acculturation) through exploration, contemplation and application.

Each section of our journey began with one of the three As. We read it aloud and let the word echo in the room. I asked students to identify words within the A word. Some found "culture" in acculturation, while others went far afield, finding words like "rat" and "late." In assimilation, they found words with interesting perspectives like "simple," "same" and "similar". Then they created and shared a few imagined definitions. We wrote these down on chart paper, which we would refer to throughout the residency.

We started with simple still images (also called frozen pictures or tableaux) related to the words, a core drama skill and a method of working with drama. We then explored two picture books about life choices—*Hey, Al!* (Yorinks, 1989), a fantasy about a man offered the chance to escape his life by becoming a bird, and *I Hate English!* (Levine, 1995), a fictionalized story of a young immigrant reluctantly discovering the need to blend her cultural worlds. To invite students into the stories and explore each main character's dilemma, I guided them through creating images, pantomimes and small role plays. I asked students to voice feelings about their own transitional lives through group reflective techniques such as the human barometer, an imaginary line across the floor on which students place themselves to express answers to reflective questions. The students then worked in common ethnic groups to identify important aspects of their cultural heritage. On the final day, small groups shared their opinions of how Americanization should be defined.

We considered the word "assimilation" through *Hey, Al!*, which asks what personal sacrifices are necessary to achieve paradise. I guided the students to explore the difficult choice the main character faced, "Which would you choose: to keep your life as it is now or give it all up if you could live someone else's life?" Using the human barometer, the students placed themselves on the line to demonstrate their opinion. Then, about half of the students walked boldly to the extreme end of the continuum showing a desire to become someone else. Josep was the most demonstrative, shouting, "Oh, yeah, I can be rich and get new friends." A few boys trailed right after him. They cheered as Josep strutted back and forth, almost chanting how he doesn't care about his life. Others followed them, though seemingly more attracted by the momentary excitement than anything else.

We then explored "acculturation" with the second text, *I Hate English*. About the struggle of merging cultural norms within one's self, this story gave students the chance to again consider the earlier question of giving up one's self. As I repeated the question, the students were a little slower to demonstrate their response on the human barometer This time, most of the students were in favor of a more balanced approach to cultural integration and more subdued about explaining their choice. More of them shifted places as they negotiated with each other, now asking each other's opinions about this question. Josep and the other initially bold students faded into the crowd this time, stating now that they like who they are but some things could be better for them. They seriously reconsidered their initial reaction to the assimilation question through their encounters with the second book.

In the next session, the students then considered the word Americanization, once more voting on their feet. Should Americanization be assimilation or acculturation? Confidently, the whole class gathered on the acculturation side. When queried about the choice, students offered, *"I want to still be me." "I like to be here, but not forget the other parts, too." "I think we can be both." "Why do I have to change? I can do all the cultures."* Having faced the same essential question several times, the students had the opportunity to think more deeply about the question and revisit their initial reactions to make changes without feeling wrong.

In their final investigation, I guided the students to reflect on what they valued about their cultures. I asked them to identify symbols of their ethnicity, aspects that uniquely represent their cultural heritage. It took discussion and clarification to consider the question of symbols, as several students struggled with understanding what a symbol is. Having gained a tentative understanding, Masos and Fred—the only two of their ethnic group—picked more recent imports: football and volleyball, elements that define their contemporary interests. I pushed them past those initial choices to consider something they could claim might be of their heritage culture only. Masos and Fred faltered, unable to identify one. Then Cheriann and Mani created a small pantomimed scene showing the use of a particular cooking tool unique to their nation. With help from the girls, Masos and Fred showed a section of a culturally specific dance.

We then expressed their cultural identifications poetically. In small groups, the students made lists of family names, places, phrases commonly used by relatives, objects they value, food, musical instruments and names of dances or songs. Titled, "Where I am From," the poem repeated the phrase, "I am from . . ." followed by insertions of the specific details. As it came directly from the students, the poem excited them; I had to stop throughout as the students scanned the room to identify the contributors of each line, or when one student, JJ, would erupt in giggles at hearing his own words read aloud. For me, this proved a good starting point for guiding the students to reflect on their own identities, ethnically and culturally. JJ's laughter of recognition expressed a sense of personal pride as he heard his voice validated through the poem.

I designed this drama residency to revisit questions and experiences, and with each visit the students engaged in deeper considerations. They assessed their reactions, revised their ideas and moved beyond the fear of answering incorrectly. The personal ownership gained over the exploratory process and the renewed appreciation of their ethnic culture is true learning. As these Pacific Islanders struggle with understanding their cultural places in "America," this experience contributed to developing a slightly clearer perspective of who they are and what they value.

★   ★   ★

Responding Critically to Literature

The above vignettes show how emergent bilingual youth engage in deep, rich, critical dialogue in response to literature, well beyond the basic tripartite response to literature outlined in the beginning of the chapter. In all three cases, students' experiences were central to the meaning-making process, and students were able to pose questions and provide connected real experiences in their lives. According to Edelsky et al. (2008), young people need such opportunities to develop critical literacy, in which they use stories to analyze what is taken for granted in mainstream. Critical literacy is about power— who has it, who does not, why and how is power taken, and the ethical implications of the inequitable distribution of that power, both within the world of the literature and relations of power thematically related to that in the readers' lives. When related to literature, such a discussion of power entails asking: whose perspectives (in the book, in our discussion as a class) are represented as normal— as the way things are? Whose perspectives are missing? (Edelsky, 2006; Vásquez, 2009). This kind of critical turn in response to literature requires questions well beyond those asked in text-to-self, text-to-text, and text-to-world sorts of connections. Teachers and students who use multicultural literature can pose questions about how literature challenges or reinforces the common-sense, the taken-for-granted in mainstream literature.

For example, in a chapter book called *Get Ready for Gabí: A Mixed-Up Spanglish Day* (Montes, 2003), the main character, ten-year-old Gabí, reflects:

> I realized I was speaking Spanish to a non-Spanish speaking teacher. I was so upset, I was crossing my brain wires . . . There's only one thing I can't stand more than Johnny Wiley: And that's mixing up Spanish and English. I only do it when I'm super stressed. I'm very proud of how well I can speak both languages. And I don't like making mistakes.
>
> (Montes, 2003, p. 20, in Chappell and Faltis, 2007)

This way of talking about mixed language resonates with many young children, who have been told by teachers and certain educated adults that mixing languages is lazy, that mixed language speech is a "mistake" that needs to be corrected, and that a language has to be pure and grammatically perfect from a monolingual perspective. This is a common-sense view of bilingualism as two separate languages, each having its own set of rules speakers should follow, lest they be labeled Spanglish speakers, who are viewed as having flawed language.

A critical response to *Get Ready for Gabí* would ask children: *Who believes that mixing English and Spanish is incorrect and who doesn't? Where do these beliefs about language mixing come from, and who promotes and benefits from these beliefs? Who in their community uses two languages for communication?* In the same literature unit of instruction, children could also be exposed to selections about language/culture hybridity such as Gloria Anzaldúa's (1999) writing:

> Until I am free to write bilingually and to switch codes without having always to translate, while I still have to speak English or Spanish when I would rather speak Spanglish, and as long as I have to accommodate the English speakers rather than having them accommodate me, my tongue will be illegitimate. I will no longer be made to feel ashamed of existing. I will have my voice: Indian, Spanish, white. I will have my serpent's tongue . . . I will overcome the tradition of silence.
>
> (p. 81)

Anzaldúa suggests that when educated Spanish speakers disparage Spanglish as illegitimate, they hurt people by attacking the very essence of their being: their language, their way of life, their history, and identity. This critical response to literatures exposes linguistic deficits based on a trickbag of *"reglas de academia"* ("academic rules") (Anzaldúa, 1999, p. 76) rather than honoring local language practices as an asset in the classroom.

As Paulo Freire (1970) and others have pointed out, engaging students in critical responses to literature instills a sense of democracy in education. Such dialogues develop young people into curious, thoughtful, and participatory citizens who question, reason, and evaluate the ideas, history, and positions they encounter. Through a critical response to literature, "you make certain principles familiar—principles of justice and equity" (Edelsky et al., 2008, p. 84), by posing questions about what is assumed to be common sense in mainstream literature and society, and looking for answers that are not readily apparent in the text, images, or the literature being read. In doing so, students participate in transforming their world through critical questioning.

One way to make responses to literature critical is to question ideas in pieces of literature, both multicultural and mainstream, assumed to be neutral or based on "common sense."

- Text-to-common-sense connections:
    - What I just read reminds me of struggles people have over . . .
    - What I just read makes me wonder whose views the author is representing . . .
    - What I just read makes me wonder what other people think about . . .
    - What I just read makes me want to ask why things happened this way . . .

Asking students to pose these kinds of questions empowers students to uncover and interrogate the normative, dominant-group understandings and views represented in much of the school literature, including the art that supports it. These questions are also particularly important for bringing in and valuing students' funds of knowledge (Moll and Greenberg, 1990), particularly in terms of the art they produce (Kendrick and McKay, 2002), and the symbolic cultural resources they bring to the classroom (Dyson, 2003). Entry into critical responses to literature promotes the creation of text—images, performances, and narratives, based on the lived experiences of children and youth, as the three vignettes in this chapter point out.

Critical Response to Literature Resources

One the best ways to learn more about how to engage your emergent bilingual students in critical response to literature is to explore the resources of organizations committed to social justice and multicultural education. For example, Rethinking Schools (www.rethinkingschools.org) publishes books and materials for elementary and secondary schools with a critical education stance about social contexts such as race, gender, class, age, immigration, language, sexual orientation, physical/mental ability, and religion. Teaching ideas and practices that promote critical responses to multiple forms of text, including children's and young adult literature, can also be found through various resources listed in Appendix B of this book. There are also a number of research articles that provide thick, rich descriptions of how students created their own literature-based art performances, and community stories (see Keis, 2006; Nathenson-Mejia and Escamilla, 2003; Riojas-Cortez, 2001; Smythe and Toohey, 2009). In the next chapter, we address ways that emergent bilingual youth can respond critically to common-sense narratives about world events produced through various news media outlets and in popular culture texts.

Questions to Consider

1. What current ways do you use literature in your educational practice? How do you make decisions about what literature to use? Which sociocultures do you want to see represented in your classroom literature?

2. How did the facilitators in these vignettes engage questions around literature that are not typically part of the classroom curriculum? Why were these questions important to their students? What decisions did they make about contemporary cultures vs the heritage cultures in the literature, and do you agree with their choices?

3. How can you use art and literature in your own classroom to engage questions of culture, belonging, identity and power with your students? What arts-based processes could you use to ask students to respond to the literature, to question common-sense notions represented in literature?

Note

1. All names in this chapter's vignettes are pseudonyms.

References

Anzaldúa, G. (1999). *Borderlands / la frontera: The new mestiza*. San Francisco, CA: Anne Lute Books.

Baker, C. (2011). *Foundations of bilingual education and bilingualism*. Clevedon, UK: Multilingual Matters.

Banksy (2005). *Wall and piece*. London, UK: Random House.

Bhabha, H. K. (1996). Culture's in between. In S. Hall and P. du Gay (Eds), *Questions of cultural identity* (pp. 53–60). Thousand Oaks, CA: Sage.

Chappell, S. and Faltis, C. (2007). Spanglish, bilingualism, culture and identity in Latino children's literature. *Children's Literature in Education*, 38(2), 253–62.

Cisneros, S. (1984). *The house on Mango Street / La casa en Mango Street*. Columbus, OH: McGraw-Hill College.

Dyson, A. (2003). Popular literacies and the "all" children: Rethinking literacy development for contemporary childhoods. *Language Arts*, 81(2), 100–9.

Edelsky, C. (2006). *With literacy and justice for all: Rethinking the social in language and education*, 3rd edition. Mahwah, NJ: Lawrence Erlbaum Associates.

Edelsky, C., Smith, K., and Faltis, C. (2008). *Side-by-side learning: Exemplary practices for English language learners and English speakers in the mainstream classroom*. New York: Scholastic.

Freire, P. (1970). *Pedagogy of the oppressed*. New York: Continuum.

Habermas, J. (2001). *On the pragmatics of social interaction: Preliminary studies in the theory of communicative action*, trans. B. Fultner. Cambridge, UK: Polity Press.

Keene, E. and Zimmerman, S. (1997). *Mosaic of thought*. Portsmouth, NH: Heinemann.

Keis, R. (2006). From principle to practice: Using children's literature to promote dialogue and facilitate the "coming to voice" in a rural Latino community. *Multicultural Perspectives*, 8(1), 13–19.

Kendrick, M. and McKay, R. (2002). Uncovering literacy narratives through children's drawings. *Canadian Journal of Education*, 27(1), 45–60.

Lee, J. S. and Anderson, K. T. (2009). Negotiating linguistic and cultural identities: Theorizing and constructing opportunities and risks in education. *Review of Research in Education*, 33(1), 181–211.

Lee, J. and Bowen, N. (2006). Parent involvement, cultural capital, and the achievement gap among elementary school children. *American Educational Research Journal*, 43(2), 193–218.

Levine, E. (1995). *I hate English!* New York: Scholastic.

Moll, L. and Greenberg, J. (1990). Creating zones of possibilities: Combining social contexts for instruction. In L. Moll (Ed.), *Vygotsky and education: Instructional implications and applications of sociohistorical psychology* (pp. 319–48). Cambridge: Cambridge University Press.

Montes, M. (2003). *Get ready for Gabí: A crazy, mixed-up Spanglish day*. New York: Scholastic.

Nathenson-Mejia, S. and Escamilla, K. (2003). Connecting with Latino children: Bridging cultural gaps with children's literature. *Bilingual Research Journal*, 27(1), 101–16.

Purcell-Gates, V. (1997). *Other people's words: The cycle of low literacy*. Cambridge, MA: Harvard University Press.

Riojas-Cortez, M. (2001). Preschoolers' funds of knowledge displayed through socio-dramatic play episodes in a bilingual classroom. *Early Children Education Journal*, 29(1), 35–40.

Rosenblatt, L. (1978). *The reader, the text, and the poem*. Baltimore, MD: Johns Hopkins University Press.

—— (1985). The transactional theory of the literary work: Implications for research. In Charles Cooper (Ed.), *Researching response to literature and the teaching of literature* (pp. 33–53*)*. Norwood, NJ: Ablex.

Shakur, T. (1999). *The rose that grew from concrete*. New York, NY: MTV.

Smythe, S. and Toohey, K. (2009). Investigating sociohistorical contexts and practices through a community scan: A Canadian Punjabi–Sikh example. *Language and Education*, 23(1), 37–57.

Vásquez, V. M. (2004). *Negotiating critical literacies with young children*. Mahwah, NJ: Lawrence Erlbaum Associates.

Yorinks, A. (1989). *Hey Al!* New York: Farrar, Straus & Giroux.

7

RESPONDING CRITICALLY
TO WORLD EVENTS

In Chapter 6, we explored how the selection and use of literature plays a critical role in the way emergent bilingual youth engage with text and make connections to themselves, other texts, and the world. This chapter will expand on the function of storytelling as a means to facilitate young people's critical engagement with world events through critical media literacy strategies. We address how learning communities in the classroom can utilize the arts to explore the ways these events relate to students' lives, rights, roles and responsibilities—past and present, local and global. As we listen to children, they tell us stories about what they care about, what bothers them, and what visions they have for making better worlds (Boyle-Baise and Zevin, 2009; Schultz, 2010).

The approaches featured in this book are critical, creative responses to a host of schooling approaches that "dehumanize" teachers, students and families in the race to improve student achievement via test scores. Discrete skill development may assist young people's skill-based school performance (as in defining and spelling words, finding the main idea in a reading passage, etc.), while standardized curriculum may assist teachers in the technical implementation of daily lessons. Yet, these approaches do not typically analyze how curricular content or instructional strategies impact students' engagement with learning. Particularly, a homogenized, skill-based curriculum does not attend to the linguistic and cultural contradictions that emergent bilingual youth encounter regularly (Pacheco, 2012) between home and school.

When schools only feature the heroes, holidays, and traditions that mainstream U.S. practices typically associate with "ethnic" cultures, emergent bilingual youth do not see themselves (their lives, their families, communities, and histories) as central to the learning process (Cruz, 2002). Focusing on token ethnic events and people usually occurs without much critical reflection or interrogation about what it means to live in a culturally and linguistically pluralistic society. Instead, we should meaningfully commit to a school year infused with discussions of the world events and policies that affect the lives of bilingual youth. This chapter explores such a commitment, featuring approaches for facilitating the development of the voices and academic skills of emergent bilingual youth to critique and act in relation to the broader world they live in.

As social constructivists, we believe that knowledge is produced through the cultural practices of sociopolitical and economic systems (Au, 2011). Students' understanding of themselves (their self-worth and self-efficacy, their cultural identities) is directly related to the social processes they encounter and interact with. Throughout our teaching lives, we make choices about social dominance: will we allow/require students to reproduce hierarchical systems (e.g. being first, speaking better, having more), or will we problematize these systems by critically examining the "metaphors we live by" with our students (Lakoff and Johnson, 2003)? Through critical media practices, we can look at the ways world events are framed, critically examine these metaphoric frames, and raise questions about the ways media and popular culture make these metaphors into common sense through the stories they tell (Barone and Eisner, 2011; McLaren, 1995; Polkinghorne, 1988). The arts are uniquely positioned as a set of disciplines to build students' consciousness through examining world events in relation to narratives of social dominance, creating a critical world curriculum based in the lives of everyday people's struggles (Zinn, 2010).

The vignettes in this chapter position difference at the center of learning and assume that systems of social dominance in contemporary life need to be addressed in schools. In the classroom, an inquiry-based curriculum allows students to pose problems and ask questions in an active, public way (Morrell and Duncan-Andrade, 2008; Smith et al., 2009). Such an inquiry process is based in consciousness–building, critique, vision and action, so that language and literacy become a tool of local, social engagement. Paulo Freire (2004) suggests that the purpose of reading the word is to read the world. In this way, teachers can build a pedagogy of hope even in a world of restrictive immigration, language, and schooling policies. Indeed, the "shocks" in the lives of young people become pedagogical possibilities (Pacheco, 2012; Renner, 2009).

We take the standpoint that various publics have constructed and continue to construct narrow, singular representations of minoritized communities in U.S. history and current events, including about immigrant, migrant, refugee, and indigenous people (Zinn, 2010; Loewen, 2007). Of particular importance to this chapter is the knowledge produced in popular historical texts (like social studies textbooks) and by news media outlets with which young people interact. Cruz (2002), for example, analyzes the ways that Latinos are represented in U.S. history textbooks as violent, lazy, and/or unwilling to assimilate. Yet, there is little coverage of how the U.S. refused to implement the Treaty of Guadalupe Hidalgo, denying civil, property and language rights to Mexican families residing in the newly arrested territory of what is now California, Arizona and Texas (Moreno, 1998). Critical student research would ask students to analyze injustices wielded by one group against another, such as the role of racial policy to deny civil rights in the histories of indigenous peoples of Native American tribes and the Hawaiian islands, as well as the denial of citizenship to Asian immigrants during the time of railroad construction (Zia, 2001).

As teachers, we can ask our students to "do history," actively uncovering the assumptions, gaps and omissions in narrative structures in school texts, news media, and popular culture that benefit dominant groups in power (Levstik and Barton, 2010; Loewen, 2007). We can identify fissures, struggles, and contestations in history and current world events in terms of how these dilemmas and their mediatized representations convey relationships between language, culture and identity. Emergent bilingual youth will learn that the difficult questions of cultural encounter and social dominance are related to their own personal choices, such as whether they should maintain their home language while learning English, or lose it in favor of English only. Conducting critical media research about world events can become part of culturally and linguistically responsive arts-based pedagogy.

Imagine, for example, that a group of seventh grade students in Santa Ana, California, are brought to the Old Orange County Courthouse in order to view an exhibition titled "A Class Action: The Grassroots Struggle for Desegregation in California Schools" (Museum of Teaching and Learning, 2011). This exhibition features the oral histories of participants in the landmark court case, *Mendez et al. v. Westminster School District et al.* In this court case, five families brought a class action lawsuit against four school districts in 1945 because 5,000 Mexican students were forced to attend segregated schools with inequitable resources. Ninety-five percent of the seventh graders on the field trip are emergent bilingual, Spanish/English, with historical family roots in agricultural fieldwork in California. The classroom teacher asks the students to observe the exhibition in relation to particular questions: *What are the conditions of schooling for Mexican students in 1945? What do you think every student deserves at school? What were the inequities in schooling then? How do the experiences of these families relate to your lives today, and, what actions will you like to take in response?* (Morrell and Duncan-Andrade, 2008).

Imagine the students listening to the exhibition's oral histories, reading the quotations, and discussing the questions. They might use mind mapping and found poetry composed through phrases selected from the exhibition text. Through these strategies, the students might begin to develop connections between the racialization of poverty and unequal school funding for migrant students in 1945 and those inequities they see in their own school. When they return to the classroom, their teacher might ask them to work in small groups to identify their own questions and ideas for action. They could decide to interview their own families, research news archives, and integrate this data into collaborative hip-hop songs about the conditions of migrant workers today. They might even perform their songs to a student-edited slide show of family photos in the main cultural plaza of their town. In this example, a critical, creative stance toward schooling creates the conditions for these young people to analyze inequities in the world and create cultural texts in response.

Such socially engaged, community-based approaches to analyzing world events have developed in the fields of service learning (Baldwin et al., 2007), youth participatory action research (Cammarota and Fine, 2008), and critical media literacy (Kellner and Share, 2005). Each discipline shares the use of problem-posing curricula to identify and critically analyze meaningful world events, as well as taking related social actions. Importantly, the students themselves are involved in locating and determining the events they want to explore, as well as the actions they want to take. These events might directly impact families and communities locally, as in the impact of restrictive immigration policies in both the vignettes of this chapter that follow. Or the world events might relate thematically because the conditions of these events might mirror those that impact your students person-ally. In a problem-posing curriculum, students often work in small groups to research root social and economic causes to these problems through online news media outlets, short articles, images, films, songs and poems.

To analyze world events, we can ask students to consider how media messages about events, groups of people, and ideas are socially constructed based on particular values and beliefs. Students can analyze the messages they hear and see based on the creative languages employed in a text (news article, story or film, school policy). They can also analyze the motivations that the authors (corpora-tions, school boards, government officials) have to tell a story in a particular way. We can ask students to listen to each other: How do we as diverse audiences decode the same message, and what in our lives informs our decoding? These questions, used often in critical media literacy (Kellner and Share, 2005), will inspire emergent bilingual youth as they make connections between themselves, texts and the world.

As you read the following vignettes,[1] note how students ask questions about their lives and relate these questions to world events, as well as how they use dialogue and creative production in response to these events. In the first vignette, Luis Garcia describes engaging his high school students in analysis of restrictive immigration policies in the Southwest through critical performance art as a form of service learning. Then, Ruth Harman, Kinga Varga-Dobai, Kelli Bivins, and David Forker utilize participatory action research and devised theatre processes to explore current world events affecting emergent bilingual youth in Arizona, culminating in a public performance and distribution of collaboratively devised texts.

Eastside High School: May Day Service Learning Project from Alumni to Future Alum

Luis Genaro Garcia, Eastside High School, Los Angeles

Introduction

This story describes an art-based project that incorporates the historical and cultural experiences of Spanish speaking students and demonstrates how culturally relevant methods of history, language, culture, politics and visual literacy can impact the academic outcome and political awareness of marginalized youth. With a growing number of Latin American students coming into the U.S. and transitioning into a new culture and language, it is important to continue developing multiple literacies through culturally relevant art-based pedagogy. In a modern post-civil rights era of political actions targeting undocumented students and workers, laws such as SB 1070 affect students of immigrant backgrounds. This socioeconomic environment impacts marginalized students both in school and outside of school (Kozol, 1992; Tierney, 1993), and a critical pedagogy focuses on empowering students to challenge the social and political limitations in their communities.

In my high school art courses, I draw from the work of Paulo Freire, and his concept of the student/teacher relationship, viewing our relationship as a collaboration of knowledge built through the teacher as a learner and the student as teacher. This allows us to work strategically and collaboratively in search of solutions to the oppressive conditions that affect students. I also work through the radical perspective of public art as a social language, influenced by the work of Mexican muralist David Alfaro Siqueiros. My focus on Siqueiros comes from the socially conscious public art he created while in Los Angeles (*America Tropical, Un Mitin Obrero*, and *Portrait of México Today*). Siqueiros' work reflects the social and economic implications of Mexican people and their connection to the United States. I use his ideology of public art with my students, which says that art speaks a different social language with a distinct style and form only understood by those who are conscious of their own limitations (Siqueiros, 1975). I want them to use public art in empowering ways that help them understand their experiences in the working class.

I wanted to develop the students' academic and artistic dialogue through "visual literacy," which is defined as the ability to think and communicate visually (based on the CA state standards). When students think visually they are able to turn their thoughts into visual images (paintings, drawings, poetry, theatre, etc.) and communicate their images verbally through dialogue. Visual dialogue can be a set of shared ideas between the artist and observer as they share perspectives through an artwork. Judith Baca (2005) suggests that public art is an antidote for the hatred and disconnectedness in society. It is a creative, participatory, critical, and analytical process of telling our stories as people and encouraging others to do the same, in any language they speak (Becker, 2004; Doss, 1992). Through the very specificity of the human experience, we learn compassion.

I believe this compassion is developed through educational acts of love, often left out of learning environments. In her experiences with ESL students, Valenzuela (1999) identifies two aspects of caring, the authentic and aesthetic. Further, Duncan-Andrade (2006) suggests the use of *cariño* (affection/love) in developing research methodologies as a way of connecting with students from poor working classes. Traditional data-driven research and teaching does not give the subjects (students) the capability of developing or contributing to their own means of social change, social mobility, or social freedom. Instead, cariño develops through student/teacher driven action research as a form of learning. In this process, we collaborate to search of social solutions. Students are not the objectified "subjects" of someone else's inquiry.

In my advanced painting class, the students and I developed a public art project that fulfilled the students' service learning requirement for California high school graduation as well as provided a structured inquiry process about issues affecting their everyday lives. This process included dialoguing about the issues and possible solutions, and actively and critically expressing these issues through aesthetic engagement inside and outside the classroom. As a former graduate of the same school, I was well aware of the limitations my students in this community experienced, and designed lessons on those they prioritized, such as the city's urban planning, gentrification, and civil rights violations. My goal as an educator was to empower my students; however, later I realized that this arts-based approach in the classroom could benefit other marginalized students from similar communities.

The Project

On May 1, 2010, seventeen students from Eastside High School, all from immigrant families, participated in the nationwide protest for immigrant rights in downtown Los Angeles. Known as "International Workers' Day," May 1 has become a day of action for immigrant rights in the city of Los Angeles. The students' participation consisted of developing a public art project and partaking in a public protest along with thousands of other Los Angeles residents. They created individual interpretations of the "Caution" (immigrant crossing) sign on the Interstate 5 freeway near the México–U.S. border in San Diego. This concept developed from an intense discussion about the controversial Arizona law SB 1070. The law, if passed, would require police to demand "papers" from people who they suspect are "unlawfully present" in the U.S. In discussing the issue, my students saw this law as a legalization of racial

FIGURE 7.1 *With Liberty and Education for All* by Luis Genaro Garcia

profiling, improper investigations, and detention in the state of Arizona. They were concerned about the possibility that the AZ law would provide momentum for other states to pass similar laws.

Based on their concerns, we discussed the idea of participating in the May Day protest. The students identified several ideas including creating a mural, stencil art, performance, papier mâché figures. Then they decided on one student's suggestion that they could do something similar to the "Education" sign I had created as an artist. I agreed, with the condition that they change the wording to reflect their own visions.

FIGURE 7.2 *Caution Sign, Interstate 5 Freeway, San Diego CA,* photo by Luis Genaro Garcia

FIGURE 7.3 *Students at the May Day March in Downtown Los Angeles,*
photo by Luis Genaro Garcia

I introduced them to the original "Caution" sign on the Interstate 5 in San Diego and required them to research the history of the sign, as well as related political propositions and actions against immigrants. After having an in-depth discussion about the sign and the stereotypes it creates culturally, I also asked the students to think for themselves and to record the first thing they thought about when they saw the silhouette of the immigrant family. Some saw this sign on their way to or from visiting families in México. From the thoughts they wrote down, they redefined the stereotypical sign by replacing the word "Caution" with a positive term or one that told a story.

In 2011, the students' projects were displayed at California State University Fullerton's exhibition "Border Inspections: Art-Based Encounters with Language, Identity, Culture and Power," curated by one of the editors of this book (Chappell). Although not all students were in my class for the following year, former students of the project went with me to the exhibition. While looking at the signs on display, they continued to reflect on their own stories with each other and other visitors about the origination of the project, its meaning to them as students and immigrants, and their experience at the May Day protest. This project's dialogue continued beyond the goals of participating in a protest as it became part of the exhibition.

Educational Significance

Developing "authentic caring" will take place when you become more than just the teacher in the students' academic spaces, as well as outside the school setting. A teacher might not be comfortable sharing their personal space with their students in the way that I describe, but for me, cariño authenticates my role as a teacher beyond the classroom. Through culturally relevant curriculum that prepared students for a culminating service learning project, students were able to connect their own experiences and background to current policies, political actions, state legislation, and education issues that directly affect their well-being.

Education needs to include social and political study with students so they may become aware and critical of the limiting factors in their schools and their environments. We need to look at art as a vital, meaningful act of education instead of an elective that takes up a period in students' daily schedules. From my own memories as a high school student, I recall being told to draw a picture from a magazine without even using real objects, considering the contexts of their production or analyzing their relationship to my life. Any subject should develop and challenge its students by looking at problems in their environment, and show them how to resolve those problems creatively. Teachers and students can work together in any multitude of subjects, raising awareness about issues surrounding their environment and working to solve them. Art for social change must begin in the classroom and continue in the streets where students live.

★   ★   ★

VIGNETTE FIFTEEN

Youth Participatory Action Research in a Middle School ESOL Classroom: Voices for Immigrant Latino Communities

Ruth Harman, University of Georgia; Kinga Varga-Dobai, Georgia Gwinnett College; Kelli Bivins and David Forker, Coile Middle School

The authors and middle school English Learners (ELs) who worked together on this project come from many different countries and speak several languages: Wolof, Spanish, Hungarian, Irish, Italian, and English. The story that we tell is about our youth participatory action research (YPAR) that explored and incorporated some of the positive and negative elements of our lives in the Southeast of the United States, especially in relation to current immigration discourses and policies. In the recent past, immigration in the United States has been the focal point of political and public debates. In April 2010, for example, Jan Brewer, Governor of Arizona, signed a bill on "illegal immigration" into law that sanctioned the prosecution and deportation of individuals without proper documentation. Understandably, such policies and practices have triggered huge anxiety among the home immigrant communities of the student participants in this study.

The one Italian/Somalian and ten Latina girls in this study attended middle school in a low-income school district that faces daunting challenges because of high stakes testing, limited financial resources, and high teacher turnover (see Gutiérrez et al., 2002). In addition, because the region does not have a history of linguistically diverse student populations, the language policies and practices in the school often failed to validate the students' rich cultural funds of knowledge or provide them with academically rigorous curricula. The home communities of the eleven girls were also often subject to arbitrary immigration raids, corrupt landlords who refused to repair or maintain the properties, and irregular and sometimes non-existent public transportation. The adult participants in this study—two ESOL teachers in the school and two university researchers—chose to engage youth participatory action research (YPAR) through arts-based processes so that the students would see themselves as agents of their own learning and as community activists.

What is YPAR?

YPAR is based on action-oriented research methods and incorporates student voices and funds of knowledge as an integral element in the research design and implementation. In other words, YPAR is a collective process that positions students as active researchers and agents of change in their schools and communities (Cammarota and Fine, 2008). One way to engage adult and youth participants in YPAR is to use arts-based processes such as theatre, poetry and dance to investigate and challenge local burning issues and concerns (Cammarota and Fine, 2008; Harman with French, in press). Distinct from more individualized reflective practices, our instantiation of an arts-based YPAR also attempted to facilitate reflexive discussion and collaborative critique of the sociopolitical context of local discursive events and of our own practices on an ongoing basis.

The research questions that guided our YPAR research over the course of nine months were the following: (1) What issues did we want to address in our action research and how could we develop a deeper knowledge of these issues? (2) How could we disseminate our research and involve local city stakeholders and community members in addressing these issues?

Our YPAR Process

As mentioned earlier, we used an arts-based approach to our research. The most important stages of our YPAR work over the course of nine months together at Chestnut Middle School included:

- history of our names through theatre games;
- sharing of student and teacher family narratives (e.g. about La Llorona);
- explanation of the goal of YPAR;
- Boal's (1979) theatre techniques used to identify social issues of student communities;
- voting and decision on what social action to use to address identified social issues;
- research, community interviews, immigration lecture, and drafting of informational texts;
- publication of newsletter and public performance for families on Cinco de Mayo;
- creation of theatrical script and PowerPoint for conference presentation at a Women Studies conference in fall 2010.

Ruth, one of the university researchers, and Kelli, the main ESOL teacher, had worked together on a previous critical literacy project with some of the girls the year before. The first goal in our new project in 2009–10 was that all participants would get to know each other. We played theatre games and told stories about how we got our names. For example, Aissatou told us her name came from the Koran, and Kinga, a university researcher who is also an English learner from Romania, discussed the complicated history of her name and country. On two subsequent storytelling days, the students, as well as Ruth and Kinga, shared stories that related to their home countries and cultures.

To identify social issues that would become the focus of our collective research together, we then used theatre techniques from the Boalian Theatre of the Oppressed (Boal, 1979) to think about burning issues that students and teachers had as community members of Chestnut Middle School and the local town. Augosto Boal used his platform as a theatre director in Brazil in the 1960s to expose many of the social inequities in Brazilian society. In image and forum theatre, through verbal and non-verbal improvisations, participants are asked to re-imagine conflicts from their everyday lives that the group sees as oppressive (Boal, 1979, 1992). In our classroom, the students re-enacted oppressive experiences related to being English learners and newly arrived immigrants.

In a post-performance discussion, the students were then asked to vote on what they perceived as the most burning social issues in regards to their status as English Learners and immigrants in the United States. The two issues that they collectively identified as the most troubling were the following: bullying and abrupt deportation of Latino communities by immigration authorities; and job discrimination against ethnic minorities. They also decided as a group that the best way to address these issues was to write to important local stakeholders such as the town mayor and city council members. The transcript illustrates this decision:

Kelli: Does anybody have any strong feelings about what you want to do next about these issues?

Roma: Write about 'em.

Kelli: Write about them. What'd you say? Who are we going to write to?

Monique: Oh, we can write to that man on local TV.

Later on in the same discussion, the girls decided that the most efficient way to disseminate research was by creating a newsletter and delivering it to their families and other community members. The task for the ESOL teachers and their university assistants was then to support the girls in finding the most relevant research related to these areas and also to support them in writing informational texts that would fit the genre of newspaper writing.

Toward the end of spring 2011, all adult and student participants in the research group collectively wrote a poem about the issues that we had researched. We all participated in a performance of the poem at a final community celebration on the Cinco de Mayo, where we also distributed the newsletter:

Deportation is wrong! Stop deportation!
Abrupt deportation is a social injustice.
When the police deport people yo me siento scared.[2]
I feel very bad when the police come and take the people away
     and deport them.
I have fears, and I am sad.
I am mad about what is happening in Arizona!
I feel like we have no rights.
My mom was very sad when she found out that the lady in
     Arizona signed the law saying that they don't want any
     Mexicans.
Immigration is bad for people that don't have papers.
No more haters!
No more discrimination.
No more broken-up families.
Before I felt confused, but now I'm strong.
I feel powerless alone but stronger as a group.
Together we are strong. We must help each other.

Later in the year, our research team, made up of one teacher, two researchers and seven of the girls (some had graduated and moved to high school) participated in a local Women Studies conference to present the research process. To prepare for the event, Ruth Harman wrote a draft of a performance ethnographic script (see below) that was based on the Boalian techniques used during our work at Chestnut and also based on the events and discussions that took place during the literacy events in spring 2011. The teachers and the girls edited the script and created a PowerPoint presentation that discussed the research process and newsletter they had created. The short scene shows the pain that the girls experienced very regularly when police officers or "La Migra" came to their communities and sometimes even to their homes at all hours of the day and night. It also represents the collective power that the girls felt after working together as a group when seeing how their words had a material effect on others (through the newsletter dissemination and women's conference).

STORY 1: First Scene

Family eating dinner (music playing)

Mom: ¿Alguien quiere más tamales?
Aissatou, Clarita: ¡Yo! ¡Yo! ¡Yo!
Mom: ¡Aquí tienen!
Clarita: ¡¡MAMA!! ¡Alguien está tocando la puerta!

LARGE KNOCKING ON DOOR. TWO POLICE OFFICERS
LOOKING ANGRY

Aissatou: I will get it. Don't worry . . .
Officer 1 (large knocking): You need to open up!!
Aissatou (opens the door): What do you want . . .?
Officer 2: Young girl, move over. We are in a hurry. I betcha have some illegal activities going on in here. Let me pass.
Mom to girls: We have no choice. We need to let them in.
Police officers (push past her): Okay, let's search the living room first.
(*Girls and Mama sobbing as they watch the police ransack the house*)
Boalian joker:[3] Okay, FREEZE! That really was powerful. Now this time, what I want you to do is play the scene again but this time someone from the audience can come in and take the place of the mother or one of the girls and change the action!

STORY 2

Family eating dinner (music playing)
Mom: ¿Alguien quiere más tamales?
Aissatou, Clarita: ¡Yo! ¡Yo! ¡Yo!
Mom: Aquí tienen.
Clarita: ¡¡Mamá!! ¡Alguien está tocando la puerta!

LARGE KNOCKING ON DOOR. TWO POLICE OFFICERS LOOKING ANGRY

Aissatou: I will get it. Don't worry.

Officer 1 (large knocking): You need to open up!!

Aissatou (opens the door): What do you want?

Officer 2: Young girl, move over. We are in a hurry. I betcha have some illegal activities going on in here. Let me pass.

Mom to girls: We have no choice. We need to let them in.

Tamara in audience: Stop! *(She taps Aissatou on the shoulder and takes her place)*

Tamara: I am sorry, officers, but do you have a search warrant?

Police officers (looking annoyed): Well, no, okay, but that doesn't stop us *(goes to push by her)*.

Tamara: You do not have the right to come in here without a search warrant!!

(Police officers leave)

Mom (hugging the two girls): ¡Qué orgullosa me siento de ti! I am so proud of you!!

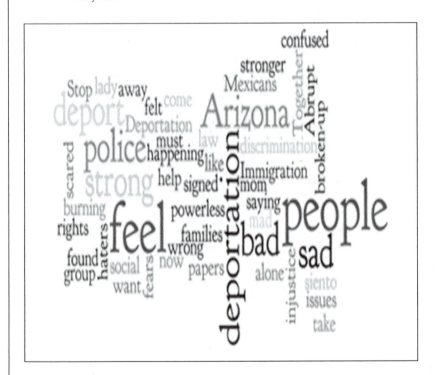

FIGURE 7.4 *Word Cloud Poem of YPAR Process*, screenshot by Kinga Varga-Dobai

To depict our YPAR endeavors and findings, Kinga created a poem using the Wordle website that represents how our work was sometimes straight and smooth and sometimes broken or jumbled up.

In sum, our arts-based YPAR provided the girls in our group with a space to embody, discuss, and write about social issues that were relevant to their lives. Language learning, in essence, became a meaningful genre-based endeavor with an authentic purpose and audience. However, there were also challenges in conducting this work. Although two of the adult participants in the group were immigrants and one was an English Learner, there were cultural and power differentials between the adults and girls that were evident despite use of theatre, storytelling, and children's literature. What was missing from our work and which we would highly recommend for others using a similar approach is to ensure that community and family members of student participants also be included in all stages of the process.

★　★　★

This chapter explores approaches for a critical world curriculum impacting the lives of emergent bilingual youth. You may have noticed elements from past chapters occurring recursively again, such as working in and between languages and cultures, utilizing cultural and linguistic responsive curricular content, engaging community collaboration, playing, and storytelling. The vignette authors used different art mediums to engage young people in a problem-posing process that involved analyzing current events in the world, relating those events to themselves and to other texts through action research, and inserting themselves and their creative expressions into public spaces. When addressing world events in curriculum, we emphasize the importance of relationship building, *cariño* that redefines schooling as a humanizing, rather than simply a socializing, agent. In the next chapter, we will discuss how such relationship building necessitates shifting emergent bilingual youth into a teaching role, as students talk back to various institutions through the use of digital media.

Questions to Consider

1. Think about the ways you acquire information about world events. What news outlets do you use? How do you "talk back" to news that frustrates you?

2. How do you currently engage students in analyzing world events? What are the limitations and challenges of your (or your school's) current approach?

3. In the vignettes of this chapter, how do the facilitators link local student experiences to world events? How do they help students critique events and envision change through different art forms?

4. How might you incorporate an approach featured in this chapter into your current social studies teaching (as an artist/classroom teacher)?

Notes

1. All names in this chapter's vignettes are pseudonyms.
2. The speaker's mix of Spanish and English perhaps highlights the intensity of her emotions about the issue.
3. The Boalian joker is the facilitator of the forum theatre scene, who controls the action being shown and calls for participation from the audience.

References

Au, W. (2011). *Critical curriculum studies: Education, consciousness and the politics of knowing*. New York: Routledge.

Baca, J. (2005). Baldwin Park press release. Los Angeles: Social Public Art Resource Center (SPARC). Retrieved December 7, 2010 from http://www.sparcmurals.org/sparcone/index.php?option=com_content&task=view&id=209&Itemid=124&limit=1&limitstart=0.

Baldwin, S., Buchanan, A., and Rudisill, M. (2007). What teacher candidates learned about diversity, social justice, and themselves from service learning experiences. *Journal of Teacher Education*, 58(4), 315–27.

Barone, T. and Eisner, E. (2011). *Arts-based research*. Thousand Oaks, CA: Sage.

Becker, J. (2004). Public art: An essential component of creating communities. *Americans for the Arts Monograph* (March).

Boal, A. (1979). *Theatre of the oppressed*. New York: Theatre Communications Group.

—— (1992). *Games for actors and non-actors*. New York: Routledge.

Boyle-Baise, M. and Zevin, J. (2009). *Young citizens of the world: Teaching elementary social studies through civic engagement*. New York: Routledge.

Cammarota, J. and Fine, M. (Eds) (2008). *Revolutionizing education: Youth participatory action research in motion*. New York: Routledge.

Cruz, B. (2002). Don Juan and rebels under palm trees: Depictions of Latin Americans in U.S. history textbooks. *Critique of Anthropology*, 22(3), 323–42.

Doss, E. (1992). Raising community consciousness with public art: Contrasting projects by Judy Baca and Andrew Leicester. *American Art*, 6(1), 62–80.

Duncan-Andrade, J. (2006). Utilizing cariño in the development of research methodologies. In J. Kincheloe, P. Anderson, K. Rose, D. Griffith, and K. Hayes (Eds), *Urban education: An encyclopedia* (pp. 451–86). Westport, CT: Greenwood.

Freire, P. (1993). *Pedagogy of the oppressed*. New York: Continuum.

Freire, P. (2004). *Pedagogy of hope: Reliving pedagogy of the oppressed*. New York: Continuum.

Gutiérrez, K., Asato, J., Santos, M., and Gotanda, N. (2002). Backlash pedagogy: Language and culture and the politics of reform. *Review of Education, Pedagogy and Cultural Studies*, 24(4), 335–51.

Harman, R. with French, K. (in press). Critical performative pedagogy and urban teacher education: Voices from the field? *Play and Culture*, 11.

Kellner, D. and Share, J. (2005). Toward critical media literacy: Core concepts, debates, organizations, and policy. *Discourse: Studies in the Cultural Politics of Education*, 26(3), 369–86.

Kozol, J. (1992). *Savage inequalities: Children in America's schools*. New York: Harper Perennial.

Lakoff, G. and Johnson, M. (2003). *Metaphors we live by*, 2nd edition. Chicago, IL: University of Chicago Press.

Levstik, L. and Barton, K. (2010). *Doing history: Investigating with children in elementary and middle schools*. New York: Routledge.

Loewen, J. (2007). *Lies my teacher told me: Everything your American history textbook got wrong*. New York: Touchstone.

McLaren, P. (1995). Critical multiculturalism, media literacy and the politics of representation. In J. Frederickson (Ed.), *Reclaiming our voices: Bilingual education, critical pedagogy and praxis* (pp. 99–138). Ontario, CA: California Association for Bilingual Education.

Moreno, J. (1998). *The elusive quest for equality: 150 years of Chicano Chicana education*. Cambridge, MA: Harvard Educational Review.

Morrell, E. and Duncan-Andrade, J. (2008). *The art of critical pedagogy*. New York: Peter Lang.

Museum of Teaching and Learning (2011). A class action: The grassroots struggle for school desegregation in California. Retrieved June 20, 2012 from http://www.motal.org/exhibits/upcoming-exhibits.html.

Pacheco, M. (2012). Learning in/through everyday resistance: A cultural–historical perspective on community resources and curriculum. *Educational Researcher*, 41(4), 121–32.

Polkinghorne, D. (1988). *Narrative knowing and the human sciences*. Albany: SUNY Press.

Renner, A. (2009). Teaching community, praxis, and courage: A foundations pedagogy of hope and humanization. *Educational Studies*, 45, 59–79.

Schultz, B. (2010). *Listening to and learning from students: Possibilities for teaching, learning, and curriculum*. Charlotte, NC: Information Age Publishing.

Siqueiros, D. A. (1975). *Art and revolution*. London: Lawrence and Wishart.

Smith, K., Edelsky, C., and Faltis, C. (2009). *Side-by-side learning: Exemplary literacy practices for English language learning and English speakers in the mainstream classroom*. New York: Scholastic.

Tierney, W. G. (1993). *Building communities of difference: Higher education in the twenty-first century*. Westport, CT: Praeger.

Valenzuela, A. (1999). *Subtractive Schooling: U.S.–Mexican Youth and the Politics of Caring*. New York: State University of New York Press.

Zia, H. (2001). *Asian American Dreams: The emergence of an American people*. New York: Farrar, Straus & Giroux.

Zinn, H. (2010). *A people's history of the United States*. New York: Harper Perennial Modern Classics.

8

TALKING TO THE SYSTEM
THROUGH YOUTH MEDIA

Thus far, we have discussed the importance of storytelling and play as mediums of creative expression, social engagement, identity and language development with emergent bilingual youth. We have explored how critical pedagogies can address the gaps and assumptions in historical and world event narratives through problem-posing inquiry. We have explored the arts-based processes emergent bilingual youth utilize to ask questions and raise concerns about the social, political and economic injustices relating to their lives, their families and communities. This chapter offers another extension of how story and play can be used with emergent bilingual youth through new media technologies, including the improvisational, strategic use of social networks, web building, digital storytelling, smart phones, tablets and apps. In this chapter, we discuss how the mediation of technology and new media can assist emergent bilingual youth in their language and identity development, as well as their sense of belonging in various communities of practice.

Engaging digital technologies in education will enable you as a teacher to be responsive to your students in new ways, in the ways of youth culture. As a teacher you may already sense a generational gap between yourself and your students in the way that they learn new technologies with ease and the references they make to various worlds constructed in and through digital media. Culturally responsive teaching includes connecting with young people as they are—in their state of being—which today is inextricably linked to the digital (Sefton-Green, 1998; Tapscott, 2008). If you consider yourself "not a technology person," perhaps the vignettes in this chapter and the following compelling statistics about youth and technology might prompt you to incorporate at least one new media strategy in your teaching.

A Pew Institute Survey (Lenhart and Madden, 2007) on youth and social media found that 93 percent of young people ages twelve to seventeen use the internet, while 64 percent of online teens participate in some form of content creation—sharing creative output and engaging in conversations about that output online (as in blogs, YouTube videos, social networking, modified photos, webpages, and online fiction). Of surveyed teen girls, 35 percent blog (write content and post it to a personal site online) regularly. Nearly half of online teens post photos and most note that these photos are commented on at least some of the time. Further, about 28 percent of all teens utilize multiple technological tools (email, texting, instant messaging, tweeting, Facebook, cell phones). By 2003, 99 percent of schools had access to the internet, with four students per computer.

The use of the internet as a communication tool is staggering: as of 2009, 100 million websites exist worldwide, while 100 billion emails are sent daily (Herrington et al., 2009). Many K–12 teachers and organizations, including the National Council of Teachers of English (NCTE), now argue that valid assessments of writing need to include the use of digital composition. Digital technologies are the mediation and cultural tools of new generations, as young people regularly build self-representational narratives through image, sound, and text in cyberspace, using sites like YouTube, Facebook, and Voice Thread and applications like iMovie and Photoshop (Tapscott, 2008). Young people today assert an ongoing social presence online, demonstrating the importance of analyzing the digital as a unique pedagogical space with a diverse set of tools. We should ensure that emergent bilingual youth have access to the use of this dynamic, multimodal means of expression.

In moving beyond the limitations of printed text, emergent bilingual youth can engage both literally and metaphorically in border crossing—moving across cultures and code switching across languages—as they apply aesthetic tools and techniques. The barrier of standing in front of the class to present one's work may be dissolved through the mediation of technology. Bilingual youth once anticipated teacher correction, even ridicule, as they spoke publically using varieties of English other than the grammar-book standard (Chávez, 2012). Yet, through ground-up, grassroots digital production, bilingual youth can wield decision-making to display their languages and experiences with confidence and pride (Curwood and Gibbons, 2009). The multimodal context of the digital requires a more flexible approach to expression, potentially leading to increased confidence in bilingual language production and cultural pride.

The multimodal quality of digital media can be explored in terms of the phases of production leading to a digital product (Nyobe and Drotner, 2008). First, teachers introduce students to the digital platform they will be using. In this phase, they might explore sample products by other young people, such as videos, PowerPoints, Facebook pages, or digital music compositions. During this phase, the media workshops focus on aesthetic criticism and social dialogue about the form and content of the example pieces. Then, students identify their own focus for production and storyboard, or visually map, their ideas. During this phase, they might conduct research much like that described in the previous chapter, with its focus on problem solving curriculum. Then, the students would produce individual or collaborative digital pieces, supported by peer mentors, teaching artists, or technology educators with prior experience in that digital medium. During this process, the teacher would introduce key mini lessons to focus their production, such as the use of emotion, rhythm, unity, exaggeration, perspectives, or framing. Students might also show each other pieces in process to receive feedback, much like they would with written work in Writers' Workshop. Finally, students would determine their pieces complete and plan for public screening or other presentation. This phase is essential to building confidence and leadership skills in young people, which you will see in more detail in the vignettes of this chapter.

Digital production for the purposes of student self-representation requires that artist/teachers pose a series of ethical questions, such as:

- How can teachers build a safe environment for the display of self through digital media?
- How and when should teachers engage language varieties as integral to digital expression, and how will this approach impact assessment of student writing?
- How can teachers prevent hurtful language, via flaming and cyber bullying, from occurring when youth digital texts are published online?
- What stories should be told?
- What is the relationship between private and public spheres in the lives of the subjects of digital stories?
- What does it mean to tell the stories of individuals in the context of social justice struggles?
- When and how should stories be contextualized by these struggles with inequity? (Bliznik, 2010; Lundby, 2008.)

As a premise of this book, we argue that narratives of the self—personal stories written by students about their own struggles and successes—should be contextualized in some way by the historical and current inequities that impact the lives of the author and audience. Goodson (1995) suggests that de-contextualized storytelling is a popular news media frame that remains in "personal minutiae and anecdotes" (p. 91) rather than cultural analysis. The proliferation of English-only education and the treatment of speakers of languages other than English intensifies a call for storytelling that moves beyond the cause and effect, hero/villain plot.

For example, a Google search for "English-only education" brings up many stories about the rise of the movement as the contemporary program model of U.S. schools for emergent bilingual youth. The story is typically told as an event (the passing of Proposition 227, and those bills like it in other states) from the perspective of a character (Ron Unz, the leader of the movement, and politicians aligned with the movement). There may be an attempt at "objectivity" with the inclusion of some counter-perspectives. But typically the news coverage concludes with a plot resolution (the inevitable adoption of English-only as the model to improve non-native speakers' chances of academic success). Yet, a local digital story produced by students might focus on subjective interpretations: *Whose voices are heard in the English-only story? Whose are marginalized or left out entirely? What happened before the event-focus of the story? What happened afterward? How else might the story be told* (Levstik and Barton, 2010)?

Local digital stories do not depend on the ratings that often limit popular news to crisis and sentimentality. Instead, self-representational digital narratives that engage lenses of critique have the power to raise questions about human dilemmas from multiple perspectives, through an exploration of competing, conflicting narratives. There are many resources and organizations to support you in honing your digital production skills, as well as your facilitation of the production process with young people, such as the Center for Digital Storytelling (www.story center.org).

The vignettes[1] in this chapter demonstrate the power of digital media for expressing the complexity of emergent bilingual youth's lives, with their peers, caregivers, teachers, and other adults they encounter in schools, their communities and the world. In the first vignette, Deborah Romero shares a youth media project she facilitated with high school students in Colorado about immigration, high school dropout and teen issues. Then, Susan Adams tells how high school students used the creation of a website to distribute their views on how ESL should be taught. As you read, consider how the projects employ digital media, the tools and techniques utilized, as well as how the youth participants negotiated public spaces to distribute their creations.

VIGNETTE SIXTEEN

Youth Media

Making It in the World!

Deborah Romero, University of Northern Colorado

> The Youth Media Project, in particular the young Latina described in this vignette, formed part of an ongoing university afterschool and summer program[2] designed to help high school students stay in school, graduate and ideally enroll in post-secondary education. Informed by the work of Goodman (2003) and others working in visual media (Zenkov and Harmon, 2009), the Youth Media Project complements and supports the tutoring and advising activities by engaging students in real opportunities to develop meaningful language and new literacies (Jewitt, 2008; Street, 2003), while also strengthening

technological and communication skills (Romero and Walker, 2010), as well as student identity (Cummins et al., 2006). Over forty students participated in Youth Media, ranging in age and grade level from fifteen to eighteen, with slightly more girls than boys. They all attended the same high school and all qualified for the program on the basis of low socioeconomic status and being first-generation college bound.

In addition, an overwhelming number of students in Youth Media were Latino, either first- or second-generation immigrants, and over 50 percent were bilingual (Spanish and English). A few other dual language students (Russian, Turkish, Somali, and Arabic) participated, and the project strove to promote students as active meaning-makers of multilingual communications. With guidance from Youth Media instructors, students selected and determined both the nature and creative content of their multimodal products, and they often worked collaboratively in filming and production teams.

The events and story portrayed here are the culmination of one year's work and activities. Under the guidance of Jason, the Youth Media instructor, and myself, the author and literacy coordinator at the program, students used small handheld digital cameras and voice recorders, professional video cameras, boom microphones, and professional editing software. Students filmed themselves and each other, then moved into the community and conducted a range of interviews in English and Spanish based on brainstorming questions and collaboratively produced scripts. Scripts included three main parts:

- General introductory questions: "Hello, could you please tell us your name and where you are from?"
- Specific questions designed to elicit details and information about student topics: "Really, can you please tell us more?" or "Could you describe what that was like?"
- Final closing statements: "Well, thank you for your time. We have learned a lot. It was a pleasure to hear your opinion or experience."

Through the interview process, students also learned the significance of listening to interviewee responses, gauging the relevance of the next question and, when necessary, being able to ask impromptu follow-up questions that allowed the speaker to elaborate further on a particular point.

After gathering footage, students worked on the university campus, in a small basement media lab with six recycled Macintosh computers, using Final Cut Pro® to log and edit video clips for the final production. As student competence and learning in youth media evolved, so too the activities and products became more ambitious. Over a course of three years, students pro-gressed from the first summer writing poetry, learning recording basics and producing short broadcast-like stories for radio and some digital narratives, to learning filming and camera techniques and principles in the fall. The following spring students engaged more seriously in recording their personal stories and illustrating these with photographs to produce digital narratives.

In the second summer in 2009, students embarked upon a series of mini documentaries on self-selected topics: Immigration, High School Dropouts and Teen Issues. They spent the summer filming and interviewing and worked during the fall on video logging, editing and rough-cut production as well as writing narratives and completing voiceovers. The final editing and production occurred in spring of 2010, with a community screening at the local cinema. By the third summer, students were researching their local community, filming and interviewing in and about town and also documenting their own filming. This work resulted in a short documentary that was screened on campus and through the local history museum's website.

Central to our work in Youth Media are the broadcasting and screening of students' completed products with different audiences. Students' early work on personal narratives was presented to friends and family at end of semester or summer session celebrations. Later, three bilingual Latino students also shared work at a local high school with their ESL peers. Then, eleven Youth Media students participated in a presentation at the National Conference on Bilingual Education (NABE) held in Denver, Colorado, in 2010. Most recently, their mini documentaries on Immigration, High School Dropouts and Teen Issues were screened at a local cinema to a wider public audience.

Lucia's Journey—Making It in the World!

On a warm May morning, with tears in her eyes, Lucia turns to Jason, the Youth Media instructor, who has unexpectedly shown up at her high school graduation with one of the project video cameras. Lucia, a vibrant young Latina, dressed out in full regalia for senior graduation, calls out to a friend, "Oh my God, Jason! You've gotta be kidding!" as she turns to hug a fellow graduate. Then, looking back at Jason, she continues, "I'm crying . . . *this* is not the best . . . movie." Jason congratulates her and continues filming. Lucia, as if seizing the moment, composes herself, takes a deep breath, touches her chest and points back to Jason and the camera. "A freaking movie of making it in the world!"

The journey for Lucia had not been easy and reaching this special day had come at the expense of many hardships and personal struggles. Many of these difficulties she shared in both private and public through her participation in Youth Media. Only some three months before her graduation, vacillating somewhere between self-confidence and that anxious nervousness, Lucia stepped forward to address the small but attentive audience at the National Association for Bilingual Education Conference in Denver. In stark contrast to her usual jeans and sneakers, Lucia dressed in a beige business suit and high heels. She was at the conference to present and share *her* digital story to the public.

"Well, I'm the lucky one, first off!" she began, as she explained that before filming their personal narratives, students had written a short paper, "a little bit about ourselves, how we are like at home, how our family is, as well as our favorite songs, and what we like to do at home in our spare time and stuff, so ..." Then she paused and turned to look at the large projection screen behind her, checking to see if her video was showing and ready to play. When she realized it was about to start she smiled and quickly explained to the audience, "Er . . . um. I really can't sit still and I—um, talk with my hands . . . so, as you can tell, I'm like bouncing around, so you try not to mind that . . ."

Entitled "My Life in Four Minutes" Lucia's short digital narrative is interspersed with colorful images of her as a baby, as a young girl in traditional Mexican dress, photographs of her Mexican grandparents and other scenes of her childhood and family, as well as more recent successes at school (see Figure 8.1). This animated visual collage formed the backdrop to her powerful narration and musing about her life. "I really don't have much of a memory with my parents, coz they were always working. I was mostly with my grandma and grandpa." Gradually, as the camera moves in to a close up of Lucia, viewers become privy to some of her innermost feelings, and all the while she talks quickly, chewing gum and moving her head.

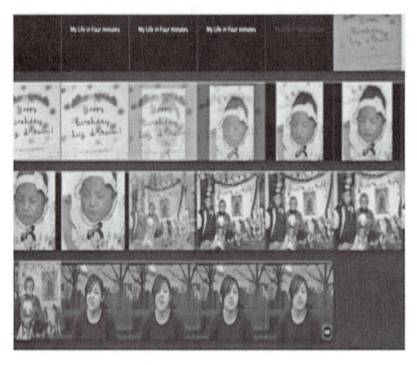

FIGURE 8.1 *Frame Shots from the Beginning of Lucia's Digital Narrative*
by Deborah Romero

"I really don't think about . . . my future, coz I've, like, seen death around me so many times. Like one of these days, it's gonna be called, my number, and I don't wanna leave any unfinished business." A little later on, she describes what she hopes to do with her life, if she does live. "I wanna go into law, coz I see all the crap that Hispanic, Latina, Chicana, or whatever race you wanna say, is dealing with. And, how lawyers that only speak English but no Spanish screw them over . . . just to make a quick buck."

After watching her digital narrative, someone in the audience asked Lucia what changes she had seen in herself since having made the recording almost a year previously. Lucia smiled and explained, "Actually, I am living longer and I caught up my credit and I'm gonna graduate this year!" The audience applauded and cheered in approval. Lucia continued, "I've gone from a straight F student, who used to go into the alley in the back to get high and sniff coke, from that to going to conferences, which is something that I really didn't see myself going to . . . there's like a big change in that, from what I used to be to how I am now."

Two months after the NABE conference, Lucia and her peers from the Youth Media Program hosted a public screening at the downtown cinema of three mini documentaries that they filmed, edited and co-produced over the course of a year. The documentaries examined Immigration, High School Dropouts and Teen Issues, all topics chosen by students. The general public and academics in attendance that night were all very impressed with the students' work. While some of her peers were nervous or shy, Lucia projected certainty and clarity in her answers. Again dressed in business attire, she confidently fielded questions and supported her classmates' discussion about how they made the documentaries. So great was the interest that about a week later, a reporter for the local city newspaper scheduled an interview with Lucia and a few of her fellow students.

Huddled in the basement Youth Media lab, Lucia reassured her peers, some of whom still seemed nervous as they sat munching on snacks and awaiting the reporter. Intermittent questions broke the silence: "What's he wanna know? What do we tell him? Who's gonna do the talking?" However, when the reporter arrived and the questions began, the students overflowed the enthusiasm and responded with alacrity. This interview marked a culmination, a coming full circle, of what had been an intense, creative project. The newspaper story took front page the following week (see Figure 8.2). All the students had something to say about their experiences in Youth Media, but in particular Lucia. She explained, "It was neat for the community to see that we're not just on MySpace or texting all day . . . We try to get into the community and see what's going on out there. Everyone who's seen what we've done is pretty amazed, because we're kids." But perhaps the words that best sum up Lucia's experiences with Youth Media are that "You learn from their [other people's] mistakes, but you are not taking the same journey as them."

FIGURE 8.2 *Front Page Story about the Students' Screening and Filmmaking Project by Deborah Romero*

And so, back to that sunny May morning, with tears still running down her cheeks, Lucia glancing at Jason and then at the camera still focused on her. Asserting her point once more, she looked not at Jason but directly into the camera lens and resumed her statement, this time with urgency and emphasis, "You guys—you guys, you can do it, if I can do it! No doubt about it . . ."

Following her graduation, Lucia spent this summer taking college credits and is now attending classes at the community college, before planning to transfer into university.

Implications for Practice and Beyond

While this youth media project was designed and developed in an afterschool setting with high school students, such projects can be adapted to school and community settings, across varying grade levels. Rather than provide a "how to" manual or guide, since many of these exist already (Baudenbacher and Goodman, 2006; Costanzo, 2008; Ohler, 2008; Porter, 2005), I list here some considerations based on my experiences in youth media and which I consider new teachers, artists and others might find useful should they decide to undertake a similar project with their own students.

1. *Start small—but think big!* Initially, it is important to keep both the scope and requirements of the project manageable. Provide students with clear

guidelines about the requirements of the assignment or direction of the product you hope to realize. It helps to have students view several finished digital products available online (useful websites for examples and further guidelines: http://www.storycenter.org/;http://youthpowered video.ning.com/, http://www.jasonohler.com/storytelling/index.cfm). Plan accordingly and allow enough time for students to complete a project, approximately five to ten hours for a short project, pending student level, ability and access to technology.

2. *Use whatever resources are available—without fear!* Depending on their level of technical savvy, teachers and adults should take time to explore the preinstalled software on the available computers. Watch online tutorials that accompany most software, and practice making your own short digital compositions. Remember, many of your students will be digital natives! Encourage them to use any technologies that they already have, such as cell phones, digital cameras, PSPs and other audio-visual recording devices. Be open to learning from them and this will become a truly collaborative experience.

3. *Connect—to students and to community experts.* You are not alone, and working in youth media is a wonderful way to break out of the classroom and collaborate with community experts or professionals, both in the field of communication technologies and in relation to the topics students may be researching. Contact local broadcasters, radio hosts, TV stations or news anchors, undergrad students of communication or film majors at a nearby university and young artists or entrepreneurs, many of whom may be willing and able to participate. Include multilingual and culturally diverse persons representative of your students.

4. *Focus on the personal, then the social.* It is important that initial digital products and stories center on students, their identities and background knowledge, as well as their personal stories. Working on familiar topics about which they have ownership allows students to focus on exploring and learning how to use the tools and technologies to compose "new narratives" using dialogue, images, sound and music in ways that extend their expressive and creative potential. This is also a wonderful way to gain insight into what is important for students and better understand how they view themselves.

5. *Build language by extending existing knowledge of writing and composing.* By all means reference students' prior knowledge on academic and creative writing from school and home, but avoid turning youth media and digital composition into a "translation" of previously written texts. There are similarities in terms of what it means to compose a narrative or story, with beginning, middle and end, but there is much more flexibility and opportunity to allow non-linguistic representations to complement or extend, not parallel, the linguistic-based text. Digital texts are dynamic and fluid, more malleable and portable.

6. *Progression through performance.* Central to youth media and digital literacies is the notion that these are hands-on, collaborative experiences. Students learn by doing and engaging in the practices of media production. Avoid long abstract tutorials or presentations. Promote small structured assignments, grounded in hands-on activities and attainable products. Encourage and promote teamwork and peer review. Products need audiences beyond the author and the teacher or artist. Work to build in critique sessions, small group viewings and public screenings. Promote students as producers of their work.

7. *Celebrate diversity by promoting student agency and success!* Fundamental elements in youth media are notions of student voice and agency. Because youth media is multimodal and affords so many creative and expressive options, even within the same class or setting, students are able to produce quite unique and different products. Value this diversity; use it as a tool for teaching and learning with other students and colleagues. It is crucial that students realize (both materially in the product and consciously in the doing) the potential and experience the power of this medium: power to project not only their voice but also to support their agency with regards to personal and social matters, to promote the dissemination of their products and their participation in local, national and global forums, both in person and across different mediums, print- based, audio-visual, and online.

★   ★   ★

VIGNETTE SEVENTEEN

Having Our Say: English Language Learners Talk Back to Teachers

Susan Adams, Butler University

Sally's high school ESL students were intrigued, yet puzzled. Perhaps they misunderstood her. Did she really just ask the students to write *to their teachers* and tell them what English language learners (ELLs) need in order to be successful in their classrooms? Slowly the truth dawned on them. Sally invited her students to write about their learning needs and the results of their work would be posted on the district's website. These students would have their say and it would be published for their teachers to read! In the past, when asked to write, these students had dragged their feet, reluctant to get started on the difficult task of writing complex thoughts and ideas in their emergent English. Today they jumped in with both feet.

Like most of us, ELLs write best when they write for an authentic audience and for authentic purposes (Atwell, 1998). With a strong sense of purpose and a deep sense of responsibility for the larger group of ELLs they represented, the students understood that, during the writing process, they would need to attend carefully to many components simultaneously. In fact, the authenticity of this assignment captivated them so completely, most of them forgot it was a class assignment. What follows are the students' accomplishments as they took on the role of real authors, instead of merely completing dry, meaningless exercises. Examples of the students' written comments and questions to teachers are italicized and represent an early stage in their writing process. The images are PowerPoint slides, in the edited, published stage, that the students showed the teachers.

A Clear, Convincing Message

Students explored rhetorical structures to create messages that were simultaneously comprehensible and persuasive to teachers. They explored the use of anger, humor, slang, and traditional Western forms of persuasive writing as they crafted the texts. The students used pathos to reach the hearts of teachers. Following a slide of beautiful photos of happy students in Mexican schools, they write this:

> *Look at the students' faces.*
>
> * *They feel happy because they are in they own country close to they family and friends.*
> * *Students don't have difficulties to learn in their own language.*

The ELLs wanted their teachers to know they were happy in their home countries, that learning is easier in one's native language, and the underlying, poignant plea for recognition of their innate intelligence.

Using Writing Conventions for Communication

In order to be understood by their readers, grammar errors were carefully examined, discussed, and corrected. While their texts are not grammatically "perfect," it is clear the students worked to transmit a clear message to teachers. As evidenced in the selected quote above, the few lingering errors in the text did not impede comprehension.

Diplomacy within Inequitable Power Structures

Students had strong feelings about what they needed from teachers, but realized that teachers have feelings, too. The writer must find a way to gently, firmly, tell the hard truth while keeping the reader engaged. How does one critique a teacher without risking failure? Word choice, length of the text, and voice or tone suddenly became urgent as students wrestled with the best way to deliver their messages. There are clearly defined roles present in this scenario. Students are attempting to speak truth to the teachers who have significant power over them. Take a look at their skill in balancing these competing demands:

- *All the students from other countries have the right to be listened and teachers need to change in ways that we can learn easier.*

  Examples:
  - *Like give us the opportunity to use a dictionary in tests.*
  - *Not to ignore us when we are asking questions.*
  - *Give us study guides and a few days before the test.*
  - *Show us films and explain them to us with patience.*
  - *Use examples not just talk because that doesn't understand, and we get confused.*

Building Empathy

The students gradually understood that most of their teachers did not grasp the complexity of classroom tasks, assignments and tests. How could the students give the teachers a taste of what it is like to be an ELL in the classroom? They decided to write a quiz for teachers:

- *Have you ever wondered?*

  1. *Read the questions and answer them for yourself.*
  2. *Read the ESL students' responses.*

  Note the differences. They might surprise you.

The students invited teachers to speculate on the ESL student experience. Question number 5 reveals the students' pain and discomfort as immigrants in a contentious political climate:

5. *Do you think we have the blame for being here in the USA?*

   Student Answer
   - *The majority of us come when we are minors, and we don't know what is happening to us.*
   - *Our parents want to give us a better life, but there are a lot of positive and negative consequences to those decisions.*

Often teachers make assumptions about the reasons families immigrate to the United States. In this same district, high school teachers are frequently surprised to learn that ELLs often long to return to their homelands, to friends, family and to familiar schools.

Utilizing the Tools of Technology

Students skillfully enlisted the supports and communication structures available through the available technology in their school. Students tapped the word processing program as an editing assistant, created sophisticated, colorful PowerPoints, and navigated internet resources to utilize existing websites as a model. They demonstrate a savvy understanding of teacher technologies in the construction of the quiz.

Collaboration and Peer Editing

Students were eager to give and receive feedback because they wanted their voices to ring loud and clear. They were inspired by the ideas, stories, and examples they heard from their peers. They brainstormed and co-wrote sections. Together they scrutinized and piloted the test they created for teachers to be sure the test accomplished their goals.

Publication Expectations

Students realized that their drafts would have to go through multiple rounds of revision and careful editing before the texts could be published on the district website. When the writers knew that an authentic audience (someone other than the teacher) would read their work, a new seriousness and pride were evident in the results.

What Students Have to Say about the Project

One of the lead students and the author of "A Survey for Teachers" from the project, Manuel, spoke passionately about his goals for the project. He stated firmly: "The project was important to me because the new [immigrant] students need more help to understand what is going on in their classes. The teachers need to cooperate with us and understand that we need to learn in different ways."

Manuel understands that ELLs often struggle to succeed when teachers expect all the adapting and transformation to come from the ELL students. His emphasis on two-way cooperation reveals his belief that offering choice, alternative assessments, multiple opportunities to master new content, and

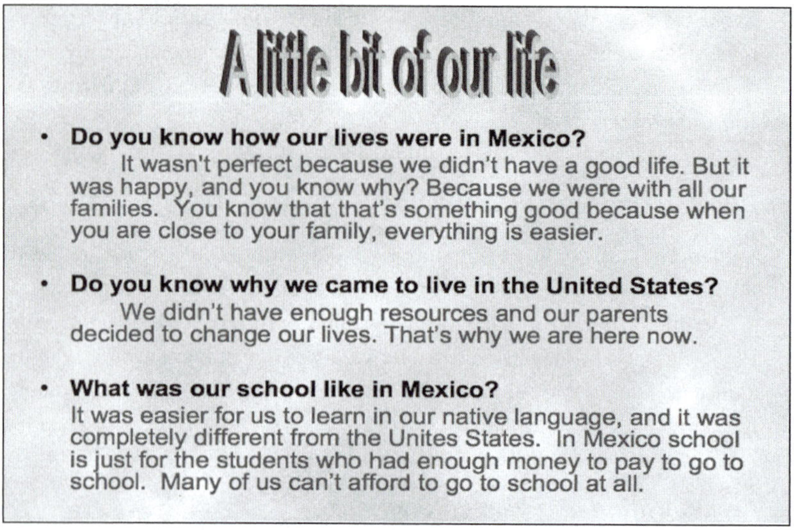

A little bit of our life

- **Do you know how our lives were in Mexico?**
  It wasn't perfect because we didn't have a good life. But it was happy, and you know why? Because we were with all our families. You know that that's something good because when you are close to your family, everything is easier.

- **Do you know why we came to live in the United States?**
  We didn't have enough resources and our parents decided to change our lives. That's why we are here now.

- **What was our school like in Mexico?**
  It was easier for us to learn in our native language, and it was completely different from the Unites States. In Mexico school is just for the students who had enough money to pay to go to school. Many of us can't afford to go to school at all.

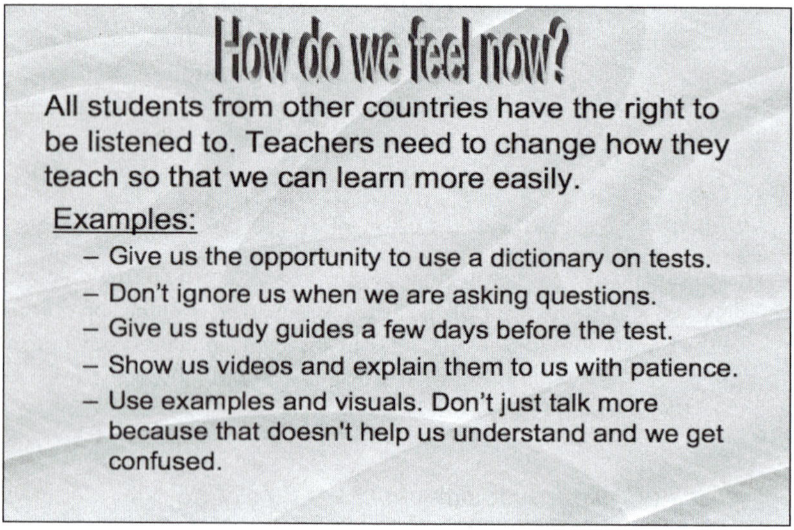

How do we feel now?

All students from other countries have the right to be listened to. Teachers need to change how they teach so that we can learn more easily.

Examples:

- Give us the opportunity to use a dictionary on tests.
- Don't ignore us when we are asking questions.
- Give us study guides a few days before the test.
- Show us videos and explain them to us with patience.
- Use examples and visuals. Don't just talk more because that doesn't help us understand and we get confused.

FIGURES 8.3, 8.4 *PowerPoint Slides from ELL Student-Authored Quiz for Teachers* by Susan Adams and students of Suburban Central High School

creative approaches in the classroom will open up learning opportunities for ELLs. And Manuel is not only thinking about his own success. Revealing a deep sense of responsibility, he reminds us: "I was thinking about all of the new students that would come after me."

Contrary to what we might expect, Manuel and his fellow students were not asking teachers to take it easy on them. They asked teachers to take time to get to know them, to understand their goals and dreams, and to see them as fully human. Manuel urges teachers to "not let us sleep in class. Just find a way to make class interesting for us to want to understand." He grins and reminds teachers, "Humor is important too, but we don't always understand it." Teachers are often unaware of the complexity of humor across multiple language groups and cultures and inadvertently leave some ELLs puzzled by the laughter of the class. ELLs wonder: *What is so funny? Who is the butt of the joke? Why don't I understand what is going on?* Missing out on classroom humor can leave ELLs feeling further isolated.

Project Alianza

The digital project featured in this vignette grew out of professional development undertaken by the students' high school teacher, Sarah. This professional development project, called Project Alianza, is a U.S. Department of Education Title III funded professional development program for teachers hosted through Butler University's College of Education with Dr Katie Brooks, the principal investigator, and Susan Adams, Project Alianza Director and the author of this text. The Project's primary goal is to prepare secondary content area teachers to support ELLs in meeting academic and English language development and proficiency standards. Brooks and Adams meet with cohorts of teachers in six local school districts in Indianapolis, Indiana, with each cohort being comprised of teachers from multiple school buildings in each district. Based on the students' digital project, Sally, their high school teacher, and a group of her colleagues created an online resource to arm classroom content area teachers with fresh ideas, deeper philosophies, a new respect, and research-based strategies for teaching ELLs. As the students remind teachers through their survey and website, ELLs are dreamers like the rest of us. They long to enter classrooms where teachers welcome them and teach with patience, humor, and empathy. ELLs reach toward academic success with an eye toward lifting up their families, the immigrant community, and the students who follow in their footsteps. Let's bring their dream to reality![3]

★   ★   ★

Digital media is a dynamic medium that allows for multiple modalities of expression (visual, written, spoken, performed, and musical). The use of technologies has the potential to raise questions not only about what is learned in schools (the knowledge and skills) but also how it is learned (the processes and practices privileged in schools). As seen in the vignettes of this chapter, multiple literacies (Curwood and Gibbons, 2009; Lankshear and Noble, 2006; New London Group, 1996) focus on student-centered identity expression in relation to academic content and the larger social world.

Additionally, the emergent bilingual youth in these vignettes produced multimodal counter-narratives that we can analyze on three levels: *refusal*, *repudiation*, and *contestation* (Curwood and Gibbons, 2009; Lindemann Nelson, 2001). These young people refused to apply dominant narrative beliefs about themselves (such as assumptions teachers and other adults made about them as ESL students). They repudiated these beliefs through counter-narratives constructed digitally with aesthetic strategies such as timing, presence, dialogue, questioning, and other text-in-use modes. Further, they contested dominant narratives through public presentation of their own stories. In the final chapter, we will further explore the importance of opening counter-narrative spaces in schools with emergent bilingual youth, their communities and other educators.

Questions to Consider

1. As a teacher, what is your current "comfort zone" with technology and digital media? What professional development might you pursue to learn more about the use of digital media in the classroom?

2. What role does digital media play in your students' lives? How can you learn more about their use of technology?

3. In the vignettes of this chapter, how do the facilitators ethically negotiate the concerns and questions their students have?

4. What practices discussed in this chapter intrigue you? How might you incorporate these practices in culturally and linguistically responsive ways in your classroom, particularly in relation to digital media already in the lives of your students?

Notes

1. All names in this chapter's vignettes are pseudonyms.
2. The Youth Media Project described here is a sub-component of the Northern Colorado Upward Bound Program, which is federally funded by the U.S. Department of Education (94 percent) and non-federal funds from the University of Northern Colorado (6 percent).
3. Vignette author's note: Susan R. Adams sends many thanks, endless respect, and much appreciation to Sarah Scholl and her amazing ELL students from Suburban Central High School, and to the Suburban Central teachers who contributed to the Alianza project. Learning from and with you is pure joy.

References

Atwell, N. (1998). *In the middle: New beginnings about writing, reading, and learning*, 2nd edition. Portsmouth, NJ: Heinemann.

Baudenbacher, G. and Goodman, S. (2006). *Youth powered video. A hands-on curriculum for teaching documentary*. New York: EVC.

Bliznik, S. (2010). We're all in this together: Framing self-representations in Disney's *High School Musical*. In D. Chappell (Ed.), *Children under construction: Critical essays on play as curriculum* (pp. 149–66). New York: Peter Lang.

Chávez, M. (2012). Autoethnography, a Chicana's methodological research tool: The role of storytelling for those who have no choice but to do critical race theory. *Equity and Excellence in Education*, 45(2), 334–48.

Costanzo, W. (2008). *The writer's eye: Composition in the multimedia age*. New York: McGraw Hill.

Cummins, J., Bismilla, V., Chow, P., Cohen, S., Giampapa, F., Leoni, L., Sandhu, P., and Sastri, P. (2006). *ELL students speak for themselves: Identity texts and literacy engagement in multilingual classrooms*. Retrieved August 27, 2010, from http://www.curriculum.org/secretariat/files/ELLidentityTexts.pdf.

Curwood, J. S. and Gibbons, D. (2009). "Just like I have felt": Multimodal counternarratives in youth-produced digital media. *International Journal of Learning and Media*, 1(4), 59–77.

Goodman, S. (2003). *Teaching youth media. A guide to literacy, video production, and social change*. New York: Teachers College Press.

Goodson, I. (1995). The story so far: Personal knowledge and the political. *International Journal of Qualitative Studies in Education*, 8(1), 89–98.

Herrington, A., Hodgson, K., and Moran, C. (2009). *Teaching the new writing: Technology, change, and assessment in the 21st-century classroom*. New York: Teachers College Press.

Jewitt, C. (2008). Multimodality and literacy in school classrooms. *Review of Research in Education*, 32(1), 241–67.

Lankshear, C. and Knobel, M. (2006). *New literacies: Everyday practices and classroom learning*. New York: Open University.

Lenhart, A. and Madden, M. (2007). *Social networking websites and teens*. Pew Internet & American Life Project. Retrieved June 9, 2012 from http://pewinternet.org/Reports/2007/Social-Networking-Websites-and-Teens/Data-Memo.aspx.

Levstik, L. and Barton, K. (2010). *Doing history: Investigating with children in elementary and middle schools*. New York: Routledge.

Lindemann Nelson, H. (2001). *Damaged identities: Narrative repair*. Ithaca: Cornell University Press.

Lundby, K. (Ed.) (2008). *Digital storytelling, mediatized stories*. New York: Peter Lang.

New London Group. (1996). A pedagogy of multiliteracies: Designing social futures. *Harvard Educational Review*, 66(1). Retrieved November 19, 2012, from http://www static.kern.org/filer/blogWrite44ManilaWebsite/paul/articles/A_Pedagogy_of_Multi literacies_Designing_Social_Futures.htm.

Nyobe, L. and Drotner, K. (2008). Identity, aesthetics, and digital narration. In K. Lundby (Ed.), *Digital storytelling, mediatized stories* (pp. 161–76). New York: Peter Lang.

Ohler, J. (2008). *Digital storytelling in the classroom: New media pathways to literacy, learning, and creativity*. Thousand Oaks, CA: Corwin Press.

Porter, B. (2005). *DigiTales: The art of telling digital stories*. Denver: BJP Consulting.

Romero, D. and Walker, D. (2010). Pushing the boundaries of writing: The consequentiality of visualizing voice in bilingual youth radio. In C. Bazerman, R. Krut, K. Lunsford, S. McLeod, S. Null, P. Rogers, and A. Stansell (Eds), *Traditions of writing research* (pp. 224–36). New York: Routledge.

Sefton-Green, J. (1998). *Digital diversions: Youth culture in the age of multimedia*. New York: Routledge.

Street, B. V. (2003). What's "new" in New Literacy Studies? Critical approaches to literacy in theory and practice. *Current Issues in Comparative Education*, 5(2), 77–91.

Tapscott, D. (2008). *Grown up digital: How the net generation is changing your world*. New York: McGraw-Hill.

Zenkov, K. and Harmon, J. (2009). Picturing a writing process: Photovoice and teaching writing to urban youth. *Journal of Adolescent and Adult Literacy*, 52(7), 575–84.

9

CREATING COUNTER-NARRATIVE PRACTICES AT SCHOOL

In the previous chapter, we explored the unique role of digital media in the lives of young people today, as well as its dynamic potential to develop multiple literacies with emergent bilingual youth through creative, critical projects. The youth and their adult mentors built communities of practice that negotiated multiple linguistic and cultural differences in their public and private lives (New London Group, 1996; Wenger, 1999). These youth-centered, community-based projects regularly negotiated cross-cultural tensions, employed new technologies of communication, and engaged immersive pedagogies that resulted in explicit skill acquisition expressed through a plurality of texts (New London Group, 1996).

With each of the approaches we have presented thus far, the question of accessibility and sustainability must be considered. What if your school does not have the funds to purchase or support the use of digital media? What if your teachers do not see the purpose of asset-based family literacy projects? What if your district views play- and arts-based learning as extraneous to the narrow, test-driven literacy and mathematics curriculum currently in use? Chapter 9 addresses the creation of counter-narrative practices at school, even among the intense pressures of high stakes testing. We focus on the power of professional learning communities among teachers with critical, culturally responsive facilitators and guided inquiry. Finding a professional learning community is vital for educators concerned with holistic, humane and justice-based pedagogies for emergent bilingual youth.

The dominant function of schooling, both historical and contemporary, is to indoctrinate young generations into an existing social system, which socially and economically stratifies people according to culturally constructed concepts of race, gender, ethnicity, language, and social class (Anyon, 1980; Freire, 1970/2000; Giroux, 1983; Spring, 2009). This implicit function, also called the hidden curriculum of schools (Apple, 2004), is not explicit in academic objectives, but instead manifests through various policies and practices that create an "opportunity gap" between student groups, such as middle class/lower class, English speaking/second languages learners, white/non-white students. According to Darden and Cavendish (2011), these gaps include less experienced teachers assigned to high-poverty schools; schools treated as units within a district rather than considering differences within those units and reallocating funds according to need, resulting in decisions to treat students "the same" as distinguished from equitably; schools with larger numbers of "disadvantaged" students receiving less of the general education fund; higher facility maintenance in poorer neighborhoods without the money available to address those needs; and a lack of culturally and linguistically responsive curriculum, instruction, and family partnerships. This book addresses the final opportunity gap in detail.

A central tenet of the dominant script of schools is that socially marginalized students are individually culpable for their persistent low academic performance because they lack the "right" language and cultural norms, knowledge, and practices that would lead to academic success. In this way, the script goes, their failure is bolstered by parents who devalue and do not support their children's education (Yosso, 2005). In response to a deficit model of assumptions about marginalized students and their families, schools resort to a banking model of instruction (Freire, 1970), in an effort to transmit basic knowledge to students in ways that enable students to fare well enough on standardized assessment. In the end, however, the dominant Eurocentric curriculum works to stratify bilingual youth into caste-like positions in society (Cruz, 2002; Ogbu and Matute-Bianchi, 1986).

Creating Counter-Narratives to Deficit Thinking and Practices

As Gloria Anzaldúa (1990) argues, "It is *vital* that we occupy theorizing space, that we do not allow white men and women solely to occupy it. By bringing in our own approaches and methodologies, we transform the theorizing space" (p. xxv, emphasis in original). As teachers, we build such theorizing spaces from the knowledge and practices we encounter in our daily lives and professional development. We then share this theorizing implicitly and explicitly with the children and youth in our schools, as we reproduce and/or rethink what counts as school-based knowledge and practice. This chapter focuses on ways to transform the theorizing space currently occupied by the dominant script. This act requires a teacher-driven creation of counter-narrative practices in schools.

In education, Solórzano (1997) has identified several theoretical ideas to frame the creation of counter-narrative practices in school that dis-invent the dominant script. To dis-invent the dominant script implies that the script is socially constructed by the dominant group as means of maintaining its power by controlling the form and content of history, as well as the curriculum of whose voices, experience, knowledge and practices count for membership in the group. In order to dis-invent, members of the marginalized groups and their allies must create counter-narratives based on lived experiences, knowledge and practices as valid and essential for participating in a democratic society. Further, as teachers, we need others in solidarity with our efforts; in this way, your counter-narrative professional learning community might not be the kind of group that meets during the school's early release time. Rather, your theorizing space of dis-invention might be a dialogue journal with a friend, a story shared in confidence with a fellow teacher over the phone, or emails with a mentor from the university.

We focus on two counter-narrative theoretical ideas for you to explore as a teacher and with your emergent bilingual students: (1) the centrality of experiential knowledge, and (2) a transdisciplinary perspective (Solórzano, 1997). The experiential knowledge of socially marginalized groups must be legitimized as appropriate and necessary to schools in order to create spaces that "denounce the faults, prejudices, and fears manufactured by the self-proclaimed center" (Gómez-Peña, 1996, p. 12). In other words, dis-inventing dominant scripts through experiential counter-narratives is a prerequisite for emancipatory, democratic education. Arts-based practices of storytelling, murals, performances, video, photography, poetry, hip-hop, ethnodrama, painting, and sculpting are means through which students can present their counter-narratives from a position of community cultural wealth (Yosso, 2005). By community cultural wealth, we mean the array of knowledge and practices owned and used by members of socially marginalized communities to create these counter-narratives to the dominant script of what counts in schools (Yosso, 2005).

The second theoretical space for dis-inventing the dominant script and creating new counter-narrative practices is building transdisciplinary knowledge that goes beyond disciplinary boundaries, such as from ethnic studies, women's studies, sociology, film, theatre, and art. Too often school-based knowledge is separated by discipline, place and time—a desk, an hour, a single-subject textbook. As early as kindergarten, young people know when it is "math time" or "reading time." Rarely will they proclaim it is "community problem-solving time" in the daily schedule! Drawing from sources and experiences across disciplines opens the possibility for hearing, viewing and reading counter-narratives of others who have been discounted within the dominant script. These narratives will show how people have harnessed their experiences and knowledge to transform their lives and the lives of socially marginalized communities in ways that "count" across subject areas (Bell, 2010; Ewick and Silbey, 1995). As Barone (2000) suggests, trandisciplinary arts-based perspectives foster *conspiratorial conversations*, dialogues across communities about possible and desirable worlds, connections that touch common emotions and question the status quo.

How does a focus on experiential knowledge and transdisciplinary perspectives promote conspiratorial conversations and counter-narrative practices? Experiential knowledge draws its power from the voices of those who live in the experience: to tell stories that are not often told, and to analyze and challenge the stories told by those in the dominant group controlling the script, tools, and practices in schools (Delgado, 1993; de la Luz Reyes and Halcón, 1988; Yosso, 2006). Arts-based processes, in particular, have the power to question the common-sense ways of interpreting and presenting the world around us through deep sensory experience. In other words, counter-narratives have emancipatory potential to disturb the conventional and orthodox ways of representing life and voice, in ways that build empathy and connection across difference. The arts have the capacity to focus on the struggles of children and families deemed both implicitly and explicitly by the dominant script as deficient, irrational, insignificant, marginal, unqualified, and undeserving of serious, sustained attention in school and society.

In the following two vignettes, each author engages in counter-narrative, arts-based practices that question the dominant script and move the conversation for awareness and action. Both vignettes focus on the importance of a teacher professional development community to support the development of counter-narrative practices. First, Masakazu Matisuma uses ethnodrama, theatre based in ethnographic research, in which teacher candidates create scripts based on real-life experiences with emergent bilingual students and their families.

VIGNETTE EIGHTEEN

Ethnodrama: Transformative Learning in Multicultural Teacher Education

Masakazu Mitsumura, Arizona State University

Teacher Education at a Crossroads

We live in contemporary America, often divided into English speaking and non-English speaking populations. In a school system where students who are non-native speakers of English are often labeled or seen as "handicapped" (Nieto, 2004, p. 214) and intellectually or cognitively inferior, students from linguistically diverse backgrounds are encouraged to abandon their native language and culture as quickly and submissively as possible so as to be functioning, if not patriotic, Americans. Students from diverse backgrounds need to be seen for the funds of knowledge they bring to the classroom, rather than the ways they are failing in schools (Moll et al., 1992; Souto-Manning, 2010; Verdugo and Flores, 2007).

Despite the fact that there are a myriad of children from diverse cultural and linguistic backgrounds who face at-risk conditions in school, teacher education programs have not succeeded in producing prospective teacher candidates who are sufficiently well prepared to confront such challenges (Ambe, 2006). Ambe maintains that conventional pedagogies prevalent in the current teacher education programs have lost their validity in responding to the changing needs of the culturally diverse student populations.

Mattai (1992) poses a more critical question, proposing that the design of multicultural teacher education programs is not sufficiently critical for eliminating institutionalized racism and providing emancipatory pedagogies to empower marginalized students who have long been excluded from the U.S. public school agenda. As a result, preservice teachers enter and exit multicultural education courses "unchanged, often reinforcing their stereotypical perceptions of self and others" (Brown, 2004, p. 325) and teachers' lack of understanding of the cultures of students of color hinders the academic success of the children from racially, ethnically, and linguistically diverse backgrounds (Ambe, 2006; Delpit, 1995). This deficit thinking is carried consciously or unconsciously into teachers' classrooms, perpetuating the status quo in which students of color are largely left behind in school.

Ahlquist (1991), however, suggests that teacher educators as well as preservice teacher candidates have never received education that is "empowering, antiracist, problem-posing, or libratory" (p. 169). A more transformative pedagogy, therefore, is necessary for today's and the future's preservice teacher education programs in order to break the cycle of the sociocultural reproduction that has trapped teacher educators and teacher education students, who are *taught* to contribute to maintaining structural inequality and systematic marginalization in so-called "post-race" America.

This vignette[1] describes one of my multicultural teacher education classroom projects through which preservice teachers engaged in the process of constructing ethnodramatic play scripts aimed at portraying critical issues pertaining to the exclusion of ELL/LEP students and individuals in school and community. I have taught nearly 400 students in a multicultural education course in a large Southwestern university's teacher preparation program for the past three years, a course based on the theoretical nexus of Freirean and Boalian critical performance pedagogy. The students enrolled in my class are asked to be "Researchers/Playwrights/Actors" (Norris, 2009) who participate in participatory theatre and sociodrama-related activities inside and outside of the classroom, such as Boalian theatre games, Image Theatre, Forum Theatre, Newspaper Theatre, Devised Theatre, and ethnodrama (Saldaña, 2010, 2011). My goal as an educator is to help preservice teachers develop Freirean "*conscientização*" (Freire, 1970/2000) or "critical meta-awareness" (Souto-Manning, 2010) that enlarges their capacity for "imaginative empathy" (Ikeda, 2010) and challenges the status quo of banking (teacher) education (Freire, 1970/2000). I have found ethnodrama to be a transformative/emancipatory pedagogical tool to promote learning in action for de/reconstructing one's own internalized ideology in relation to hegemony.

What is Ethnodrama?

An *ethnodrama*, the word an amalgam of two words or social science fields: *ethnography* and *drama*, is a dramatized script that is constructed by transforming qualitative data collected through ethnographic data sources, such as ethnographic interview transcripts, participant observation filed notes, hand-written or online journal entries, retrospective memories, and/or printing or media artifacts (Saldaña, 2005). An ethnodrama "may not be an exact rendition of lived reality; however, it is most certainly a powerful translation of lived experience" (Nimmon, 2007, p. 384).

The ultimate goal of ethnodrama, according to Nimmon (2007), is "social transformation and emancipation" (p. 392). Through constructing ethnodrama play scripts, ethnodramatic researchers affirm the "voices" of informants, striving to make such marginalized, silenced voices heard through a dramatic art form/piece and found and recognized as legitimate voices in an oppressive society. Nimmon (2007) continues:

> An ethnodrama can create an opportunity to promote critical reflection and empathy about real-life situations that often are silenced. It provides an outlet for audience members to discuss the possibilities of transforming the oppressive elements of the experience of others, culminating in collective social action. This involves a dynamic form of reflection and action or praxis and ultimately is linked to the concept central to Freire's participatory processes.
>
> (p. 394)

Ethnodrama in Action

In my multicultural preservice education class, students create ethnodrama play scripts. They interview ELL or non-native speakers of English, asking them about their school and life experiences after immigrating to America, and then create an ethnodramatic play script based on the analyzed interview data they collected. Many ELL interviewees share their experiences of frustration, isolation, and exclusion based on their limited language proficiency or public language usage including pronunciation, accent, and/or intonation. As ethnodrama is not recognized as entertainment purposes, at least in my class, I have no expectation for technical profession in students' constructing play scripts; rather, the processes of experiencing dialogical interactions are of greater importance, interactions that take place between interviewees and interviewers during assigned ethnographic interviews as well as among students in classroom discussion or on interactive online journal entry attempting an analysis of ethnodramatic play scripts.

In our ethnodramatic play scriptwriting project, an ELL/LEP student or non-native speaker of English is chosen as an interviewee/informant, mainly because of the sociopolitical context of Arizona where there are a myriad of Mexican immigrant students who are attending schools without demonstrating adequate English proficiency, suffering from the English-only instruction requirement that has been mandated since 2000. An interviewee/informant may need to be carefully chosen considering their unique geographical, demographic, cultural, societal, and political identities for a more critical exploration illuminating and confronting issues faced by specific local contexts.

The student constructed ethnodrama play scripts are later used in Forum Theatre (see Boal, 1985; Rohd, 1998) or Readers Theatre (see Donmoyer and Yennie-Donmoyer, 1995) formats in order to enhance critical reflection and analysis in-class and online journal entry. Forum Theatre focuses on *a moment of decision* usually located in the last part of the script that provides the audience with a catalyst to think of alternative endings or interventions that, to them, are more ideal and just. Through this participatory interaction in Forum Theatre, the audience members (i.e. spectators) are transformed into what Boal terms "Spect/Actors," as they begin to discuss their own experiences and ethnographic research in relation to the ethnodrama they have just observed (Tobin et al., 1984), collaboratively experiencing a critical meaning-making process. Sleeter et al. (2004) emphasize the importance of having prospective teacher candidates develop a sense of ownership over their own learning:

> In addition to empowering students as authors, creating class books makes students' efforts and insights a permanent product rather than a disposable one. It also is an opportunity to influence others with their own awakenings, which may constitute a transforming action in itself.
>
> (p. 95)

As readings in our class, I often share the student constructed ethnodrama play scripts as *alternative* texts compiled from actual testimonials and inherited over time in my multicultural teacher education class. The following dramatic texts are excerpts from three of my students' constructed ethnodramatic play scripts assigned in my multicultural preservice teacher education class.

Student Constructed Ethnodrama Play Scripts

Act 1

> *Teacher (excited with a big smile on her face)*: Hi, welcome to class! I'm your teacher, Mrs Goodwill, tell me what your name is and I will help find where your seat is.

Student (does not understand a word she says, except for the word "name," and replies in a Spanish accent): Eduardo?

Teacher (with a weird expression on her face): Eduardo, this is your seat and welcome to class . . . I am assuming that you are probably used to speaking Spanish at home, but while you are here at school let's use English, okay?

Student (feels scared, alone, and confused; does not understand a word that she says, so remains silent).

Teacher: Eduardo, I know that today is the first day, but here at school when the teacher is talking to you, you have to answer them . . . It is the polite thing to do.

Student (gaining some courage; replying in Spanish): I do not understand English.

Act 2

Student (with her soft Spanish accent): I am having trouble doing my assignment . . . Can you help me?

Teacher (with a stern voice): My job is to teach you during school hours.

Student: But I still do not understand how to do it.

Teacher: You should have learned all of this in elementary!

Student: But I was never taught this material when I attended elementary in México.

Teacher: What do you mean you were never taught this?

Student: In my hometown, our classrooms were overcrowded and the students were loud and not used to the classroom environment so I never got to learn all of the material.

Teacher: What does this have to do with your situation?

Student: I was trying to explain why I did not have a chance to understand the material.

Teacher: I told you, I went over it in class.

Act 3

Teacher: Okay, everyone: pull out a sheet of paper so that you can write notes on the guidelines for the assignment. *(Looks around the room)* I know I have already gone over them, but it seems as if some of you didn't understand me the first time.

(Jose notices that the teacher is staring at him; turns his head away, embarrassed and ashamed; class start laughing because they realize that the teacher is looking at Jose.)

Teacher (addresses the class again): I'm going to show you an example of what not to do on your paper! You see, Jose over here forgot to check his spelling in his paper before he turned it in, and his sentences are not grammatically correct. His paper overall doesn't make sense!

Jose (with an accent): I really tried *(stutters)* my hardest *(stutters)* do the assignment right. *(Jose starts to get teary-eyed; feels ashamed, looking away because he doesn't want anyone to see him crying. Class laugh again.)*

Teacher (addresses the class again): This is why we need to make sure to check our work before we turn it in because you don't want to sound like this in your paper.

Tom (speaks in a condescending tone): It's probably because he's Mexican and doesn't know English! *(Looks at Jose)* Maybe you should learn English before you decide to move here. Don't you know that we speak English in America?

Jose (silent; feels completely degraded).

Teacher (wants to get back on task): Okay, everyone, now that we have gone over the guidelines, start working on your papers.

(Jose leaves the classroom silently; feels ashamed to be in the room with everyone making fun of him for not knowing English.)

Ethnodramatic Exploration: Empathy Development and Ideological De/construction

An ethnodrama play script as "evocative, contextual, and vernacular" (Barone and Eisner, 2006, p. 97) text enhances Bakhtinian dialogic interactions (Mienczakowski, 2006), offering "multiple interpretations of text, multiple points of view" (Styslinger, 2000, p. 185): that is, the ethnodramatic exploration of script construction and analysis enables one to examine the binary perspectives of the characters portrayed: the antagonist and the protagonist. The scripts above developed through script writing and script analysis phases based on interviews the multicultural education teacher candidates conducted with English learners. Reading the scripts in class facilitated a critical dialogue about assumptions, stereotypes and biases held about English learners. This dialogue led to empathy development and ideological de/reconstruction.

On the one hand, by examining protagonists' inner (*emic*) perspectives and listening to their inner voices that are marginalized in schools and society, one may develop *imaginative empathy* by awakening "the ordinary unseen, unheard, and unexpected" (Greene, 1995, p. 28). On the other hand, by analyzing antagonists' (oppressor) attitudes, belief, and values, comparing them to one's own, one may self-reflectively examine one's own unacknowledged privilege, prejudice, and power as well as "the oppressor consciousness embodied in the social institutions of power" (Styslinger, 2000, p. 196).

Examining protagonists' viewpoints portrayed in ethnodramatic play scripts helps preserve teacher candidates nurture imaginative empathy through scrutinizing ELL voices that are silenced through their limited language proficiency and/or their teachers' lack of understanding of linguistic and cultural diversity. Using student-constructed ethnodramatic play scripts as generative, localized texts that pose educational questions and problems prevalent in local schools and community, preservice teacher candidates can explore creative approaches to building a supportive learning environment for ELLs from an empathetic standpoint. A previous study has confirmed that monolingual teachers, even though they do not understand students' native languages, can create such a positive school climate supportive to linguistic diverse students (Gollnick and Chinn, 2004). However, ELL students are often demotivated and disheartened, eventually dropping out of school, when they experience unfair treatment by their teachers (Verdugo and Flores, 2007). In my own personal experience as an ELL and working with Asian immigrant students, ELL students are very sensitive to their teachers' facial expression and nonverbal tactics, as they excel in visual cognitive development to compensate for their lack of listening comprehension.

Ethnodramatic script analysis would have a potential pedagogical benefit in helping preservice teacher candidates to de/reconstruct their own internalized ideology, or values and beliefs that guide behavior. Hall (2000) elaborates an idea of individual level ideological consumption, stating: "We have to 'speak through' the ideologies which are active in our society and which provide us with the means of 'making sense' of social relations and our place in them" (p. 272).

I ask preservice teacher candidates to experience the critical process of examining their internalized ideology (Assaf and Battle, 2008), through building *ideological clarity* (Trueba and Bartolomé, 2000). During this cognitive, emotional, and cultural process, teachers self-reflectively and dialectically examine our own internalized ideology in relation to dominant ideological discourse. As we analyze ethnographic texts about the lives of English learners, we have a critical opportunity to examine/analyze our own internalized social dominance that manifests through values and beliefs about speakers of languages other than English.

Final Thoughts

We as teacher educators play a pivotal role in encouraging preservice teacher candidates to examine and confront their own internalized domination by providing them with transformative/emancipatory teaching/learning approaches developed through our daily teaching/research efforts. Through empathy development and ideological de/reconstruction as a consequence of ethnodramatic exploration, we as teacher educators may be able to help change the way that teachers view their students' language diversity (Nieto, 2004). These changes would exert a significant influence on the academic achievements of linguistically diverse students. Through inner transformation, prospective teacher candidates in turn may be able to "transform the school environment in which they work" (Ambe, 2006, p. 694), if not through a single multicultural education experience, through commitment to such ethnographic work in small doses over time.

★　★　★

In the following vignette about teacher professional development, Marguerite Lukes and Calder Zwicky share their experiences with New York teachers exploring how emergent bilingual children can be deeply impacted through critical analysis of modern art at the Museum of Modern Art. This vignette serves as a sharp counter-narrative to the dominant view that poor immigrant children are academically unprepared to access rich and complex content. As you will see, upon engaging with modern art via MoMA programs, these students engaged in critical discussions about their own invisibility in society, using writing and discussion with others about the importance of their experiences.

VIGNETTE NINETEEN

Seeing Art, Seeing the World: Modern Art and Literacy Development with English Learners K-12

Marguerite Lukes, LaGuardia Community College, City University of New York; Calder Zwicky, The Museum of Modern Art, New York; contributions by Louise Edman, Kim Constantine, and Rachel Lindsay, New York University

Project Description

> Modernist culture can make a practical difference to us.
>
> (Arcilla, 2009, p. 9)

Starting in fall 2007, two institutions whose missions converged around the goal of promoting access for underserved students in pre-K through adult education began a project to address the needs of immigrant students in New York. Too often, immigrant families consider art museums and other cultural institutions as off-limits to them. The cost of a museum visit, the location, the perception by many immigrant families—due in part to their unfamiliarity and in part to museum policies—that museums are not places where they are welcome, and the failure of some museums to make themselves accessible to culturally and linguistically diverse audiences results in the perception that museums are, in the words of one student, "places where rich people drink wine." However, we believe that through pedagogical engagement with modern art, these families are able to take part in deeply meaningful conversations about themselves and the world. In the spirit of educator Paolo Freire (1970/2000), they are both "reading the word, reading the world," or, more accurately, *seeing art, seeing the world*. A small beginning, but for the teachers and students who have participated, it is a model of existential pedagogy with great transformative potential.

From 2007 to 2011, the New York State Spanish Bilingual Education Technical Assistance Center (NYS SBETAC) at New York University and the Community and Access Department within the Department of Education at the Museum of Modern Art (MoMA) in New York City began a collaborative project to bring art and critical literacy skills together for K-12 English language learners. Throughout multiple professional development sessions held over the course of the past three years, English as a Second Language (ESL) and bilingual teachers from New York City and State schools have engaged in guided conversations about modern art that go beyond the traditional constraints of art history, with the goal of fostering personal reactions to works of modern art, analysis, connection to classroom themes, personal writing, critical reflection, and continued museum-going. Participating teachers have been immersed as students in a process in which they engage with modern art, not to "understand" it *per se*, but to start by exploring what they see and what it reminds them of, to use works of modern art as thematic starting points for discussion and critical analysis, and to connect the artwork from MoMA's collection to pertinent classroom lessons and themes. As will be described below, the resulting classroom-led projects have included explorations of identity using art, literature, art–making, writing, and publishing.

Why Modern Art and Immigrant Students?

As arts funding is cut in schools across New York and more emphasis is given to test preparation, museum visits are often moved to the bottom of a teacher's or school's list of priorities. The MoMA/SBETAC professional development series was designed to target teachers of English language learners in both K-12 and adult education contexts whose students view museums neither as comfort zones nor as familiar visiting places. Most of the immigrant students of the participating teachers had never been exposed to modern art in a formal way through their school curriculum, nor had most visited an art museum prior to their involvement in this program. Most participating teachers, we found, were nervous and unsure about how to begin a discussion about art in the classroom because they did not view themselves as "experts" on the subject of art history, criticism, or interpretation.

The intersecting goals of NYS SBETAC and MoMA's Community and Access Programs created a synergy. Housed in the Metropolitan Center for Urban Education at NYU's Steinhardt School of Education, Culture and Human Development, the NYS SBETAC seeks to improve the quality of services for English language learners throughout New York State and to create equity and access in schools. MoMA's Community and Access Programs work closely with a variety of community-based organizations to bring arts-based curricula to previously overlooked and underserved audiences throughout the New York City metro area.

The foundational goal of all of our professional development is to improve instruction and, in the long run, to promote student learning. In this collaboration we have sought directly to help classroom teachers and students reflect, promote critical thinking, encourage productive language, express themselves freely, and explore self and life's essential questions. All of these skills connect directly with state blueprint standards including Art-Making, Literacy in the Arts, Connections, Community and Cultural Resources, Careers and Lifelong Learning. At the center of this pedagogy is a concern for *access*: access to art, to the museum, to mainstream cultural capital, and to conversations about what we see and how we interpret it. In this process the prerequisite is not a broad knowledge of modern art or art history, but the importance of taking time to look and to reflect. Teachers who have participated in these inquiry learning sessions report that most of the English language learners in their classrooms rarely visited museums other than the Museum of Natural History. Yet these same students are avid consumers, and readily access YouTube, Facebook, all manner of graphics, advertising, and various other forms of visual media.

As educators and art-lovers, we planned, designed, and conducted these multi-session professional development series grounded in the belief that modern and contemporary art is accessible to English language learners precisely because it lends itself to an analysis that is somewhat more open-ended than that evoked by classical or representational art. Time and again, teachers reiterated that art is iterative, and that repeated viewings evoke different and deeper interpretations. Teachers began to see the skills of engagement with art as parallel to those of engagement with literature, while the former may suggest a "seeing" or interpretation of something specific (and often recognizable). We entered into the project as a team: an artist/museum educator and an art-lover/bilingual educator. Although conceptual and modern art can be confounding to many adults—teachers among them—who feel inhibited by not being art historians or are hampered by the nagging question of "What does it *really* mean?", for students new to art-based interactions, this open-endedness was freeing and served to validate their views, interpretations, and opinions.

But . . . I Don't Understand it! And Isn't Modern Art Too Weird?

The potentially transformational role that modernism can have in moving us beyond the distractions of entertainment to engage more with life's key questions (Arcilla, 2009) will remain merely hypothetical for students to whom museum culture is a closed door. We define modernism as a movement away from strictly literal representation and towards an abstraction of form and a connection to emotional expression and the personal lives of the artists and the sociopolitical realities in which they lived. Using modern art (rather than classical or more strictly representational art) lends itself to building upon students' innate ability and desire to communicate personal views, investigate subjective themes, and express lived experiences, in the most Freirian (1970/2000) sense. Freire (1970/2000) critiqued traditional pedagogy from a Marxist perspective, criticizing the "banking model" that seeks to fill students' heads with knowledge. His "pedagogy of the oppressed" seeks to build upon students' knowledge and lived experiences, and sees learners and teachers as partners in the creation of knowledge. Our inquiry-based strategy for using art as a springboard begins with a basic question of viewing: "What are we looking at?" and thus welcomes students' personal impressions and culturally rooted interpretations into the classroom. As New York City ESL teacher Rachel Lindsey expressed:

> My attempts at using art to guide instruction was one of the first times I felt the idea of differentiating instruction crystallize for me. In other words, the notion of "Differentiating Instruction" went from jargon to a critical tool for my teaching.
>
> Taking the four modalities of ESL (listening, speaking, reading, and writing), I started to notice that kids who were previously struggling oral language, suddenly were given a voice due to the need they seemed to feel in order to express themselves . . . These observations were the most striking because the shift from near muteness to vociferous expression in these students was exciting and rapid progress. However, I noticed gradual change in the other modalities as well. I have been practicing Inquiry Study in my class and one of the fundamental principles is to guide content instruction through student-driven interest. The reasoning behind this is that if students have an inherent interest in what they are studying, the other concepts can be integrated with seamless transition. The child will actually learn the information for life rather than forgetting what they have seen as soon as the new unit chunk is introduced. I feel that my Inquiry Study and the work I did with MoMA are analogous in that they both allow the student to invest interest in the subject first and then a natural desire to learn more inevitably

follows. Therefore the students did not need a dictated assignment as a follow-up activity, but rather enthusiastically illustrated their learning on their own through self-directed reading and writing. This coming from students who had to have a pencil thrust into their hands and watched over continually to keep them reading and writing before.

Art as a springboard into the classroom has great potential to link with thematic instruction for ELLs and build upon students' lived experiences, as Louise Edman, an elementary school art teacher from the Hewlett Woodmere School District on Long Island, writes:

> The Art and Literacy workshop inspired me to introduce the artwork of Marc Chagall to fifth grade students. Using questioning strategies, students were asked to spend time looking at his painting *I and the Village* (1911), and to write five "dreamlike" elements that they saw in the work. Students shared their responses, while I repeated back what each had said. This open forum helped them feel confident sharing their observations, and gave them a feeling of ownership that a teacher-led discussion of the work might have missed. Next, students completed a handout that asked them to recall their youngest memories—a favorite toy, their house, a favorite snack, etc. Using these written responses, students created paintings using oil, pastel and watercolor in the style of Chagall. The Art and Literacy workshop helped me to formulate ideas for combining writing and art-making. The combination allowed for a greater depth of understanding of Chagall's work, and greater engagement of students in their art-making.

Visual arts are essential tools for all types of learners, and using the arts within a classroom environment acknowledges the different strengths of students and the different intelligences being drawn upon at any given time. For new immigrant students from low socioeconomic backgrounds in under-funded urban schools, many cultural institutions are closed or symbolically "off-limits" by virtue of students' (and teachers') lack of understanding of what it means to participate or partake of them. In many cases, this schism has been the fault of the museums themselves, as high ticket prices, confusing in-gallery rules, and a lack of bilingual advertising and labels have created a disconnect between emergent English speakers and the cultural institutions. MoMA devotes an entire department to increasing access to underserved groups, and their visitors represent an increasingly non-English speaking audience (63 percent of yearly visitors are from other countries); creating bilingual resources has been a high priority for years.

However, it became apparent that, while initiatives such as multi-language gallery tours, multi-language audio guides, and an in-gallery emphasis on art from multiple cultures were helpful in welcoming these audiences, these new initiatives were not well known among educators or students from these underserved communities. Also, in the context of the curriculum for ELLs, art museums are often seen as *separate* from resources useful or helpful to language acquisition—because museum education is often approached with the knowledge of art history as a goal, rather than using art as a tool to promote thematic instruction. ELLs are often not exposed to museums until they reach advanced levels of proficiency, if this exposure comes at all. This project has shown the power that accessing museums and viewing of art as a critical literacy tool can have in transforming the classroom.

This professional development series for teachers proposed an unusual, non-traditional approach to the use of art and art-making in the curriculum: rather than seeing art as something static to be learned "about," art could link into thematic instruction and promote discussion and student self-expression. Teachers participated as students in a tour of the museum that focused not on art history but on thematic and critical analysis. They then practiced talking about art using a series of inquiry-based, scaffolded questions:

- Drawing students' attention to the artwork: *"What do we see here?"*
- Connecting students' prior knowledge and experiences to the artwork: *"What does this remind you of?"*
- Creating a narrative or thematic understanding: *"What is the person doing in the painting?"*
- Expressing personal reactions: *"People seem to like this painting less than the one we just saw. Why is that?"*
- Paraphrasing and reflecting back all students' comments about the works.

In the course of this instruction, students unfamiliar with having conversations about art would be introduced to freeing ways to talk about and engage with modern art. Kim Constantine, high school ESL teacher in the Bronx, describes her experience:

> As a result of my professional development, I used the photograph *After "Invisible Man" by Ralph Ellison, the Prologue* (Wall, 1999). The class read the Prologue from *Invisible Man* (Ellison, 1952). Then students were asked to write: "Have you ever felt invisible? Where? Why?" This confused the students but I allowed them to struggle with the answer. The fact they were intrigued enough to struggle was refreshing. We discussed invisibility in all its forms. Then I gave them Wall's photo and we began questioning: *Why is he there? What are those light bulbs? He's in a basement, isn't he? Why isn't he looking at us?* I did not answer; they began to answer each other. We then paired for further inspection

of the picture and to answer the probing questions proposed by the class, slightly directed by me.

I began to group them and working with extending their adjective usage. They strained to capture the elements of the art in words. Basic words worked but didn't really give you "the flavor" as I was told. So they worked and posted their adjectives on the board. We had an extensive word pool now. We began to look for clues, to delve deeper into the art as we mixed the groups again. They forgot about differences and related through a human theme: invisibility. Without effort, students inferred, predicted, analyzed, synthesized and so on. Incredible! It is never work when it's inspired. We did a lot of freewriting and also journaling about their invisible experiences within their families and cultures and within their new surroundings. Societal invisibility eventually emerged, something they are intimately confronting. In my class, they had socially isolated from each other trying to be invisible, not to connect, and now I watched this community emergent based on an awareness prompted by a piece of artwork. Eventually we reread the *Invisible Man* prologue and deepened our conversation about the people society forgets, the ones that no one wants to see. We talked about the responsibility of the invisible one and that of those who make him invisible.

Students began to write extensively, and with their new word pool, at much higher levels. We went from a personal experience, to an art piece, to a literary piece and moved into social graphs, psychology articles and even scientific writings. With this content we could answer any of the essay tasks on the ELA Regents with one lesson anchored in one art piece. It naturally scaffolds and enriches. It is so vital to higher level thinking skills, challenging students to independently think and synthesize information in a thoughtful manner. Formal essays were produced that mimicked the ELA Regents but instead of these being dreary, repetitive assignments they became invigorated academic challenges. We coherently did cross-curriculum related to the topic vividly depicted by the artist.

What art did was create a community in a class that had no common ground. Lessons are easy but creating a responsive team is not easy when the surface differences seem enormous and the motivation to bond is nil. I would say there is an art piece for any classroom challenge, any challenge! But for me, this was the miracle. I had tried everything I knew and everything suggested to me. The students were not relaxing their boundaries and I knew very little movement would occur if they did not connect. It was one of those teaching moments when you step back and sigh with relief, knowing that it is done and the rest is easy. I had a class! My ESL students progressed to all but one passing the

NYSESLAT and all scheduled for the ELA Regents passed, lest you think art-based lessons are non-productive in the standard sense. I am a believer in art for all the classes I teach, but with this experience, I was privy to the "miracle" of art. A picture is worth a thousand words and those words can be uttered in any language and still have a common understanding, a humanity. It can inspire language and learning. It can turn obstacles into challenges and in doing so create a confidence so essential to higher learning, inquiry, delightful inquiry.

Conclusion

The synergy created in the partnership between museum education, community access, and professional development for teachers of emergent bilinguals has grown over the three years in which it has been developed. We have been repeatedly amazed and gratified by teachers' enthusiasm, spirit of adventure, and the creative energy created by putting teachers in the position to experience modern art as their students would. The Freirian principles have opened up a new world for the educators who have participated and for their students as well. When teachers returned for a follow-up session, we were repeatedly wowed by the creative projects upon which they have embarked with their students. For many, the work to reclaim art as part of the curriculum is not only fun, but it is energizing and thought-provoking as well.

MoMA has one of the most active and generous community outreach programs of any cultural institution in New York City and seeks to bring new audiences into the world of modern and contemporary art. Students whose teachers have participated in the Art and Literacy Development for English Language Learners series with NYS SBETAC and MoMA are now museum goers and have experienced conversations in which they see that their views about art *truly* matter. They have learned to interpret and experience art in a way that no quick gallery tour of glancing at paintings could afford. The experiences that they have in the Museum, or viewing the artwork on their own, transcend questions of nationality, economics, politics, and even education. We are connected in the subjectivity of human experience and creative vision.

That is what seeing the world is all about.

★   ★   ★

In the era of NCLB educational policy, many educators, researchers and community members seek solutions to the opportunity gap that prevents education from being inclusive, just and equitable for every child. From a social constructivist perspective, this book commits to the idea that people's identities are formed and forming through daily interactions with dynamic communities of practice.

Further, we negotiate our subjectivities through language—and the values and beliefs constructing our use of language—in local practices. In this way, communities of practice have the power to change the monologic hold that dominant/master narratives have on the curriculum and instruction in our schools. Instead, each teacher's daily choices of what we teach, as well as critical, ongoing reflection with others about these choices, is a strong source of change.

Counter-narrative practices are easier when they are done in solidarity with others via a professional learning community. These allies—such as educators befriended online or found through a resource shared in this book—can provide the support you need as a teacher to make small changes every day. What will you do, for example, when a parent says she wants to officially change her child's name from one in her native language to an "American" one? When you read a story aloud that mocks a child who speaks Spanglish? When your school provides forms to go home to families only in English, or in English and Spanish when other languages are spoken by families in your community? Or, when the school year starts and you have Week One's homework pre-prepared from last year: will you keep it the same and run off thirty copies? Or, might you make a change, however small or large, based on a principle from this book?

We hope that you will.

And, as authors and educators, we promise to do the same in our own lifelong journeys to be/become culturally and linguistically responsive. Then, we hope you will share your own counter-narrative stories with someone new, building a broad movement of critical, creative education with emergent bilingual youth. In the final chapter, we consider ethical implications of working with young people about sensitive and controversial issues as well as working with communities across differences. We also consider the impact of young people's art-making on community memory, as in the responsibility of teachers to the process as well as to the artworks themselves.

Questions to Consider

1. Think about the teaching materials and instructional practices you use with your students. What assumptions do your materials and practices make about what is "natural," "normal," and "common sense"? Whose experiences are/might be left out based on these assumptions?

2. Examine the environment print and images in your school hallways, offices, and classrooms. Whose cultural knowledge and practices are represented and how can you work to make your school more experientially arts-based?

3. How can you assist your students in responding critically and producing their own counter-stories to dominant forms of knowledge and practice?

4.   How might ethnodrama facilitate research, writing and presentation about a current or past sociopolitical issue your students face or are concerned about?

5.   The vignettes in this chapter focused on professional development with teachers about the creation of counter-narrative stories and practices. What professional development might you seek to build your knowledge of counter-narrative pedagogy?

Note

1.   All names are pseudonyms.

References

Ahlquist, R. (1991). Position and imposition. Power relations in a multicultural foundations class. *Journal of Negro Education*, 60(2), 158–69.

Ambe, E. B. (2006). Fostering multicultural appreciation in pre-service teachers through multicultural curricular transformation. *Teaching and Teacher Education*, 22(6), 690–9.

Anyon, J. (1980). Social class and hidden curriculum of work. *Journal of Education*, 162(1), 67–92.

Anzaldúa, G. (1990). *Haciendo caras/Making faces, making soul: Creative and critical perspectives by women of color*. San Francisco: Aunt Lute Press.

Apple, M. (2004). *Ideology and curriculum*, 25th anniversary 3rd edition. New York: Routledge.

Arcilla, R. V. (2009). *Mediumism: A philosophical reconstruction of Modernism for existential learning*. Albany, NY: State University of New York Press.

Assaf, L. C. and Battle, J. (2008). Reading teacher educators' ideologies and instructional practices about multicultural teaching and learning: An evolving vision of one field-based teacher education program. In Y. Kim, V. J. Risko, D. L. Compton, D. K. Dickinson, M. K. Hundley, R. T. Jiménez, K. M. Leander, and D. W. Rowe (Eds), *57th yearbook of the National Reading Conference* (pp. 94–106). Oak Creek, WI: National Reading Conference.

Barone, T. (2000). *Aesthetics, politics, and educational inquiry: Essays and examples*. New York: Peter Lang.

Barone, T. and Eisner, E. (2006). Arts-based educational research. In J. L. Green, G. Camilli, and P. B. Elmore (Eds), *Handbook of complementary methods in education research* (pp. 95–110). New York: Routledge.

Bell, L. (2010). *Storytelling for social justice: Connecting narrative and the arts for antiracist teaching*. New York: Routledge.

Boal, A. (1985). *Theatre of the oppressed*. New York: Theatre Communication Group.

Brown, E. L. (2004). What precipitates change in cultural diversity awareness during a multicultural course: The message or the method? *Journal of Teacher Education*, 55(4), 325–40.

Cruz, B. (2002). Don Juan and rebels under palm trees: Depictions of Latin Americans in U.S. history textbooks. *Critique of Anthropology*, 22(3), 323–42.

Darden, E. and Cavendish, E. (2011). Achieving resource equity within a single school district: Erasing the opportunity gap by examining school board decisions. *Education and Urban Society*, 44(1), 61–82.

de la Luz Reyes, M. and Halcón, J. (1988). Racism in academia: The old wolf revisited. *Harvard Educational Review*, 58(2), 299–314.

Delgado, R. (1993). On telling stories in school: A reply to Farber and Sherry. *Vanderbilt Law Review*, 46, 665–76.

Delpit, L. (1995). *Other people's children: Cultural conflict in the classroom*. New York: New Press.

Donmoyer, R. and Yennie-Donmoyer, J. (1995). Data as drama: Reflections on the use of Readers Theatre as a mode of qualitative data display. *Qualitative Inquiry*, 1(4), 402–28.

Ellison, R. (1952). *Invisible man*. New York: Vintage.

Ewick, P. and Silbey, S. S. (1995). Subversive stories and hegemonic tales: Toward a sociology of narrative. *Law and Society Review*, 29, 197–226.

Freire, P. (1970/2000). *Pedagogy of the oppressed*. New York: Herder and Herder.

Giroux, H. (1983). Theories of reproduction and resistance in the new sociology of education: A critical analysis. *Harvard Educational Review*, 55(2), 257–93.

Gollnick, D. M. and Chinn, P. C. (2004). *Multicultural education in a pluralistic society*, 6th edition. Upper Saddle River, NJ: Pearson Merrill Prentice Hall.

Gómez-Peña, G. (1996). *The new world border: Prophecies, poems and loqueras for the end of the century*. San Francisco: City Lights.

Greene, M. (1995). *Releasing the imagination: Essays on education, the arts and social change*. San Francisco: Jossey-Bass.

Hall, S. (2000). Racist ideologies and the media. In P. Marris and S. Thornham (Eds), *Media studies: A reader* (pp. 271–82). New York: New York University Press.

Ikeda, D. (2010). *A new humanism: The university addresses of Daisaku Ikeda*. New York: I. B. Tauris.

Mattai, P. R. (1992). Rethinking the nature of multicultural education: Has it lost its focus or is it being misused? *Journal of Negro Education*, 61(1), 65–77.

Mienczakowski, J. (2006). Ethnodrama: Performed research—limitations and potential. In S. Nagy Hesse-Biber and P. Leavy (Eds), *Emergent methods in social research* (pp. 235–52). Thousand Oaks, CA: Sage.

Moll, L., Amanti, C., Neff, D., and González, N. (1992). Funds of knowledge for teaching: Using a qualitative approach to connect homes and classrooms. *Theory Into Practice*, 31(2), 132–41.

New London Group. (1996). A pedagogy of multiliteracies: Designing social futures. *Harvard Educational Review*, 66(1). Retrieved November 19, 2012, from http://www.static.kern.org/filer/blogWrite44ManilaWebsite/paul/articles/A_Pedagogy_of_Multilite racies_Designing_Social_Futures.htm.

Nieto, S. (2004). *Affirming diversity: The sociopolitical context of multicultural education*, 3rd edition. Boston, MA: Pearson Education.

Nimmon, L. E. (2007). ESL-speaking immigrant women's disillusions: Voices of health care in Canada: An ethnodrama. *Health Care for Women International*, 28(4), 381–96.

Norris, J. (2009). *Playbuilding as qualitative research: A participatory arts-based approach*. Walnut Creek, CA: Left Coast Press.

Ogbu, J. U. and Matute-Bianchi, M. (1986). Understanding sociocultural factors: Knowledge, identity, and school adjustment. In Evaluation, Dissemination and Assessment Center, California State University (Eds), *Beyond language: Social and cultural factors in schooling language minority students* (pp. 73–142). Los Angeles: California State University, Evaluation, Dissemination, and Assessment Center.

Rohd, M. (1998). *Theatre for community, conflict and dialogue: The hope is vital training manual.* Portsmouth, NH: Heinemann.

Saldaña, J. (2005). *Ethnodrama: An anthology of reality theatre.* Lanham, MD: Rowman & Littlefield.

—— (2010). Playwriting with data: Ethnographic performance texts. *Youth Theatre Journal,* 13(1), 60–71.

—— (2011). *Ethnotheatre: Research from page to stage.* Walnut Creek, CA: Left Coast Press.

Sleeter, C., Torres, M. N., and Laughlin, P. (2004). Scaffolding conscientization through inquiry in teacher education. *Teacher Education Quarterly,* 31(1), 81–96.

Solórzano, D. (1997). Images and words that wound: Critical race theory, racial stereotyping and teacher education. *Teacher Education Quarterly,* 24(1), 5–19.

Souto-Manning, M. (2010). Teaching English Language Learners: Building on cultural and linguistic strengths. *English Education,* 42(3), 248–62.

Spring, J. (2009). *Deculturalization and the struggle for equality: A brief history of the education of dominated cultures in the United States.* New York: McGraw-Hill.

Styslinger, M. E. (2000). Relations of power and drama in education: The teacher and Foucault. *Journal of Educational Thought,* 34(2), 183–99.

Tobin, J. J., Wu, D. Y. H., and Davidson, D. H. (1984). *Preschool in three cultures: Japan, China, and the United States.* New Haven: Yale University Press.

Trueba, H. T. and Bartolomé, L. (2000). Beyond the politics of schools and the rhetoric of fashionable pedagogies: The significance of teacher ideology. In H. T. Trueba, and L. Bartolomé (Eds), *Immigrant voices: In search of educational equity* (pp. 277–93). New York: Rowman & Littlefield.

Verdugo, R. R. and Flores, B. (2007). English-language learners: Key issues. *Education and Urban Society,* 39(2), 167–93.

Wall, J. (2001). *After "Invisible Man" by Ralph Ellison, the prologue.* New York: Museum of Modern Art. Retrieved June 13, 2012 from http://www.moma.org/collection/object.php?object_id=88085.

Wenger, E. (1999). *Communities of practice: Learning, meaning, and identity.* Cambridge, UK: Cambridge University Press.

Yosso, T. (2005). Whose culture has capital? A critical race theory discussion of community cultural wealth. *Race Ethnicity and Education,* 8(1), 69–91.

—— (2006). *Critical race counterstories along the Chicana/o pipeline.* New York: Routledge.

10

EPILOGUE

Building Sustainability in/with Multilingual Communities

ARTS ARTIFACT SIX

Inspecting Borders

Sharon Chappell, California State University Fullerton

"We're here to stay"
A poster lay defiantly at the feet of the Tucson school district
Arms crossed after lighting candles of mourning and hope
Young people demand better worlds than
Adults boxing books in front of their faces

A girl takes a sip of water

Megaphone resting against the tree
Throat burning from demanding to be heard
The linguistic landscape
Stretches far in front of her
A sidewalk of English-only school policies
A secretary's desk of reluctantly translated school newsletters

"I am Latino"
A boy whispers behind her
He is inspecting borders too

The water slides down the girl's tongue and she can feel
The words rolling
Her taste buds perked to fresh, mad, hopeful words
She had no idea were poised inside her

The girl turns and grabs the boy's hand
A little squeeze, just firm enough
Let's do this thing
She grabs her sign and passes it to him
Imagines a community better than this

The sign is shaking
The girl looks at the boy, his trembling the source of its movement
Words not rolling yet

If only I could unfurl my tongue, she thought.
If only I could open my mouth and deep from the cavern of my
     throat
The words wrapped in blankets of determination would soothe
     him
Today is the day

We are here to stay

In this poem, how are language, culture and politics interrelated in the lives of these emergent bilingual youth? What assets would these young people bring to the classroom? How might you use an arts-based practice from this book to engage their assets and everyday acts of resistance?

This book focuses on building critical, creative and caring education with emergent bilingual youth in community and school contexts. Taken together, the chapters represent interconnected facets of this practice: understanding the research and theory about bilingual and arts-based learning; becoming a culturally and linguistically responsive educator; collaborating with families; and developing counter-narratives through play, storytelling, literature, world events, and digital storytelling. In this final chapter, we consider several issues around the sustainability of critical, creative, caring education with multilingual communities. Such sustainability suggests a commitment on the part of all participants to pursue social change and art-making over time. In order to achieve sustainability, we must consider ethical questions about working with young people on sensitive, controversial issues as well as working with communities across differences and power dynamics. We must also consider how young people's art-making can impact communities over time, such as through memories, histories, and commentaries made through the projects. What, then, is the responsibility of teachers to the artworks themselves—texts, objects, recordings— toward their future use in constructing local knowledge?

Ethics and Art-making with Emergent Bilingual Youth

As young people participate in communities of practice (Lave and Wenger, 1991), they learn specific perspectives, discourses and conditions of work that have been collectively agreed upon, although with new membership and new situations, these practices adapt and change. According to Wenger (1998), practice is both individually subjective and collectively experienced through matrices of power that must be negotiated and navigated. Because membership is constrained by norms, rules and values, people might sometimes respond with nonparticipation and dis-identification (Hodges, 1998). In this way, as we work across differences about sensitive issues of personal and political importance, such as struggles in the face of social dominance, teachers should consider questions about the norms of our communities of practice:

- How do schools and community organizations represent young people and their artworks?
- How much influence should adult facilitators have over the content and production of young people's artworks?
- What sorts of products would young people create if left on their own without adult guidance or intervention?
- Who benefits from the artworks created and how?
- What kind of knowledge(s) are young people developing, and how do schools and organizations honor this knowledge, even when it is not what adult facilitators anticipate or judge as effective, good, or of quality?

As communities of practice change over time and generations, their boundedness may also be transformed based on their members (Wenger, 1998). This includes the shared and conflicting experiences of community members as well as the conditions of practice that affect a community's present dynamics. The community defines legitimate participation and regulates competency, producing inclusions and exclusions that impact what young people think and how they express themselves. These inclusions (during school, in art-making, with peers out of school) are enforced through rules and norms about practices of engagement among the community, during making meaning, and through use of the community's repertoire of resources.

Local art-making and artworks have the power to facilitate varying and oppositional uses of art on the part of the artists and audiences. Teachers can reflect on how we as "experts" might impose our outside values, facilitation styles, and resources on a population (such as an indigenous, migrant, or immigrant youth community) (Ballerini, 1995; Turner, 1992). This question is of particular importance given the Western trajectories of colonialism and imperialism, as in the forced removal and/or assimilation of indigenous peoples of the Americas, the near-erasure of their cultures and languages, as realized through past missionary work and boarding schools to current practices of English-only public schools (Margolis, 2004).

Instead, the arts as education should facilitate critical expression about issues in the lives of emergent bilingual youth, one that provides a framework for structuring feelings about difficult issues (Dewey, 1938/1997; Williams, 1977). As teachers, we should look at their artworks for qualities of activated, conscious experience, assessing student growth in terms of language development, community engagement, and aesthetic expression in their social contexts. What kinds of questions do we ask about the process and product that move beyond traditional schooling practices that evaluate discrete skills? How does the art-making process or viewing of artworks affect change in a community? How do the young people's arts processes inspire them to participate further in their communities, even when the project is done? How do we track and celebrate this long-term critical, caring, creative engagement?

As teachers, we must reflect on our roles with/in a bilingual community, considering the goals and objectives of our work in relation to principles of mutual engagement, collaborative decision-making, and community funds of knowledge. This conscious mindfulness can stop cycles of cultural and linguistic erasure that have plagued the history of U.S. education (Spring, 2009). We can consider, for example, the implications of maintaining traditional cultural knowledge versus engaging youth cultures, such as those emergent from hybrid integration of the old and new (Paris, 2012). We can reflect collectively on how young people make sense of their inherited "authentic" heritage cultural identity in relation to the youth cultures and mainstream consumer cultures they encounter regularly.

Artworks as Community Memory

Throughout the book, we have identified culturally and linguistically responsive principles for critical, caring, creative projects with emergent bilingual youth. One impact of these projects is their contribution to local community memory—a remembering process that is informal (that is, not recorded in the history books) but strongly present in the space of community. Through their artworks, young people can contribute to laying memory and/or re-narrating histories for future use by their peers, younger children in their community, and others outside the community who take up these narratives as a textual resistance to mainstream histories and visions. In archiving and utilizing their artworks as curricular texts, young people position diverse storytelling trajectories and aesthetic languages as valuable in schools. As Connerton (2004) suggests:

> The oral history of subordinate groups will produce another type of history: one in which not only will most of the details be different, but in which the very construction of meaningful shapes will obey a different principle.

Different details will emerge because they are inserted, as it were, into a different kind of narrative home.

(p. 19)

This is not to naively romanticize or valorize the roles of young people or art-making in exacting large-scale social change. Instead, it is a pragmatic proposal that stems from young people's assemblages of relationships, knowledge and resources already at work in their daily lives. Young people often position themselves along historical trajectories of activism, referencing other activists or activist art forms that also contest marginalizing narratives and actions. As emergent bilingual youth produce ruptures in social hierarchies and inequitable social institutions through their resistance, they participate in a not-so-quiet, grassroots historic movement. Their efforts emphasize the importance of what Connerton (2004) calls "personal memory claims" (p. 22): memories, critiques, and creative expressions that can construct important knowledge in school. Rather than being the "outside curriculum" (Schubert and Melnick, 1987), these artworks can become central to the ways young people construct knowledge in school and their communities over time.

In many of this book's vignettes, the emergent bilingual youth demonstrate their desire to participate in community dialogue and to change public perceptions being bilingual and bicultural through art-making. This contributes to community-based memory quite unlike that of the traditional curriculum in history textbooks and professionally published biographies. Through the use of young people's artworks as curricular text, new culture is produced while social memory is maintained, reflected, and changed (Kuftinec, 2003). Young people's artworks impact the language and behavior, use of space, relationships between artists and audience, values and beliefs that build local community memory.

The critical, creative, caring pedagogies we have featured in this book look very different than the traditional curriculum and instruction of formal schooling. Under the pressures of No Child Left Behind and its high stakes testing, many teachers struggle to structure their curriculum through their students' lives, critiques and hopes for the world.[1] Yet, the vignette authors in this book persevere, facilitating young people's art-making on social change issues and producing their work for the general public. We call for readers to experiment with these pedagogical approaches, examining how emergent bilingual youth "educate your desire" for better worlds through their art-making and artworks (Thompson, 1977).

We close the book with a vignette and a poem[2] that perform the strong counter-narrative work of critical, creative, caring education that emergent bilingual youth need. As you read, reflect on ethical questions the authors consider, as well as the impact of the young people's artworks on community memory. Also imagine how you might make curriculum change in your own contexts based on the ideas of these artists/educators.

It Is *NOT* What It Is: A Multidisciplinary Approach to Critical Pedagogy, Cultural Production, and Youth Development in the Youth Roots Program

G. Reyes, Oakland Leaf and University of California Berkeley

> Break free break free
> Ain't it obvious Youth Roots Oakland Leaf
> We social activists
> Now put yo fist up and listen to this
> > > Danilo, eleventh grader

Youth Roots is an eight-month critical media production, leadership, and rites of passage fellowship program for thirty high school students in inner-city Oakland, California, where I am both the Program Director and Lead Teacher. Students, primarily Black or Latino, can come from any high school in Oakland to enroll in the Youth Roots program. Youth Roots is one of the high school leadership branches within Oakland Leaf with the aim of cultivating ARTivists who fight oppression By Any Medium Necessary (Asante, 2009). As ARTivists, students combine their art with activism. According to Asante, an ARTivist does not focus on art for art's sake, but rather on art for the uplifting, provoking, and inspiring of people.

As an out-of-school-time program, Roots meets a minimum of two days per week for 2.5 hours/day during what is called a "Seed Session." Seed Sessions are intended to "plant seeds" of criticality, community, wisdom, self-confidence, and agency through opportunities in anti-oppression work, critical inquiry, media production, visual arts, performing arts, video arts, rites of passage, adventure education, event production, and workshop facilitation/conference presentation. Students can earn a Roots fellowship multiple times, returning back for a second year or a third if they choose. Otherwise, they may apply for an internship in any of the other Oakland Leaf programs or within Youth Roots. The program runs from October through June.

To cultivate the ARTivist, the Roots program focuses on nurturing four roles: (1) Word Warriors, (2) Image Infiltrators, (3) Just Journalists, and (4) Cyba Souljas (a.k.a. Cyber Soldiers). A student can focus on working to cultivate one or a combination of these roles within themselves over time. At the most basic level, Word Warriors write and speak. This can happen in poetry, rap, singing, presentations, outreach literature, and youth-led workshops. In relation to the music they co-create, they can learn the artistic, technical, and business side of making a music CD. They learn the structure of a song, how to arrange music, how to record/engineer vocals, and how to promote their CD. Image Infiltrators use digital photography and graphic design to take photos, create print and online flyers and posters, and t-shirt designs. The Image Infiltrators partner with the Word Warriors to co-create the entire artwork for the annual CD, which includes a twelve-page booklet of lyrics and photos. Just Journalists work with the medium of video. They can produce documentaries or music videos. Cyba Souljas use internet technologies such as Myspace, Facebook, and YouTube to reach others on the web. The Cyba Souljas also get involved with the CD/DVD project. To promote the content of the CD/DVD, they use the social networking technologies to get the Youth Roots message out.

Regardless of the identity that any Roots youth gravitates more towards, there is always the element of performance present. Spry (2006) argues that performance is personal, political, and professional. In an academic context, it may be viewed as heretical, yet performance liberates us from the normalized scripts that dictate how an intellectual is supposed to produce knowledge. It has allowed us to examine ourselves as "others" who have evolved our definitions of ourselves to have multiple facets. This act gives us an agency needed to confidently be the border crosser of which Anzaldúa (1999) speaks.

Performance also acts as a site for struggle and an enactment of power (Wa Thiong'o, 2002). It is both being and becoming, a struggle of control on the part of the artist and on the part of the state (or other institution in power). Within Roots, "performance" is a rite of passage. In particular, it is a way to support the cultivation of what Gramsci (1971) calls the organic intellectual or, more appropriately, what Neal (2003) calls the "celebrity Gramscian." Gramsci introduced the concept of the organic intellectual, who emerges from what he called the un-unified, working "subaltern" classes. The organic intellectual, from this perspective, serves as an organizing intellectual force for the working classes. The celebrity Gramscian, intersects his or her fame and political agenda to bring the "message" to the mainstream. The youth in Roots function as organizers, conveying their messages to various publics through performance.

As a rite of passage, performance places a Youth Root in front of an audience—whether physical or virtual—becoming more elaborate and in-depth over time as one gains more and more experience and skill. It includes, but is not limited to, performing a poem, song, or theatre piece on stage; performing a dynamic multimedia presentation in front of teachers at a conference; producing (i.e. performing) a personal poetic piece, music video, or documentary on iMovie; or wearing a thought-provoking t-shirt designed by a Youth Root. Whatever the performance, there is always an audience; there is always a goal (Wa Thiong'o, 2002). In this light, the audience makes the performance a site to struggle for power.

As a theoretical framework, Youth Roots has six intersecting inputs that determine its pedagogy, curriculum, and structure: (1) Digital Literacy and Knowledge of Self as a Critical Pedagogy frame, (2) Critical Social Theory as a Sociological Analysis frame, (3) Theatre of the Oppressed and Gender

FIGURE 10.1 *Youth Roots Singers Performing the Song, "Oakland State of Mind,"* photo by G. Reyes

Circles as an Anti-Oppression frame, (4) Hip-Hop and Media as a Culture Production frame, (5) Rites of Passage as a Continuous Improvement frame, and (6) Youth Development as an Organizational frame. Separately, each of these components can serve a particular interest in a particular way. Intersected together as a multidisciplinary framework, they act in what Sandoval (2000) calls a *differential coalitional consciousness*. From this space, people can utilize different frameworks to develop a collective agency that is dynamic, mobile, and acts as an oppositional strategy against dominant ideologies. We focus on the *process* towards the consciousness through the unique six components of the Roots framework, forming what I call *Critical Youth Cultivation*. In this process, nurturing and cultivation, rather than "development," is intended for students of Youth Roots over an extended period of time (i.e. multiple years with sustained direct interaction). During that time, the Roots program intends to not only nurture critical tools for students to focus "inside-out," but also provides support for students' mental and emotional health. Focusing "inside-out" asserts that in order to change the outside world, one must be willing to start inside oneself. Similarly, it is intended that teachers who work within Roots also act in a capacity to know and support each unique student in this process.

From this point of departure, what is the nature of the conditions, practices, and cultural products that nurture youth within Youth Roots? How might Youth Roots move from the passive and apathetic expression "It is what it is" to the more critical "It is NOT what it is"?

Sirens, gunshots
They put me to sleep
Not exactly memories that I wanna keep
But the graph of homicides grows every year so steep
Now I'm wonderin if we'll ever meet some peace
Shit that goes down will make you sicker than the flu shot
Does it give you comfort though?
Knowing who's hot and who's not?
"It is what it is" first thought on the spot
[Juan] and B on the track gon make it real hot

> Excerpt from "Inured" by Juan (eleventh grade)
> and Blanca (ninth grade)

In the song, "Inured," Juan and Blanca, youth from Oakland, California, are referring to an internalized state of being that they name: "it is what it is." Bourdieu (1977) might refer to this normalized phenomena as *habitus*. However, this particular habitus that Juan and Blanca refer to is more localized than those commonly associated with the larger social structures and is specific to an often marginalized and pathologized *field*. According to Bourdieu (1977, p. 95), a *field* is the larger container for the structured set of social relations that determine how human activity functions and reproduces. Individual agency exerted through habitus or otherwise within a field is still constituted by the structures of that field. In the case of Juan and Blanca's song, some may label the field to which they refer as the "street" (Asante, 2009). Some might call it "urban" (Hill, 2009; Morrell and Duncan-Andrade, 2008). Some go so far as to call it "ghetto" (Anyon, 1997). Whatever the case, there is no denying that this field has its own ideologies, dispositions, and structures that are relevant and unique to itself. Take for instance the idea that the sounds of sirens and gunshots put them to sleep. Normally, these sounds would be considered alarming. However, Juan and Blanca poetically refer to them as a sort of nighttime lullaby, because they are heard so often at night. At the same time, they reflect an underlying tension that those sounds are undesired, yet normalized memories. Their dulled responses to the sounds, although undesirable, are still automatic; they are *habitus*.

Likely, this is not the *habitus* that Bourdieu (1977) spoke of when he theorized how various "fields" are structured to contain dominant dispositions that its actors internalize, while also struggle to control. He was speaking more of what happens within particular *fields* of power in society—"high" society, education, business, politics, etc. This "street" field contains its own habitus that its actors arguably believe they need to possess in order to survive. How does one cope within a place where "the graph of homicides grows every year"? Certain ways *have* to be normalized. (Or do they?)

"*Things don't feel right over here. Lately I ain't been seeing clear,*" rapped the world renowned hip-hop band, The Roots (not to be confused with Youth Roots). The suggestion to the internalized disposition of "it is what it is" refers to a common-sense saying, where people in all walks of everyday life know that things are not right, but do not know what to do and so become complacent. In some ways, it is another way of saying, "that's just how it is."

> I saw a fight on the bus today . . . it is what it is.
> Our English teacher quit . . . it is what it is.
> Another person got shot in East Oakland . . . it is what it is.

"It is what it is" reflects a powerlessness and/or an apathy toward doing anything about "it," whatever "it" is. In a way, perhaps it is a safety mechanism that protects us from feeling too frustrated about what we think we cannot do to make change.

Juan and Blanca are students who recently finished their second year of Youth Roots. They wrote and produced the song "Inured," whose title is also an S.A.T. word infrequently known by adults, let alone youth in Youth Roots. Juan and Blanca continue their analysis by naming what that normalized attitude is, *inured*. They illuminate what *Inured* is meant to do: *get people used to unpleasant conditions*. In reality, *inured* is a descriptive term that is related to the "it is what it is" attitude. Nonetheless, they then provoke the listeners by challenging their attitudes:

> That's just what it's meant to do (meant to do)
> Get used to it (that's inured)
> Now you walk through the Town
> And you hear a gunshot
> You find that it's normal
> I guarantee that it's not
> The spot's real hot 5.0 on the block
> You got a chain on ya mind
> Ya need to take a look inside

With all that can influence an "it is what it is" mentality, Juan and Blanca then counter these forces. They reveal a subtext of "It is NOT what it is" when they say, "I guarantee that it's not." Juan himself went through quite a journey in the time he has been in Youth Roots. On so many levels, his process in life mirrors the structured processes within Youth Roots that act to counter the larger social structures. He reflects:

> I feel I have always thought about all these things . . . I just didn't feel
> the need to do anything about it . . . I feel that I've always known there

was something holding me back . . . Not just physically . . . But structurally-wise . . . In society like in schools . . . And in stereotypes . . . And I always knew it . . . It always hit me in the face . . . And I just always took it . . . And coming into youth roots . . . It helped me find an outlet . . . Which is music . . . And I definitely found a part of me . . . Was yet to be awakened which was my musical and artistic side . . . And my passion for music and for writing . . . Has definitely expanded a lot more . . . And now I feel like I have more of a purpose . . . And more of an understanding of what I need to do . . . And what are some of my obligations . . . To do here . . . To just help better society for all of us . . . And to help break stereotypes . . . And that's been my biggest epiphany.

As Juan illuminates, the journey into the core of the self is a process of discovering, especially in the midst of harsh social conditions. "It is what it is" was not acceptable. Today, Juan sits alongside me as the first Youth Roots alumni staff member.

In "The rose that grew from concrete," Tupac Shakur (1999) tells how, despite being surrounded by toxic conditions where a thriving life should not occur, it still does. And not only does life occur, but it is beautiful. It is a rose. Through the Youth Roots Seed Sessions, the goal is not to grow a rose. Rather, it is about cultivating a process by which we can grow gardens.

★   ★   ★

ARTS ARTIFACT SEVEN

Language Lessons I

Melisa Cahnmann-Taylor

> **Proud**, *adj.* conceited, arrogant, high-minded, vain (PRIDE)
> (Roget's Thesaurus)

Her first sentence reads: *I am proud,*
conceited, and vain. Julia loops
handwriting, wears a Puerto Rican flag emblazoned
on jacket's black satin.

And what is wrong with a little conceit
and vanity? She taught me truth
betrayed by synonyms, and I taught
what I knew about learning a second language:

errors of translation differ from mistakes.
The errors are missed links, repeated unchanged
unless language variations
are distinguished one from the other.

There's no word for *lend* in Spanish, only *borrow*.
One day she wavered, then
"Can you borrow me a pencil?"
when she didn't bring her own.

An error can be coached,
guided, explained. Mistakes
can be careless, gauging laziness,
and should be corrected and marked wrong.

On Mondays we discussed current events.
A student brought a newspaper clipping: *April 1999.*
A Navy F/A 18 Hornet missed its target. A U.S. citizen,
a Puerto Rican, was killed on the island of Vieques.

They protested in D.C.,
blocked bridges in Miami. We searched the web,
learned Vieques has been a base
and training ground since 1941. The Marines

tested napalm; the Navy, live fire. "Our mistake"
a U.S. Senator wrote,
as if another's death could be rectified
with an "X" from one's own red pen.

And what's wrong with a little pride
crossed over the border to conceit? I talked
about grammar and word choice, but couldn't explain this:
our thesaurus, like our treaties and referendums,

was not to be trusted. She erased words,
accidentally tore paper. Like a small island
with defiance on her back, she leaned over,
started again.

What does the teacher learn from the student in this poem about her world of language, culture, identity and power? How does the student's personal response metaphorically relate to the power held by schools and other institutions? What might the teacher do as a next step in her interactions with the student based on this reflection?

This book is about principles of practice, informed by interdisciplinary research, theories and daily experiences that build a humanizing pedagogy for emergent bilingual youth. Through play, story, creative production and critical thinking—each at the heart of language learning—the pedagogy we propose is about raising questions rather than finding answers. Teaching and learning come through a process of inquiry with no singular approach or ideal set of tools. Instead, this critical, creative pedagogy asks how we should invite and sustain the participation of emergent bilingual youth in diverse educational contexts (Faltis, 2005). This pedagogy asks teachers to analyze the issues that schools, families, communities and youth grapple with individually and collectively in daily cross-cultural interactions. This pedagogy asks what assets and concerns your emergent bilingual youth bring to the classroom, and how you encounter them.

Some may think that it is easier to raise questions than to find answers. Yet, as arts-based teachers and researchers, we believe that questioning, problematizing, and probing for uncertain, unfinalizable depth across a breadth of learning experiences is the hardest and bravest work we can do. The act of problem-posing reminds us that the struggles we have privately deserve public space and attention, that we are not alone in our desire to change power structures and their ideologies of social dominance. These questions remind us that multicultural and multilingual communities of practice are tender spaces forged from histories of devastation that deserve ideological clarity, ethical vigilance and care. The stories of this book demonstrate that emergent bilingual youth are beyond dissatisfied—they have visions for better worlds that they can and will realize. And, as teachers reading this book, you too can be a part of this critical, caring, creative work.

Questions to Consider

1. In the poems and vignettes of this chapter, how do the worlds of the arts, social engagement, and language intersect?

2. Based on your reading of this book, what might your next steps be as a teacher toward developing a critical, creative, caring educational practice with emergent bilingual youth?

Notes

1. For an analysis of curricular control, see Au, 2007.
2. All names in this chapter's vignettes and poem are pseudonyms.

References

Anyon, J. (1997). *Ghetto schooling: A political economy of urban educational reform*. New York: Teachers College Press.

Anzaldúa, G. (1999). *Borderlands/la frontera: The new mestiza*. San Francisco: Aunt Lute Books.

Asante, M. K. (2009). *Erasing racism: The survival of the American nation*. Amherst, NY: Prometheus Books.

Au, W. (2007). High-stakes testing and curricular control: A qualitative metasynthesis. *Educational Researcher*, 36(5), 258–67.

Ballerini, J. (1995). Flip: The homeless child as auteur. *Yale Journal of Criticism*, 8(3), 87–101.

Bourdieu, P. (1977). *Outline of a theory of practice*, trans. R. Nice. Cambridge, UK: Cambridge University Press.

Connerton, P. (2004). *How societies remember*. Cambridge, UK: Cambridge University Press.

Dewey, J. (1938/1997). *Experience and education*. New York: Free Press.

Faltis, C. (2005). *Teaching English language learners in elementary school communities: A joinfostering approach*, 4th edition. Upper Saddle River, NJ: Prentice Hall.

Gramsci, A. (1971). *Selections from the prison notebooks*. New York: International Publishers.

Hill, M. L. (2009). *Beats, rhymes and classroom life: Hip hop pedagogy and the politics of identity*. New York: Teachers College Press.

Hodges, D. (1998). Participation as dis-identification with/in a community of practice. *Mind, Culture and Activity*, 5(4), 272–90.

Kuftinec, S. (2003). *Staging America: Cornerstone and Community-based Theatre*. Carbondale, IL: Southern Illinois University Press.

Lave, J. and Wenger, E. (1991). *Situated learning: Legitimate peripheral participation*. Cambridge: Cambridge University Press.

Margolis, E. (2004). Looking at discipline, looking at labour: Photographic representations of Indian boarding schools. *Visual Studies*, 19(1), 72–96.

Morrell, E. and Duncan-Andrade, J. (2008). *The art of critical pedagogy*. New York: Peter Lang.

Neal, P. (2003). *Urban villages and the making of communities*. New York: Taylor & Francis.

Paris, D. (2012). Culturally sustaining pedagogy: A needed change in stance, terminology, and practice. *Educational Researcher*, 41(3), 93–7.

Sandoval, C. (2000). *Methodology of the oppressed*. Minneapolis, MN: University of Minnesota Press.

Schubert, W. and Melnick, C. R. (1987). Study of the "outside curriculum" of students' lives. *Journal of Curriculum and Supervision*, 2, 200–2.

Shakur, T. (2009). *The rose that grew from concrete*. New York: MTV.

Spring, J. (2009). *Deculturalization and the struggle for equality: A brief history of the education of dominated cultures in the U.S.* New York: McGraw Hill.

Spry, T. (2006). A "performative-I" copresence: Embodying the ethnographic turn in performance and the performative turn in ethnography. *Text and Performance Quarterly*, 26(4), 339–46.

Thompson, E. P. (1977). *William Morris: Romantic to revolutionary*. London: Merlin Press.

Turner, T. (1992). Defiant images: The Kayapo appropriation of video. *Anthropology Today*, 8(6), 5–16.

Wa Thiong'o, N. (2002). Enactments of power: The politics of performance space. In B. Jeyifo (Ed.), *Modern African Drama* (pp. 434–57). New York: W. W. Norton.

Wenger, E. (1998). *Communities of practice: Learning, meaning and identity*. Cambridge: Cambridge University Press.

Williams, R. (1977). *Marxism and literature*. Oxford: Oxford University Press.

Appendix A

A PROCESS FOR BUILDING CRITICAL, CREATIVE, CARING EXPERIENCES

Drew Chappell, California State University Fullerton

Use the following framework to support you throughout the phases of building critical, creative education in school or community contexts with emergent bilingual youth. This framework is organized as a series of questions and action steps about planning, implementation, and evaluation of your project. The questions and actions steps have been developed considering the contexts of art-making, social/cultural study, and bilingual language development. The questions and action steps also refer to three intersecting dynamics: learning about the community and the content of the project, learning about your participants, and learning about yourself as a teacher/artist.

During each phase of your project, consider how you might engage the components we address in this book toward critical, creative education in school or community contexts with emergent bilingual youth. These include:

- Ongoing efforts toward cultural and linguistic responsiveness
- Collaborative engagement with families and communities
- Development of arts-based counter-narratives with young people through:

  - Play
  - Storytelling
  - Literature
  - World event analysis
  - Digital media and other technology.

Planning

Developing ideas for a program, project or curriculum; collaborating with participants; finding funding or other support; establishing goals and objectives.

Questions

- What community(ies) is this project geared toward? What community members and organizations could be potential partners?
- What are the community assets you might utilize? How can you learn more about them?
- What languages are in use in the community? How will you ensure these languages are utilized and presented through the project?
- What ideal goals do you have in mind at the start of the project? How will the community (families, students, other stakeholders) collaborate to develop these ideals into attainable and mutual goals?
- What arts medium(s) are you interested in using or learning more about alongside the participants?
- What topic(s) might the population be interested in exploring? How can you find out their interests, questions and concerns?
- What funding will you need in order to implement the project? Where might this funding come from?
- How will you regularly reflect on your own assumptions, values, and beliefs about the population and about yourself as a facilitator? How do you imagine your perspectives might shift and change?

Possible Actions

- Map the participants' community funds of knowledge (interests, expertise, other resources, networks, and relationships).
- Develop and administer a survey or questionnaire.
- Meet with stakeholders.
- Apply for funding.
- Secure and train staff and volunteers.
- Secure participant commitment.
- Develop a timeline for action.
- Pursue professional development in the arts medium.
- Pursue background knowledge in the participants' home languages and cultures.

Implementation

Putting the project into action, including introducing the project, student research of topic, student production of work, student dialogue, and student public presentation.

Questions

- How will you mutually plan the objectives of your project with your student participants in both English and their home languages?
- How are student interests guiding the research process? The creative process?
- How does student engagement in the project directly relate to their communities?
- How will you and the students reflect on their learning along the way?
- How will you regularly reflect on your own assumptions, values, and beliefs about the students during the project and about yourself as a facilitator? How do you imagine your perspectives might shift and change?
- How do the students plan to have a public showing/dialogue in their community at the end of the project?
- Whom will you invite to the showing? (Close friends and family only? Members of the community only? Others?)
- How will the funders interact with the students during the art-making process and at the showing? Why/when/how might this be important?

Possible Actions

- Bring facilitator(s) and young people together in one space.
- Outline project goals and objectives.
- Develop procedures for engaging in multiple languages.
- Hold conversations around mutually selected topic(s).
- Research ideas based on student and family conversations.
- Bring research findings into the group setting.
- Discuss arts-based expressions of findings: analyze, comment on, and revise creative work.
- Divide roles and responsibilities in creative process(es).
- Show/feed back creative work with community.
- Allow response from community to the creative work.
- Brainstorm or choose next steps for project with the participants.
- Thank participants and community in a meaningful way.

Evaluation

Determining whether goals and objectives were met, communicating with funders or other stakeholders, determining next steps.

Questions

- What were the outcomes (quantitative and qualitative) for each of these stakeholders: students, community, facilitator(s), funder(s)?
- How do you know if the outcomes meet the goals and objectives, based on criteria you developed in the planning stage?
- What data did you collect? In what language(s)?
- How will you decide which data to include in your evaluative process?
- Do you have permissions for the use of student commentary or work?
- How will you report the outcomes of your project? To whom? In what languages?
- Does your project have another cycle? If not, how will you continue to be present in the lives of your participants?

Possible Actions

- Gather data (student feedback, ethnographic descriptions, testimonials, student work, numbers) and store carefully and ethically.
- Translate data as needed, but keep original language intact to use side by side with English translation.
- Assess and evaluate all components of program (curriculum, community interactions, facilitators, student interactions and outcomes) based on criteria developed during planning.
- Report to funder(s) and/or other stakeholders.
- Decide when and how to repeat the project (or not), and how to change it.
- Create pathways to keep in contact with participants, especially if the project will not be repeated.

Appendix B

RESOURCES FOR EDUCATORS AND ARTISTS

Arts Education Service and Advocacy Organizations

American Alliance for Theatre and Education
A professional organization of educators, artists, and researchers dedicated to theatre education in the US.
www.aate.com

Art for Change
An organization in East Harlem, New York, that provides space and facilitates participation of communities and artists toward social change.
www.artforchange.org

ArtCorps
An arts partnership organization placing artists in Central American communities to build sustainable development with local organizations.
www.artcorps.org

Artists Against SB1070 and Poets Responding to SB1070 (Facebook)
Artists who use their art to communicate concerns about the Arizona restrictive immigration law SB1070.
http://www.facebook.com/#!/pages/Artists-Against-Arizonas-SB-1070/1141 60971948532
http://www.facebook.com/#!/PoetryOfResistance

Arts Education Partnership
A national coalition of education, arts, government and philanthropic organizations dedicated to arts education research and advocacy.
http://www.aep-arts.org/

Asian American Arts Alliance

An organization strengthening Asian American cultural groups through the arts.
http://aaartsalliance.org/

Center for Art and Public Life

Part of California College of the Arts, the Center facilitates community partnerships based on creative practice in Oakland, San Francisco and beyond. http://center.cca.edu/

Community Arts Network (CAN)/Art in the Public Interest

CAN was a project within API that promoted dialogue about critical community arts practices. Archived at:
http://wayback.archive-it.org/2077/20100906194747/
http://www.communityarts.net/
www.apionline.org

Critical Art Ensemble

A group of tactical media practitioners focusing on the intersections of media, technology and political activism.
www.critical-art.net

Imagining America

A consortium of universities and colleges dedicated to advancing the public and civic purposes of humanities and the arts.
www.imaginingamerica.org

International Journal of Education and the Arts

An open-access online journal for scholarly dialogue about education and the arts.
www.ijea.org

National Art Education Association

A professional organization of educators, artists, and researchers dedicated to art education in the U.S.
www.arteducators.org

National Association for Music Education (formerly MENC)

A professional organization of educators, artists, and researchers dedicated to music education in the U.S.
www.nafme.org

National Council of Teachers of English

A professional organization devoted to improving the teaching and learning of English and the language arts at all levels of education.
www.ncte.org

National Dance Association
National Dance Education Organization
Two professional organizations of educators, artists, and researchers dedicated to dance education in the U.S.
http://www.aahperd.org/nda/
http://www.ndeo.org/

Native Arts and Cultures Foundation
A philanthropic organization dedicated to revitalizing and appreciating indigenous arts and cultures.
http://www.nacf.us/

Pedagogy and Theatre of the Oppressed
An organization focused on challenging oppressive systems by promoting critical thinking and social justice through the works of Paulo Freire and Augusto Boal.
www.ptoweb.org

Prison Creative Arts Project
A project committed to the arts in correctional facilities, juvenile facilities, urban high schools, and communities across Michigan.
www.lsa.umich.edu/pcap

Radical Art Caucus
An organization that promotes art and art history scholarship that addresses historical and contemporary problems of oppression and possibilities for resistance.
http://radart.squarespace.com/about/

Social and Public Art Resource Center (SPARC)
Founded by muralist Judy Baca, SPARC is an arts center committed to public art in Los Angeles, California.
http://www.sparcmurals.org:16080/sparcone/

Tucson Arts Brigade
An arts and education organization dedicated to participatory community arts in Tucson, Arizona.
http://www.tucsonartsbrigade.org/about.html

Social Justice, Diversity and Multicultural Education Organizations

Center for Applied Linguistics
A research organization dedicated to improving communication through better understanding of language and culture.
www.cal.org

Center for Education Organizing at the Annenberg Institute for School Reform

A project that focuses on educational justice in underserved communities, including support for education organizing.

http://annenberginstitute.org/project/center-education-organizing

Centre for Social Justice

An organization that conducts policy research to fight poverty and other social injustices in the U.K.

http://www.centreforsocialjustice.org.uk/default.asp?pageRef=44

CREATE

(National Center for Research on the Educational Achievement and Teaching of ELLs) A research organization focused on supporting educational outcomes for English language learners in grades four to eight.

http://www.cal.org/create/about/mission.html

Gay and Lesbian Alliance against Defamation (GLAAD)

A media organization that works with news, entertainment and social media to bring culture-changing stories of LGBT people through storytelling, media watch, and advocacy.

http://www.glaad.org/

Institute of Humane Education

An organization providing professional development about human education, living and parenting.

http://humaneeducation.org/home

MN Neighborhoods Organizing for Change

A member-led, grassroots organization committed to fighting for racial and economic justice in neighborhood communities of Minneapolis, Minnesota.

www.mnnoc.org

National Association for Bilingual Education

A national professional organization devoted to representing bilingual learners and bilingual education professionals.

www.nabe.org

National Association for Multicultural Education

A national professional organization devoted to equity and social justice through multicultural education.

http://nameorg.org

NYC Coalition for Educational Justice

A parent-led organization working toward educational equity and excellence in New York City.

www.nyccej.org

Rethinking Schools
A publishing organization with a magazine and books committed to social justice, written by teachers and researchers.
www.rethinkingschools.org

Teachers 4 Social Justice
A teacher support and development organization based in San Francisco, providing opportunities for leadership and community building toward social justice.
http://www.t4sj.org/

Teachers of English to Speakers of Other Languages (TESOL)
A professional organization for advancing expertise in English language teaching and learning for speakers of other languages worldwide.
www.tesol.org

Teaching Tolerance
An education support center through the Southern Poverty Law Center that provides a magazine and online resources dedicated to equitable school experiences for all children.
http://www.tolerance.org/

Zinn's Education Project
A curriculum support organization focused on teaching a people's history, based on Howard Zinn's *A people's history of the United States*. Educational materials focus on the roles of women, people of color, working people, and organized social movements in shaping history.
http://zinnedproject.org/

Community and Family Partnerships

Harvard Family Research Project
A research group helping communities to evaluate strategies in three areas that support children's learning and development—early childhood education, out-of-school time programming, and family and community support in education.
www.hfrp.org

Parent Center Network
An organization focused on parent–professional partnerships, particularly for parents with student disabilities.
www.parentcenternetwork.org

Parent Institute for Quality Education
An organization facilitating parent education, taught in sixteen languages, for involvement in K-12 schools, colleges and universities.
www.piqe.org

Parent Teacher Association
Find PTA offices by state: http://wdcrobcolp01.ed.gov/Programs/EROD/org_list.cfm?category_cd=PTA

U.S. Department of Education—Parent Training and Information Centers
Search by type of parent support organization:
http://wdcrobcolp01.ed.gov/Programs/EROD/org_list.cfm

Parent Resource Centers (by state)
http://wdcrobcolp01.ed.gov/Programs/EROD/org_list.cfm?category_cd=PRC

Parent Training and Information Center
http://wdcrobcolp01.ed.gov/Programs/EROD/org_list.cfm?category_cd=SPT

ABOUT THE CONTRIBUTORS

Dorothy Abram, Ed.D., is a playwright and Associate Professor in the Social Sciences Department of Johnson & Wales University, Providence, Rhode Island. Focusing on global concerns of human rights, her plays serve to articulate the experiences and celebrate the cultures and sources of strength of recently arrived refugees.

Susan R. Adams is currently an ESL teacher educator and was most recently the Project Alianza Director in the College of Education at Butler University, where she teaches ESL courses for preservice and practicing teachers. A former high school Spanish and ESL teacher and instructional coach, Susan is a doctoral candidate in Literacy, Culture, and Language in Education at Indiana University at the School of Education in Indianapolis. She is a national facilitator and Critical Friends Group Coach with the School Reform Initiative and a Teacher Consultant with the National Writing Project, and a site leader of the Hoosier Writing Project. Her research interests include equity, teacher transformation, and ELL student writing development.

Alicia Apodaca is an English teacher at El Centro High School in El Centro Unified School District. She received her teaching credential from San Diego State University-IV Campus. Her teaching practices are built to decrease the number of long-term English language learners. Her methodology seamlessly balances the instruction on fundamental skills as well as the challenge to reinforce critical thinking and creativity among her students.

Dalida María Benfield, Ph.D., is an artist, scholar, educator, and advocate for social justice in and through media art and information technologies on local, national, and global scales, with a particular emphasis on youth and women. Her work is focused on creating and supporting open access to media and information technology through innovative education and activist initiatives. Dalida has worked in community arts and development organizations, cultural institutions, and foundations, and taught widely in education contexts ranging from public schools, senior centers, centers for adults and children with developmental disabilities, and colleges and universities. In 1994, she co-founded the media collective Video Machete, focused on youth, women, GLBTQ (gay, lesbian, bisexual, transgender and queer), and racialized communities in Chicago. She is currently a Fellow at the Berkman Center for Internet and Society at Harvard University, where she researches questions of digital media, gender, race, and social movements.

J. David Betts is a Professor of Practice in Literacy, Technology and the Arts in the Department of Teaching, Learning and Sociocultural Studies, University of Arizona. His research focus is the integration of literacy, technology, and the arts in in-school and out-of-school settings with diverse populations. Recent work includes a longitudinal study of After School Multimedia Arts Education, an artists-in-the-schools project in theatre arts in a seventh grade writing class, a community computing study with a local Native American tribe, and an investigation of the integration of computer game-making software in an afterschool writing workshop.

Kelli (Kiki) Bivins proudly serves the families of Athens, Georgia, as a middle school ESOL teacher and friend. There are currently five generations alive in Bivins' family; four of those five worked in poultry plants. This personal knowledge of poultry work helps her form deeper relationships with the families she serves, because most of them are poultry laborers themselves. When not serving her students, Bivins enjoys laughing and living with her husband and two sons.

Shannon Burgert is a teacher at Fireside Elementary School in Louisville, Colorado. She is a doctoral candidate in Curriculum and Instruction at the University of Denver, and her research interests include aesthetic education and ecological education. Shannon is an arts integration specialist for Think360 Arts Education. She is also a freelance writer, with a focus on science and health issues.

Melisa "Misha" Cahnmann-Taylor is Professor of Language and Literacy Education at the University of Georgia. She is the winner of Dorothy Sargent Rosenberg Prizes and a Leeway Poetry Grant, and has co-authored two books, *Teachers Act Up: Creating Multicultural Learning Communities Through Theatre* (with Mariana Souto-Manning and Kris D. Guiterrez; Teachers College Press, 2010) and *Arts-Based Research in Education* (with Richard Siegesmund; Routledge, 2008). Her research examines creativity and multilingual–multicultural education, including Spanish workshops for non-Spanish speaking educators. Follow her articles, poems, and blog at http://teachersactup.com/.

Louisa Castrodale is the Visual and Performing Arts Specialist for Palm Springs Unified School District, where she coordinates art, music, dance, drama, film and fashion programs for 25,000 students in twenty-six schools. She is a poet, and author of three poetry chapbooks, as well as an artist. Her collaboration with fellow artist, Luis Fausto, produced many wonderful pieces, and *La Noche* is her favorite.

Drew Chappell teaches at California State University Fullerton in the department of theatre and dance. He is a performance studies scholar with research interests in popular performance forms, enculturation, globalization and cultural export, as well as visual and narrative research methods. His edited book, *Children Under Construction: Critical Essays on Play as Curriculum,* was published by Peter Lang in 2010. Drew holds an M.F.A. from the University of Texas at Austin and a Ph.D. from Arizona State University. He is also an award-winning playwright.

Sharon Verner Chappell is Assistant Professor in the elementary and bilingual education department at California State University Fullerton. She is an arts-based researcher interested in teacher education and youth art-making toward social justice. Sharon holds an M.A. from the School of the Art Institute of Chicago and a Ph.D. from Arizona State University. Sharon taught K-8 multilingual, multicultural young people in Texas and California for six years before becoming a teacher educator. She has recently mounted the international bilingual arts exhibition at CSUF titled *Border Inspections: Arts-based Encounters with Language, Culture, Identity and Power.* She learns how to live through social justice practices of care, creativity and critique with her daughter Gillian and husband Drew.

Mary Carol Combs is a Professor of Practice in the Department of Teaching, Learning, and Sociocultural Studies, University of Arizona. She teaches graduate and undergraduate courses in bilingual and ESL education, sheltered content instruction and ESL methods, Indigenous language revitalization, and language policy and planning. Her research interests include bilingual education policy and law; sociocultural theory; indigenous language revitalization and development; immigration and education; and bilingual and ELL teacher preparation. She is the co-author (with Carlos Ovando) of *Bilingual and ESL Classroom*, 5th edition (McGraw-Hill, 2011) and has authored numerous articles and book chapters on Arizona's language policies.

Kim Constantine is a Network Achievement Coach for ELA/ESL/iLearnNYC in the Division of Academics, Performance and Support of the New York City Department of Education.

Dafney Blanca Dabach, Ph.D., is currently an Assistant Professor in the University of Washington's College of Education. Situated in the field of immigrant education, her work examines the nature of opportunities for immigrant-origin youth in urban secondary school settings. Before conducting academic research, Dabach was a professional photographer, and continues to be interested in photography as a medium for engaging with social issues. From 2005 to 2007, Dabach worked on an innovative collaboration (between Harvard's Project Zero, the Alameda County Office of Education, and Oakland's Center for Art and Public Life at the California College of the Arts) to integrate the arts in K–12 public schools. Her photographs have been exhibited in the U.S. and México.

Marilyn Dike-Dunn is an aspiring poet who resides in Riverside, CA. She received her Bachelor of Arts degree in English at California State University, Fullerton; a multiple subject teaching credential from the University of California, Riverside; and is currently pursuing a Master's degree in Education at Cal State Fullerton. She is currently an elementary school teacher and writes poetry about her experiences as an educator.

Louise Edman is an Art Educator at the Hewlett Elementary School, Franklin Early Childhood Center, in Hewlett, New York. She currently teaches art to students from kindergarten through fifth grade. Louise believes that art is an essential component of student learning, and art-making broadens and deepens learning when students reflect on other cultures. She develops young artists as members of a global community.

Christian J. Faltis is the Dolly and David Fiddyment Chair in Teacher Education and Professor of Language, Literacy and Culture in the School of Education at University of California, Davis. He is author and editor of eighteen books, and more than sixty scholarly journal articles and book chapters on bilingual education and Latino students. In 2001, Christian was recognized by AERA as a Distinguished Scholar of the Role and Status of Minorities in Education. He is an artist and activist who studies oil painting in México.

Luis Fausto is a Guatemalan-born artist who was raised in the U.S. from the age of six. His work ranges from life drawing to socially motivated pieces. In the painting *La Noche* featured in Chapter 3, he and Louisa Castrodale capture the experience of an immigrant family newly located in the U.S., and the strong bond formed from their common struggle to assimilate. Luis studied Graphic Design and currently owns a design firm located in Palm Springs, California. He works with non-profit clients and makes time for photography, his newly found passion.

Paul Fisher has been a master teaching artist in theatre for over thirty-five years throughout the U.S., Europe, Africa and Russia. He has provided theatre and arts integration training for educators in K through post-graduate studies. Paul is also an accomplished actor, director, researcher and writer. He is the recipient of both the Arizona Daily Star/Tucson-Pima Arts Council "Lumie" Award, and the Community Foundation of Southern Arizona/Buffalo Exchange Arts Award for outstanding contributions to arts and education. He is currently teaching "Bootcamp for the Brain"—a series of lectures and workshops in critical thinking and problem-solving skills.

David Forker earned his B.A. in Philosophy from High Point University in North Carolina and his M.A.T. in Secondary English Education from Piedmont College in Athens, Georgia. He teaches English to speakers of other languages (ESOL) at Coile Middle School in Athens, Georgia. His passions include learning, language, and music.

Luis Genaro Garcia is a local artist and art teacher in Los Angeles and a doctoral student at Claremont University's School of Educational Studies. He earned his B.A. in Art Education from California State University and an M.A. in Public Art Studies from the University of Southern California. He uses methods of civic engagement and critical pedagogy to develop student-based arts projects that address issues faced in urban schools.

Ruth Harman is Assistant Professor in the TESOL and World Language Program at the University of Georgia. Irish-born and raised, she uses performance, children's literature and genre-based pedagogies with ESOL teachers and students to support critical academic learning communities.

Daniel A. Kelin II is the Director of Drama Education for the Honolulu Theatre for Youth and on the national roster of teaching artists with the John F. Kennedy Center for the Performing Arts. A 2009 Fulbright–Nehru Senior Research Scholar in Education, Daniel has served as a consultant with theatres and social service agencies in several countries. A regular contributor to journals, his most recent book is *In Their Own Words: Drama and Young English Language Learners* (New Plays, 2009). Daniel is currently co-authoring *The Reflective Teaching Artist* for Intellect Books. He is President of the American Alliance for Theatre and Education from 2011 to 2013.

Joo Ae Kim obtained a Master's degree in the Art Education program at the University of Georgia. She completed her B.A. in Fine Arts at the University of Kentucky. Currently, she is an elementary art teacher in South Korea. She is interested in therapeutic art education programs for multicultural adolescents and families.

Sandra Kofford is the Director of the Migrant Education Program in Region 6-Imperial Valley County. Her projects focus on creating access to college for migrant students. Her research analyzes the importance of educating migrant parents to better understand how educational systems work within sociocultural contexts.

Elizabeth Lewis is an Assistant Professor in the Department of Education at Dickinson College in Carlisle, PA. She teaches courses in social foundations of American education, educational psychology, and methods of teaching secondary English. Her research focuses on adolescent literacy, new literacies, and the literacy development and instruction of English language learners.

Rachel Lindsay is the ESL Coordinator at PS 112, Manhattan in the New York City Department of Education.

Marguerite Lukes, Ph.D., is Assistant Professor at LaGuardia Community College City University of New York. Throughout her career, she has taught in, led, supported and evaluated English as a Second Language and bilingual education programs. Her research on educational language policy, immigrant education, and language acquisition has been published in *TESOL Quarterly*, *Journal of Latinos and Education*, and *International Multilingual Research Journal*. She can be reached at marguerite.lukes@gmail.com.

Jessica Mele is Executive Director of Performing Arts Workshop in San Francisco, CA. Jessica joined the Workshop in April 2006, and became director in 2011. Prior to this position, she worked at Harvard's Kennedy School of Government as a project coordinator and organizer for the Harvard Union of Clerical and Technical Workers (AFSCME, AFL-CIO). In the community, Jessica currently serves as the Advocacy Co-Chair for the Arts Provider's Alliance of San Francisco and as a member of the steering committees of Teaching Artists Organized and the Alameda County Office of Education's Alliance for Arts Learning Leadership. She holds a B.A. in Anthropology and French Studies from Smith College and an M.Ed. in Education Policy and Management from the Harvard Graduate School of Education.

Masakazu Mitsumura is a Ph.D. candidate in Curriculum Studies at Arizona State University's Mary Lou Fulton Teachers College. His teaching/research interests include multicultural teacher education, critical (performance) pedagogy, and critical race theory. He is currently working on his doctoral dissertation, "Participatory theatre as transformative pedagogy in preservice multicultural teacher education," aimed at examining how preservice teachers develop Freirean "critical consciousness" in multicultural practice through experiencing participatory theatrical activities in his classroom.

Elizabeth Renner is an accomplished kindergarten and first grade teacher, and has taught in urban schools in Omaha, Nebraska, and Denver, Colorado. Blending her passions of early literacy and the arts, Ms Renner has devoted her practice to engaging young English language learners and their families in vibrant, multimodal learning environments. Elizabeth received her B.S. in Elementary Education and Spanish from Creighton University and completed her graduate studies at the University of Nebraska at Omaha with an M.S. in Education and English language development.

G. Reyes is co-principal at ARISE High School in East Oakland, California, focusing on critical education practices in K–12, youth development, and teacher development. He is the former Executive Co-Director and Youth Leadership Director of Oakland Leaf, an arts and social justice youth organization. He founded and taught high school age youth in the critical media program, Youth Roots, and has co-presented with the youth in this program at many conferences and workshops. He is a doctoral candidate at UC Berkeley in Language, Literacy, Culture and Society.

Fernando Rodríguez-Valls is Associate Professor of Teacher Education at SDSU-IV Campus. In the Imperial Valley, he is developing community-based literacy programs involving parents and students on dialogic reading practices that explore the linguistic symmetries between English and Spanish. His research focuses on sociocultural factors affecting second language learners and their academic achievement.

Deborah Romero is an Associate Professor in English as a Second Language and Bilingual Education in the Hispanic Studies Department at the University of Northern Colorado and currently serves as Associate Director for Faculty Development at the Center for Enhancement for Teaching and Learning. Dr Romero's research focuses on multilingualism and multimodal communication with underrepresented students and is informed by sociocultural theories of human development, critical pedagogies and a commitment to equity and diversity in education, coupled with a background in linguistics and digital literacies. For several years now, she has been committed to developing action research projects with teachers and adolescents in both print and multimedia projects as vehicles for student empowerment and agency.

Karena Salmond is Program Director at Performing Arts Workshop. She joined the Workshop in 2007 following the completion of an M.A. in International and Multicultural Education from the University of San Francisco. Before graduate school, she taught visual art and workshops in afterschool programs and with Chicago Children's Museum. With Performing Arts Workshop, she sits on the Community Based Organization Advisory Board of the San Francisco Unified School District. Karena holds a B.A. in Fine Arts from Kalamazoo College.

Lizzet Samaniego is an elementary school teacher at Heber School in Heber Elementary School District. She received her teaching credentials from San Diego State University-IV Campus. She holds a multiple subject credential and a single subject credential in Mathematics. Her pedagogy and methodology underscores the idea of developing multidimensional lesson plans to meet the needs of a full range of students.

Daphnie Sicre holds a B.A. in Journalism, History and Theatre from Lehigh University, an M.A. in the Teaching of Social Studies from Columbia University, and an M.A. in Educational Theatre from New York University. Formerly a Swortzell Scholar, she is now a Ph.D. candidate in Educational Theatre at NYU. In addition to her doctoral work, Daphnie works as an adjunct at NYU, Borough of Manhattan Community College and Marymount Manhattan College. She is also a teaching artist for the George Street Playhouse, and NJPAC. Prior to her Ph.D. work she directed over twenty-five productions with high school teenagers in Miami, Florida, and since commencing her studies in New York she has directed *AfroLatino~Ism*, *NuYork Pastorela*, *Collateral Bodies*, and *Not About Eve*. Raised in Madrid, Spain, but born in Guayaquil, Ecuador, to Peruvian and Spanish parents, Daphnie shares a deep passion for discovering multiple Latino and African American perspectives in drama.

Saskia Stille is a Ph.D. candidate in the Department of Curriculum, Teaching, and Learning of the Ontario Institute for Studies in Education at the University of Toronto. Her research focuses on language learning in multilingual school contexts, and she works with students and teachers to understand how cultural and linguistic diversity and rapid technological change are re/shaping language and literacy practices in schools.

Kinga Varga–Dobai is an Assistant Professor of Literacy Education at Georgia Gwinnett College. Her research interests include sociocultural approaches to literacy education, multigenre writing practices, children's literature and feminist qualitative research methodologies.

Eva Rose B. Washburn–Repollo, Ph.D., is Assistant Professor in the Communication Department of Chaminade University of Honolulu. She teaches in the doctoral program in curriculum and instruction and intercultural communication. She also performs as a storyteller of Filipino stories for children and cultural events.

Calder Zwicky is the Associate Educator of Teen and Community Programs at the Museum of Modern Art, where he has worked since 2006. In this capacity, he oversees the Museum's Community Partnership Program, which seeks to create programming throughout New York City for a wide range of underserved and historically overlooked community audiences. In addition, he runs the MoMA's multiple-session programming for teens including their Cross-Museum Collective as well as their long-running In the Making program. He has worked for a variety of museums and arts institutions including the Walker Art Center, the Bronx Museum of the Arts, the Queens Museum of Art, and the Studio Museum in Harlem.

INDEX

Page numbers in *italics* denotes an illustration.